MUSIC OF THE AFRICAN DIASPORA
Edited by Samuel A. Floyd, Jr.

DEAD MAN BLUES

Detail from the visa Morton obtained in 1921 in order to work in Mexico. Courtesy Historic New Orleans Collection.

Dead Man Blues

Jelly Roll Morton Way Out West

Phil Pastras

UNIVERSITY OF CALIFORNIA PRESS

Berkeley   Los Angeles   London

CENTER FOR BLACK MUSIC RESEARCH

Columbia College Chicago

THE PUBLISHER GRATEFULLY ACKNOWLEDGES
THE GENEROUS CONTRIBUTION TO THIS BOOK
PROVIDED BY SUKEY AND GIL GARCETTI, MICHAEL
ROTH, AND THE ROTH FAMILY FOUNDATION.

University of California Press
Berkeley and Los Angeles, California

University of California Press, Ltd.
London, England

Center for Black Music Research
Columbia College Chicago

Library of Congress Cataloging-in-Publication Data

Pastras, Philip.
    Dead man blues : Jelly Roll Morton way out West / Phil
Pastras.
        p.   cm.—(Music of the African diaspora ; 5)
    Includes bibliographical references and index.
    ISBN 0-520-21523-0 (cloth : alk. paper)
    1. Morton, Jelly Roll, d. 1941. 2. Jazz musicians—
United States—Biography. 3. Morton, Jelly Roll,
d. 1941—Relations with women. 4. Gonzales, Anita.
I. Title: Jelly Roll Morton way out West. II. Title. III.
Series.

ML410.M82 P37 2001
781.65′092—dc21
[B]

2001027291

Printed in the United States of America
08 07 06 05 04 03 02 01
10 9 8 7 6 5 4 3 2 1

The paper used in this publication meets the minimum
requirements of ANSI/NISO Z39.48–1992 (R 1997)
(*Permanence of Paper*).

To my son, Chris Pastras

To paraphrase Henry David Thoreau: You have had the courage to advance confidently in the direction of your dreams and to live the life you had imagined.

O make me a mask.

—*Dylan Thomas*

CONTENTS

ILLUSTRATIONS

PREFACE

When Ferdinand "Jelly Roll" Morton sat at the piano in the chamber music auditorium of the Library of Congress in May 1938 and began to tell his story to Alan Lomax and his recording machine, few people in the United States would have understood the significance of what was about to unfold, even had they known about it. As May turned into June and Morton continued to spin his tale, with every word he spoke and every note he played he saved from oblivion another piece of American cultural history. The focus was on his own colorful life and on his important contributions to American music, but in the course of the interviews he called up much more from his tenacious memory: New Orleans funeral customs; life in the legal red-light district called Storyville; the ambiguities and absurdities of race and color in America; the Robert Charles riots; an assortment of gamblers, thugs, and street people like Aaron Harris, Chicken Dick, Sheep Eye, Nigger Nate, and Toodlum and Toodoo Parker; the styles of rival pianists long dead and unrecorded; a cameo portrait of the legendary trumpet player Buddy Bolden, also unrecorded; voodoo practices in New Orleans and New York; the early stirrings of a jazz scene in Los Angeles, San Francisco, Seattle, and Vancouver; and, certainly not the least of all, his reminiscences of the woman who called herself Anita Gonzales, who served as wife and companion in his odyssey up and down the West Coast. As Ralph Ellison once said, "It is well that we keep in mind the fact that not all of American history is recorded. And in some ways we are fortunate that it isn't, for if it were, we might become so chagrined by the discrepancies which exist between our democratic ideals and our social reality that we'd soon lose heart. Perhaps that is why we possess two basic versions of American history: one which is written and as neatly stylized as ancient myth, and the other as unwritten and chaotic and full of contradictions, changes of pace, and surprises as life itself."[1]

In the Library of Congress interviews, Jelly Roll Morton has saved some of that unwritten history for us, and the recordings have not only all of the qualities that Ellison enumerates but something else: brilliant performances, at the piano, of his landmark compositions. Most of the music had been recorded already in the 1920s, but a handful of pieces had not and would have otherwise remained part of unwritten history forever. When Lomax edited the interviews and added his own chapters filling in some of the gaps Morton left, unwritten became written history; and to some extent it also became "as neatly stylized as ancient myth" when the book, *Mister Jelly Roll*, appeared in 1950. At times, Lomax succumbs a bit too uncritically to the legendary, mythic elements of his subject. But even there, when Morton speaks, his words carry with them the poignant reminder that all of it could have been lost.

Another great loss would have been his carefully articulated views defining the elements of the music called jazz. In one chapter of the book, "Sweet, Soft, Plenty Rhythm," Lomax has pulled together all of Morton's comments on jazz and thereby performed a valuable service. Jelly Roll was not only the first great jazz composer and one of its greatest practitioners but also, as the chapter makes clear, an intellectual of sorts who was able to turn his experience of the music into clear concepts and definitions. One by one, he names the qualities essential to jazz, at least in his view: syncopation, the "Spanish tinge" (Morton's term for the habañera-tango rhythms that appear in some pieces), the importance of riffs and breaks and of "medium slow tunes" to the development of jazz, the jazz piano as "an imitation of a band," and the use of what he calls "novelty" effects like wah-wah mutes on trumpets and trombones.[2] Where most musicians of his generation—and later, for that matter—would have balked at defining jazz ("Aw, man, if you can't *feel* it, what's the use of defining it?"), Morton shows that he has thought long and hard on the subject and has developed at least a loosely coherent set of ideas about how the music works at its best. Perhaps his various claims to have "invented" or "originated" jazz are not as preposterous as they might seem. At the very least, he appears to have been one of the first jazz musicians to see it as a distinct art form and to articulate its basic principles.

However, many readers will find aspects of his life distasteful at best, morally onerous at worst: for long stretches he supported himself by gambling, bootlegging, and pimping. Often he was even unsure whether music was really his main focus in life. And many who knew him have said that prostitution was his special forte. Today, feminists, health workers, those who consider themselves moral arbiters of society, and others would single out prostitution as his most damnable activity. The modern idea that prostitution is nothing more than the rank exploitation of women's bodies, along with the spread of the AIDS virus, put prostitution high on the list of threats to the moral and physical health of the nation—indeed, of the world.

But the historian must be careful about reading modern ideas and values into the world that Jelly Roll Morton inhabited just after the turn of the twentieth century. Certainly, even then there were many who vigorously condemned prostitution, and for reasons similar, if not identical, to those stated above. The AIDS virus, of course, was not to appear until decades after Morton's life, but before the advent of penicillin the ravages of syphilis could be almost as devastating, especially in the final stages. However, the moral issue was somewhat more complex back then. Although prostitution was condemned as much as, if not more than, it is now—from the pulpit, on editorial pages, and in political oratory—at the same time many of the major cities in the United States experimented for various lengths of time with legalizing prostitution and containing it within clearly demarcated districts like Storyville in New Orleans, where the ordinance creating the district was not repealed until 1917. However many citizens of the city considered prostitution to be immoral, it was nevertheless legal. And it was in that context that Morton began his life as a professional musician, at about age fifteen, playing piano in the legally sanctioned bordellos in the red-light district of New Orleans. And it should be noted that, whatever the legal status of prostitution in various cities on the West Coast when Morton was there (1917–23), the West was still wild, still virtually a frontier where there were often far more men than women. This was especially true of Las Vegas, where Anita Gonzales was running the Arcade saloon when Jelly arrived in Los Angeles. To this day, prostitution is still legal in the state of Nevada, and, though the red-light district in Los Angeles had been outlawed in 1909, the fact that red-light activities were still thriving when Morton arrived in 1917 should surprise none but the most naive.

It was around 1909, give or take a year, that Morton made his first trip to California, a brief visit that he mentions in passing in *Mister Jelly Roll*. He makes a comment in that passage that can be explained only in reference to the close connection in his early years between his piano playing and prostitution, along with other illegal activities. Morton was persuaded to make the trip by a friend called Nick, who "wanted to get in with the sporting-women through me," according to Jelly, who sums up the trip very quickly: "California was a nice place at the time, no discrimination, but I played very little piano except in Oxnard, a very fast-stepping town. In fact, things was so dead that I headed back to New Orleans."[3] The statement about Oxnard puzzled me at first—after all, the town lies in the middle of Ventura County, where antialcohol sentiment was so thick that the citizens voted in their own countywide prohibition ordinance in 1913, six years before the nationwide ban went into effect. As it turns out, Oxnard literally sprang up, at about the turn of the century, around a sugar beet–refining plant built by Henry T. Oxnard and his brothers in the middle of the fields that grew the crop. The hastily improvised town quickly became a haven for gambling, prostitution, and opium dens that served the factory workers and field hands—mostly Chinese, Japanese, and Mexicans. According to Judith P. Triem in her book *Ventura County: Land of Good Fortune*, "In 1903 Oxnard incorporated so that ordinances could be passed to control the saloons and gambling halls."[4] The wording—"to control," not "to ban"—suggests that Oxnard's approach was one of tolerant control rather than rabid prohibitionism, and Morton's comment indicates that there was still, at the end of the decade, enough of a lively nightlife to support a man of his background and interests.

It needs to be said too that the choices of occupation available to African Americans in Morton's day were severely restricted. The vast majority were cooks, servants, maids, and manual laborers simply because they could not find other kinds of work. A small but significant minority were entertainers, but at the cost of being considered disreputable by ministers and churchgoing African Americans. And, then as now, the chances of having a secure, well-paying livelihood as an entertainer were slim. The only lines of work readily available to an ambitious black person, man or woman, who wanted to make a lot of money were illegal underworld activities of the kind that Morton practiced. In a community where most people work long hours and earn little, it is hard not to envy those few who dress well, always have plenty of money, and seem to be living the good life. This is, alas, true today in the inner cities of our nation, where in some neighborhoods the good life seems to be open only to crack dealers. But there are other choices, and there are prominent African Americans who have prospered by taking advantage of those choices. That was not true in Jelly's day.

Also, Morton was not alone among black entertainers of his day, especially the musicians, in taking advantage of the fact that their livelihood put them in direct contact with opportunities to make money from illicit underworld activities. Making a living as a musician has always been difficult and insecure. Today, musicians often have to secure some sort of steady income by working what they call "day gigs"—that is, working during the day, full- or part-time, at an ordinary, salaried job.

Some musicians of Morton's generation had their day gigs too, but often these entailed hard physical labor not compatible with doing what it takes to be a highly skilled musician. The chance to make easy money doing something convenient to the nightlife in which they played their music must have been very appealing. And many of them did just that, especially the piano players—as anyone familiar with the biographies of pianists knows. That kind of thing became less and less common in the post–World War II era, but even there one can find isolated instances of it: both Charles Mingus and Miles Davis have admitted to working as pimps for short periods of time to ease the financial strain of trying to make it as jazz musicians.

A historian's responsibility to his subject matter is not primarily—perhaps not even secondarily—to make moral judgments, but to provide insight into the motives and movements of people and events of the past, thereby making them present once again. In *Dead Man Blues* I have done my best to bring Jelly Roll Morton and Anita Gonzales back to life in the minds of my readers—a daunting task, but one that has been well worth undertaking. Whether I have succeeded is for the reader to decide, but I regard the completion of this task as only repaying a debt I have owed for some time now to one of the great masters of American music for the delights, the laughter, the flights of romantic fancy, and, yes, the occasional moments of poignant melancholy he brought into my life—into all our lives—through his music. The fact that his kind of music grew and developed where gambling, prostitution, and saloons prospered, or that his style of piano playing was once dubbed "whorehouse piano," was not a matter of choice for Morton or any of the early jazz pianists. It was a reality, and the only choice was to make the best of a bad environment or to quit playing—or in the case of a few, like Thomas Dorsey, to make the switch to church and gospel music, not a very lucrative occupation at that time.

As for the debt we all owe Alan Lomax, it is obviously huge. But as my research progressed I became dismayed by the number of errors and omissions in the text of *Mister Jelly Roll*. Some of these errors I have pointed out in my own text, when necessary: the confusion of the names of Bill and Dink Johnson that continues for three pages in the chapter "The Cadillac in Bloom" (Morton first says "Bill" but immediately corrects that to "Dink," while Lomax has Jelly continue to say "Bill" until he mysteriously changes it to "Dink"); after his heart attack in 1939, Morton was hospitalized for three weeks, not three months, as Lomax has Jelly's wife, Mabel, say; and there are others, some of which I have let stand because they are not essential to the story I tell. Also, there are omissions that, while perhaps not of great interest to the general reader, are essential for the researcher: most notably, the name of Anita's saloon in Las Vegas.

In addition, Lomax's methods are at times questionable. For example, Morton talks about a vocal quartet that used to sing spirituals at wakes, where there would always be "plenty ham sandwiches and cheese sandwiches slabbered all over with mustard, and plenty whiskey and plenty of beer"; when he begins to sing the words *"Nearer, my God, to thee,"* Lomax has him interject some comments: "very slow and with beautiful harmony, thinking about that ham—*Nearer to thee* . . . plenty of whiskey in the flask and all kinds of crazy ideas in the harmony."[5] On the recording, it is Lomax who suggests to Morton that his mind was on the ham and the whiskey; Jelly simply goes along with the joke. No modern researcher in the field of oral history would put words into a subject's mouth like that. Nor would a modern researcher have stage-managed the interviews as Lomax does when he asks Morton to play some chords on the piano while he is talking. Even worse, according to the discographer Laurie Wright, Morton, who did not want to record the whorehouse tunes from the Storyville period—and there are quite a few of them—with their lurid and obscene language, did so at Lomax's urging. In Wright's words, "Morton was not very happy about this, but gave Lomax what he wanted."[6] Creating that kind of a situation must rank high on the list of an interviewer's cardinal sins.

Having said all of that, however, we must remember that the field now called "oral history" was practically nonexistent when the Lomax-

Morton interviews took place and when Lomax and his father, John, made their recordings in the 1930s of Mississippi Delta blues musicians as well as musicians of other styles of American folk music. Like most pioneers, they had no road maps, no guidelines to go by, and mistakes were inevitable. Perhaps we should be surprised that there were not more. And we should most definitely be grateful for their unerring sense of what was authentic in American music. Needless to say, had they not done their work when they did, the loss would have been tremendous: much of the history of American music would have remained unwritten.

I was first alerted to Alan Lomax's errors and omissions in *Mister Jelly Roll* by the writer Peter Pullman, who has transcribed all of the Lomax-Morton interviews literally and plans eventually to publish the results. He quite generously sent me photocopies of the pages having to do with Morton's West Coast years and has given me permission to use them in my text. Naturally, the transcripts have none of the literary polish that Lomax attempted to give Morton's words in *Mister Jelly Roll*. I have therefore decided to quote Lomax wherever possible but to cite Pullman's transcripts where Lomax errs. Since the transcripts are still in manuscript, I have cited not Pullman's page numbers but the relevant American Folklore Society (AFS) catalogue numbers for the recordings themselves. Readers interested in pursuing my documentation further should consult Laurie Wright's excellent discography, *Mr. Jelly Lord*.

Also, it was my good fortune while I was researching *Dead Man Blues* to find a collection of Jelly Roll Morton memorabilia in Portland, Oregon. The collection includes a scrapbook of some fifty-eight pages that Morton himself evidently put together, probably at the end of 1938, along with a pile of unorganized clippings, documents, receipts, and so on that is equal in size to the scrapbook itself. For reasons that I explain later, the assortment of memorabilia is called the Henry Villalapando Ford Collection; in addition there is a smaller collection contributed by Mike Ford. Both collections are now in the Historic New Orleans Collection, in New Orleans, and the material is now being catalogued. I am therefore unable to supply any catalogue numbers for the material I cite.

ACKNOWLEDGMENTS

I had no intention of writing a book about five years ago when I began to do some rather informal research on Ferdinand "Jelly Roll" Morton's West Coast years. Dick Hyman's compact disc *Jelly and James* had renewed my interest in Morton's life and music. I bought a brand-new copy of Alan Lomax's *Mister Jelly Roll* and began to collect all the compact discs of Jelly's music I could get my hands on. I included the book on the reading list of one of my courses at Pasadena City College and soon found myself trying to answer questions from my students, who responded to the man and the music with great enthusiasm and curiosity, especially concerning his life in Los Angeles. Once my own curiosity had been piqued, I began to poke around, somewhat casually at first. I remember the Saturday afternoon when, following up on Jelly's statement in Lomax's book that the Anita Hotel was "on the corner of Central, near Twelfth," I drove to that spot to see what I might find. When I looked north, I saw an old hotel, now called the Tokyo, on the corner of Eleventh Street and Central Avenue. I took some Polaroid snapshots and, later, determined that the building was indeed old enough to have been the Anita. I have never been able to prove that it once carried that name, but no matter: I was hooked. I cannot help wondering if I ever would have begun work on this project if there had been no Dick

Hyman compact disc, no Lomax, no students to help fuel my curiosity. But there they were, and here I sit, trying to make sure I don't forget anyone who has helped me along the way.

I have to begin with my wife, Elaine, who listened for countless hours, before, during, and after dinner, as I tried to make sense of the bits and pieces of evidence I kept accumulating. She was more than just patient about my growing obsession with the story as it unfolded and about the amount of time the project has consumed over the years: she has unflinchingly and enthusiastically supported my every effort and has often gone far beyond simply cheering me on from the sidelines.

Though I called the writer and collector Floyd Levin without any kind of introduction, formal or informal, he immediately invited me to his home. When I arrived, he sat me down in his study, turned over his extensive Morton file, and said he would photocopy anything I thought I might need. And I have been the beneficiary of that kind of generosity from Floyd many times since that day.

At about the same time, I was introduced to Steve Isoardi, then in the last stages of putting together that monumental work *Central Avenue Sounds: Jazz in Los Angeles.* We were soon exchanging manuscripts, discussing future projects, and sharing our enthusiasms. It so happened that Steve also knew Floyd, and at some point one of us suggested that we three meet for lunch on the first Saturday of each month to talk shop. Our talks have been freewheeling and wide-ranging—nothing that had to do with the music was deemed too trivial; and nothing can ever replace the bonds of friendship and trust that were forged during those wonderful conversations. This work would not be the same without their help and encouragement.

Also, both sides of Anita Gonzales's family made generous contributions to my work in progress. On the maternal side, Anita's granddaughters, Rose Mary Johns (executrix of Anita's estate) and Tommie Fuller, at first a bit wary of the stranger who wanted to write about their grandmother, soon came to support my work in every way they could. Special thanks go to Rose Mary, who patiently answered whatever questions she could over many hours of telephone conversations. On the paternal side of the family, Jeanne, Mike, and Patti Ford made tremendous contributions to my work: Jeanne, Anita's daughter-in-law, quickly understood that the Morton memorabilia in her possession needed to be placed in some sort of institution, and, though she had known me for little more than the long weekend I had spent in Portland, Oregon, to view the collection, she trusted me to take it back to Los Angeles to have its value assessed and to eventually get it to the proper institution. Mike and Patti, Anita's grandchildren, shared with me the photos they had of their grandmother and grandfather, as well as their recollections of Anita. Mike also trusted me to take the few pieces of memorabilia that had come into his possession to be assessed with the rest of the collection.

The scholars James Dapogny, Lawrence Gushee, and Peter Pullman were especially kind and supportive of my project from the moment I contacted them—Gushee in particular, whose patient criticism of my theories as I developed them was very helpful, and who generously shared the fruits of his research on the Creole Band with me when they were at all relevant to my work. Both Dapogny and Gushee served as readers of the entire manuscript, and their comments, corrections, and overall appraisals were very helpful in getting the work done. And at a crucial point, Peter Pullman sent me copies of the relevant pages of the literal transcription he made of Morton's 1938 interviews with Alan Lomax at the Library of Congress.

Many others have made contributions, both large and small, to *Dead Man Blues*, but the following have been especially helpful: Babette Ory, who supplied the information that led to Rose Mary Johns and, ultimately, the Ford family; Tim Fitak, who sent me copies of Morton family photos from his archive; Gordon O'Dell, for his efforts in trying to find out if the building at the corner of Eleventh and Central really was the Anita Hotel; the New Orleans musician Don Vappie and Dr. Alfred E. Lemmon, Director of the Williams Research Center at the Historic New Orleans Collection, for the information they shared with me about some of Morton's late arrangements, especially that strange and wonderful piece, "Gan-Jam"; Rick Corrales, who photographed most of the Ford Collection of Morton memorabilia without charging me a cent; Harry Smallenburg, friend, fellow musician, and office mate at Pasadena City College (PCC), who read and commented astutely on an early version of my first chapter, as did Isabelle Perez, a former student at the college; Anna Maria Gonzalez, student in the Scholars Option program at PCC, for her very helpful research in old microfilms of the *Chicago Defender*; and Mark Wallace, Director of Public Relations at the college, who helped get the word out on my discovery of the Ford Collection, publicity that led to the letter from Joe Marvin with the wonderful tale of his and Dick Russell's chance meeting with Jack Ford.

Special thanks go to the writer and jazz enthusiast Mimi Melnick for compiling the comprehensive index.

I am grateful to the Hal Leonard Corporation for permission to reprint lyrics from the following Jelly Roll Morton compositions: "Dead Man Blues" by Ferdinand "Jelly Roll" Morton, © 1926 (renewed) Edwin H. Morris & Company, a division of MPL Communications, Inc. All rights reserved. "Winin' Boy Blues" by Ferdinand "Jelly Roll" Morton, © 1939, 1940, 1950 Tempo Music Publishing Co. Copyright renewed by Edwin H. Morris & Company, a division of MPL Communications, Inc. All rights reserved.

Finally, I owe a tremendous debt of gratitude to the staff of the University of California Press, especially Associate Director Lynne Withey and the editor Mary Francis for their warm enthusiasm and professional support from the time when the book consisted of no more than one chapter and a proposal for the rest.

CHAPTER I

Prelude to a Riff

1

Ferdinand "Jelly Roll" Morton could brag almost as well as he could play piano—and, as the world knows, he played piano very well indeed. His most famous boast was provoked by a broadcast of Robert Ripley's *Believe It or Not* radio program, which introduced W. C. Handy as the originator of jazz and the blues. "W. C. Handy is a liar," Morton announced in a long letter addressed to Ripley and published in the *Baltimore African-American* and *Down Beat* magazine. The letter goes on to claim, "It is evidently known, beyond contradiction, that New Orleans is the cradle of jazz and I, myself, happened to be the creator in the year 1902."[1] That was not the only time he made that claim or something like it. The guitarist Danny Barker recalls that Morton would announce, "I created jazz and there's no jazz but Jelly Roll's jazz."[2] According to the musician and entrepreneur Reb Spikes, "[Jelly] would hear a piece and say, 'They're stealing that from me. That's mine.' Or 'That guy's trying to play like me.'"[3] The trumpet player Lee Collins remembers going to see Morton in his hotel room: "He asked me to come work with him. 'You know you will be working with the world's greatest jazz piano player . . . not one of the greatest—I am the greatest.'"[4]

But if in his boasting Morton appeared to pass fool's gold off as the real thing, he was actually passing along some golden nuggets. Comments by the bassist Bill Johnson echo what many musicians have said over the years: "You could go by a house where Jelly would be playing and you'd know it was him because nobody did and nobody does play just like him. He wasn't afraid to admit it, either. . . . 'Nobody playing I can't cut,' he used to say. The thing was he could really do what he said. He was the best, the very best." [5] Even his seemingly outrageous claim that he created jazz, surprisingly enough, has the faint but golden ring of truth to it. Of course, his statement to Ripley is at the very least an exaggeration; no one person "created" jazz—it evolved out of a long tradition, and there were many people involved in its development. But in another, more considered statement, made during the same year (1938), Morton suggests where the truth might actually lie: "All these people play ragtime in a hot style, but man, you can play hot all you want to, and you still won't be playing jazz. . . . Ragtime is a certain type of syncopation and only certain tunes can be played in that idea. But jazz is a style that can be applied to any type of tune. But *I started using the word in 1902 to show people the difference between jazz and ragtime.*" [6]

A rather extraordinary and revealing statement, to say the least: it shows an intellectual bent in Morton that few writers have discussed. Unlike most other musicians of his generation, he could not only perform the music, but he could also discuss the performance analytically, as he did at some length in response to Alan Lomax's questions during the recording of his interviews at the Library of Congress in 1938. In Lomax's *Mister Jelly Roll*, based largely on those interviews, Morton spells out with great precision his view of the essential elements of jazz. The statement above is musically, etymologically, and historically accurate with respect to the words *ragtime* and *jazz*. When the ragtime compositions of writers like Scott Joplin became popular in the 1890s and 1900s, everyone wanted to cash in on the fad, and all kinds of tunes were labeled "ragtime" that were nothing of the sort: Irving Berlin's "Alexander's Ragtime Band," for example. Also, early jazz orchestras were often called ragtime bands, for lack of a better term. According to the *Oxford English Dictionary*, the first appearance in print of the word *jazz* to describe the music was in 1909; however, the term was not in general use until about 1917. In the Library of Congress statement, Morton does not claim to have invented jazz but to have been the first to use the term to distinguish the new music from ragtime—a credible if unprovable claim, especially credible because of its accuracy: the difference between the two does lie in jazz's greater range of tempos, styles, and emotional textures, just as he says. And it would have been just like Morton to choose a term that, in its original manifestations (spelled *jass*), meant *sexual intercourse*. But more about Morton's sexual persona later.

It is tempting to compare Morton's bragging to that of Benvenuto Cellini, the great Renaissance artist, and indeed Lomax does just that when he says that in Jelly Roll he "had encountered a Creole Benvenuto Cellini."[7] Like Morton, Cellini could both talk the talk *and* walk the walk. More to the point, however, would be to compare Morton's bragging to ancient epic traditions that expect heroes like Odysseus to proclaim their virtues loudly and clearly. Comparing Morton to figures in epic traditions may seem far-fetched, but actually it's not: Morton was a good storyteller, and storytelling strengths like his are evident elsewhere in oral tradition; his story can be read as an American odyssey, with its particularly American brand of near misses and narrow escapes, of Sirens, Circes, and monsters, of far-flung travels and homecomings. And, as we shall see, Jelly Roll faced his own death with a degree of courage that can only be described as heroic. We should remember, too, that the African American oral tradition allows mock-epic heroes like Stagolee the same privilege as Odysseus when he shouts out his true name to the Cyclops, having tricked him first with the phony name Noman. That kind of verbal one-upmanship has always been an essential ingredient in the black linguistic experience, from the ballads of Stagolee to blues lyrics, from street talk to rap and hip-hop—even in such forms as "playing the dozens," in which the combatants try to outdo each other by insulting the opponent's mamma, starting with something as simple and straightforward as "Your mamma don't wear no drawers." Morton mastered those traditions, just as he mastered the musical forms of blues, ragtime, and jazz. In New York City, one of his favorite spots for practicing his verbal skill was the street corner outside the Rhythm Club on West 133rd Street, as clarinetist Barney Bigard recalls:

> Jelly was kicks. He was never a bitter person right up to the end. He always loved to fuss and argue with somebody. He knew it all. He was a big shot at that time [circa 1930] and could always talk a good fight. He and Chick Webb would stand on a street corner and argue so bad you could have become rich selling tickets. Chick would just rile him to get him going. Jelly would tell Chick he was the greatest and Chick would tell him[,] "Yeah? Well come around to see my band tonight. We just got a new arrangement on so and so," and Chick would hum him the whole thing out of his head. Top to bottom. Jelly would say: "That ain't shit. Listen to this one," and he'd go to humming his stuff. People would all gather around. They thought there was a fight going on I guess. It was a show, those two guys, Chick with his little crooked back and Jelly with that damned great diamond stuck in his teeth. I guess ordinary people had never seen nothing like that before.[8]

They thought there was a fight going on I guess. Bigard implies that, really, there was no fight, just verbal jousting and good acting. In fact, though, the two men really were rivals: in 1930 Morton represented the older generation of New Orleans pioneers, Webb the younger generation that created the swing era; Morton's fortunes were about to take a nosedive; Webb's were about to soar. Hard to imagine there was no real venom in the verbal darts the two aimed at each other, just as it's hard to imagine that the exchange of cutting insults about "your mamma" in playing the dozens never draws blood. But to play the game means to pay the price, and that means maintaining the fiction that it's just a game. Only sore losers get angry. Morton's bragging occasionally had the bitter overtone of jealousy or even of defeat, especially toward the end, but its basis was the sweet babble of black street talk, the poetic license that allowed the combatants to think the unthinkable and say the unsayable, like the Fool in Shakespeare's *King Lear*, whose comic persona gives him license to tweak the king with the truth. In his autobiography, the trumpeter Rex Stewart remembers a typical Jelly Roll performance:

> Sometimes one of the guys would needle Jelly just for the fun of it. Then he would really perform, pulling out his clippings, his contracts and his photos of himself with the greats of that era. He always had an audience, and, to our uninitiated ears, his pronouncements and declarations were way out. "You little pipsqueak," he would yell, "who the hell do you think you're talking to? I'm the 'Jelly Roll.' I invented this music . . . See these diamonds? My music bought 'em. There's enough dough in these stones to buy and sell your whole damn family! Don't you try to tell me nothing about my music, you little no-blowin', hardshirt-wearin' sapsucker." And the crowd would roar.[9]

Stewart and Bigard quite rightly portray Morton's street-corner oratory as a performance tailor-made for a specific context and audience. In both anecdotes, someone "needles" or "riles" Jelly to get the game going. Stewart's comment—"Then he would really perform"—suggests that Morton was already performing and that goading him would merely kick him into high gear. And, in both instances, the crowd reacts with delight and fascination. However, outside of that context, minus that audience, Morton's bragging could come off as abrasive self-aggrandizement. Kenneth Hultsizer, a fan who wrote a brief reminiscence of his conversations with Morton in Washington, D.C., astutely warned Lowell Williams, a young man taking notes for an article on Jelly Roll, that "it was fun to listen to Jelly Roll talk but that he was given to exaggeration. That his conversation was enjoyable and amusing to listen to but if reproduced in impersonal print without Jelly Roll's warm personality it was certain to make Jelly Roll sound like a paranoiac."[10] Viewed in the wrong light, the distortions of the comic persona can make it appear as a grotesque rather than as a caricature.

Morton was a man of many masks, especially at the beginning of his career: pool hustler, card shark, pimp, vaudevillian, pianist, composer, bandleader. He did not focus exclusively on music until after his five-year stay on the West Coast, from 1917 to 1923. When he left Los Angeles for Chicago in 1923, he was thirty-two years old; he had less than twenty years to live, but for the first time his focus was clearly on music. The reasons for that rather dramatic shift make up the main theme of this book, but the years before his stay on the West Coast provide valuable insights into Morton's complex personality, into the personae that preceded the great shift and in some ways laid the groundwork for it.

Before 1917–23, music served either as a front for Morton's various illegal activities, as we shall see, or as an adjunct to his work in vaudeville. Lawrence Gushee's chronology of Morton's early years shows that Jelly Roll served a fairly long apprenticeship in vaudeville, where, among other roles, he performed as a blackface comedian—a persona if there ever was one. As onerous as the blackface stereotype seems by today's measure of political correctness, it actually involved a highly ironic interplay of racial identities: it began among white minstrels as a racial caricature of blacks, but it was quickly picked up by black minstrels as a caricature of white people's stereotyped notions about blacks. The irony implicit in that kind of manipulation would not have been lost on Morton, as sensitive as he was about the issue of race. For him, the experience must have been a kind of initiation into the role or roles he was expected to play as a black performer. His performance as a comedian received mixed reviews, though. It was evidently not his most successful role. His old friend Reb Spikes once spoke of this period: "I met Jelly in Tulsa, Oklahoma, in 1912[,] and we had a show. He thought he was a funny man and, my god, he was as funny as a sick baby. He never made nobody laugh. He'd black up (he was very light, you know) and come out and sit at the piano and tell jokes and play some rags and nobody ever laughed and so one day I told him to cut out the funny crap and stick to the piano crap and he'd do all right."[11] Morton was much funnier in his role as street-corner braggart than he was as Stepin Fetchit.

His most successful and most carefully crafted persona was the one called Jelly Roll Morton. The bragging was a part of that, but there was a good deal of onstage showmanship too, which he must have picked up in vaudeville. In *Mister Jelly Roll*, Morton's wife, Mabel, describes a typical performance with the Red Hot Peppers, as his 1920s band was called: "The band all wore black tuxedos, but Jelly Roll wore a wine-red jacket and tie to match, white pants and white shoes. He directed the band himself, used to cut a lot of capers, then sit down at the piano with that great big smile of his, and, I'm telling you, he was a sensation. . . . He took the solos on piano[,] and then the rest of the band . . . would just stop dead and all the people would gather around the stand to hear."[12] Even in his heyday, when he was performing before mostly white audiences, his sense of stage presence came straight from the same tradition that has informed the work of black artists from vaudevillians to Cab Calloway to James Brown and beyond. (See fig. 1.) The great pianist James P. Johnson once recalled a solo performance by the great Jelly Roll in a New York nightclub during the 1920s:

> I've seen Jelly Roll Morton, who had a great attitude, approach a piano. He would take his overcoat off. It had a special lining that would catch everybody's eye. So he would turn it inside out instead of folding it, he would lay it lengthwise along the top of the upright very solemnly as if that coat was worth a fortune and had to be handled very tenderly.
>
> Then he's take a big silk handkerchief, shake it out to show it off properly, and dust off the stool. He's sit down then, hit his special chord (every tickler had his special trademark chord, like a signal) and he's be gone! The first rag he'd play was always a spirited one to astound the audience.[13]

Morton approaches the piano here with an air of solemn ritual, like a priestly celebrant approaching the altar for a High Mass.

Figure 1. Flyer for Jelly Roll Morton, "the originator of jazz and stomps," 1927. Courtesy Historic New Orleans Collection.

Certainly, the priestly persona would not have been foreign to Jelly Roll, born and baptized a Roman Catholic, like most New Orleans Creoles. The phrase *priestly persona* fits the previous scene particularly well because of its associations with myth, ritual, and drama. In "Remembering Jimmy," a lovely, nostalgic, elegant essay on singer Jimmy Rushing, Ralph Ellison writes,

Rushing, along with the other jazz musicians whom we knew, had made a choice, had dedicated himself to a mode of expression and a way of life no less "righteously" than others dedicated themselves to the church. Jazz and blues did not fit into the scheme of things as spelled out by our two main institutions, the church and the school, but they gave expression to attitudes which found no place in these and helped to give our lives some sense of wholeness. Jazz and the public jazz dance was a third institution in our lives and a vital one; and though Jimmy was far from being a preacher, he was, as official floor manager or master-of-the-dance at Slaughter's Hall, the leader of a public rite.[14]

The writer Albert Murray confirms Ellison's insight into the ritual basis of the tradition: the "mission" of performance "is not only to drive the blues away and hold them at bay . . . but also to evoke an ambiance of Dionysian revelry in the process"; and, Murray adds, even though performers like Morton worked mostly in dance halls, nightclubs, and vaudeville theaters, "they were at the same time fulfilling a central role in a ceremony that was at once a purification rite and a celebration the festive earthiness of which was tantamount to a fertility ritual."[15] Symbolically, the performer becomes the hero of the myth, the priest of the ritual, the protagonist of the drama— in Ellison's phrase, "the leader of a public rite." What we know of Morton's approach to performance confirms the insights of both Ellison and Murray into the ritual basis of music and dance in the African American tradition, and the persona known as Jelly Roll Morton was his response to the demands that the role placed on him. Even his performance as street-corner braggart was a kind of miniature ritual, with definite roles assigned to both the congregation and the celebrant.

Ironically, the only photograph of Morton performing on stage shows him in his Stepin Fetchit mode with a light-skinned woman partner. In later years, Jelly Roll's publicity posters and ads would extend the connection between his performances and blackface imagery, though most often it is his sidemen, tiny in comparison to Morton's large, smiling face, that wear the blackface. In the 1930s, Morton managed a Washington, D.C., nightclub called the Jungle Inn, and ads for the club in the local papers have as a kind of logo a cartoon of a piano player in blackface. Oddly enough, in many of his regular publicity photos of the 1920s he looks somewhat formal and even solemn. Only in the informal photos taken by Danny Barker and others on the streets of Harlem in the 1930s does Jelly Roll look relaxed and at ease with the camera.

Anyone who has ever posed for a photo or taken one gets a sense of posing as a kind of miniperformance, as a presentation of a persona. Morton's photos show him to be light-skinned, his nose long and straight and just a hint of a dimple on his chin. Two small creases between his eyebrows suggest a permanent frown, but, as if to offset that impression, he has two sets of doubled smile lines framing his mouth and making his broad, warm smile seem even broader and warmer—though in some photos, when he forces a smile, they make it seem even more forced. In the 1920s photos, his hair looks straight and slick. In the 1930s (hard times must have taken hair treatments out of the budget), his hair looks to be something between curly and kinky.

As his appearance suggests, Morton lived his life in the no-man's-land of color and race in America. In 1923, when the famous New Orleans Rhythm Kings, an all-white band, brought him to Richmond, Indiana, to record with them, they passed him off as Cuban to get him lodgings in the rooming house where they were staying. Born and baptized Roman Catholic, he died having been anointed with oil consecrated by a Roman Catholic priest; but there was fear gripping his failing heart because he believed his bad luck and ill health had come from a voodoo curse. He thought of himself as Creole, and, as with most Creoles, that meant he did not think of himself primarily as a Negro. Lomax claims that "Jelly Roll's whole life was constructed around his denial of his Negro status,"[16] and at the end of the Broadway hit musical *Jelly's Last Jam*, George Wolfe has Morton carried off to hell for that denial. In Lomax's book, Mabel Morton says, "Really, Jelly Roll didn't like Negroes. He said they would mess up your business. And Negroes didn't like him." [17] But Mabel, too, was a Creole, and Creoles have good reason to consider themselves a distinct ethnic group: their French (sometimes Spanish) names, their Creole brand of the French language, their cuisine, their particular blend of French, Spanish, and African ancestry and culture all distinguish them from other African Americans as well as from whites. Jelly complained loudly about some of his musicians, calling them "niggers acting rowdy" who messed up his gigs by drinking on the bandstand. [18] But he certainly knew he was not white and must have heard himself called "nigger" on many occasions. In fact, he once had to leave a small Mississippi town in a big hurry because rumor had it that he was sleeping with the white woman who ran the roadhouse where he was playing piano; and more than once in his travels through the Southeast he heard about lynchings. [19] His ambivalence on the subject of race and color is not so much a "denial" as it is a recognition that, in America, the color of your skin is a kind of destiny.

At this point it may be tempting to ask, "Can we ever know the *real* Jelly Roll Morton?" But that is the wrong question. For one thing, masks have a reality of their own, just as dramas do. People who ask, "Is *Oedipus Rex* a true story?" miss the point: in one sense it is a fiction; in another, more important sense, the story is more "true" than the headlines in today's newspapers. For another thing, if by "the *real* Jelly Roll" we mean the private as opposed to the public person, the evidence is too scanty. Even the Library of Congress interviews are a public performance, with the persona fully formed and in place. The mask slips only on occasion—for instance, saying that he only "half believed" in voodoo, Jelly admits "in a confiding moment of weariness" his belief that the decline of his career in the 1930s was brought about by a voodoo curse. [20] If he really only "half believed" in voodoo, the half that believed was far stronger than the half that did not. Lomax presents the story as an extraordinary moment of self-revelation, but neither he nor subsequent writers have given the subject of voodoo in Morton's life the attention it deserves. The story Morton tells about his attempts to exorcise those

demons helps to put his bragging and his brash self-confidence in a surprisingly poignant light.

Another moment of self-revelation comes in the excerpts from letters
he wrote to his friend Roy Carew at about the time of the Lomax interviews. Sick and at times dispirited, Morton somehow found the courage
and energy to forge ahead in spite of the odds stacked against him. Perhaps the most touching passage occurs in a 30 May 1939 letter, which describes the moment he learned just how sick he was: "I went to the hospital for my check up and tried to explain all I could concerning myself,
well, I was examined again, hardening of the arteries of the heart and was
told that it was incurable, but that if I did not exert myself I would . . .
do all right. I was very sad over the report at first[,] 'but' [*sic*] after a second thought, I had a different decision. I was not expecting to live when
I went there, and I am at least living yet. Then again we have a much
greater power that has something to say about those things—that's the
Supreme Power above."[21] Mabel Morton's version of the story supports
Jelly's: the doctors told her that he could live another ten or fifteen years
if he stopped performing—in other words, if he stopped playing the piano.[22] But Morton could not accept life on those terms. This courage
and intense dedication to his art in his final years have been sadly over-
shadowed by the persona of Jelly Roll the braggart.

But if Ellison and Murray are right, wearing the mask is not simple
masquerade: if the performer's role is as vital as Ellison says it is, it can
perhaps tell us more about the "real" Jelly Roll than a mere recitation of
facts and historically verifiable dates and figures. The real question is not
"Can we ever know the *real* Jelly Roll Morton?" but "What does the creation tell us about the creator?" Or, put another way, "What does the
mask tell us about its maker?" To answer that question, we must first
avoid a pitfall marked by Ellison in another essay, a review of *Bird: The
Legend of Charlie Parker*, edited by Robert Reisner. After reminding the
reader that the word *legend* originally meant "the life of a saint," Ellison
remarks that Reisner "prefers to participate in the recreation of Bird's
legend rather than perform the critical function of analyzing it."[23] In

other words, we should not confuse the mask and the man, but neither should we dismiss the mask as an artificial barrier to knowing the "real" man. To paraphrase Ellison, we should resist merely re-creating the legend of Jelly Roll and instead perform the critical function of analyzing the complex relationship between the mask and the man.

Nothing expresses the complexities of that relationship better than the name itself: like the persona, the name "Jelly Roll Morton" was a deliberate creation. Jelly's "real" name was discovered only recently, in the 1980s, thanks to the diligent research of Lawrence Gushee. In Lomax's transcriptions of the interviews, Morton's last name is spelled La Menthe, but that was evidently a transcriber's guess at a phonetic spelling of what Morton said. His first name, Ferdinand, was bestowed upon him by his godmother, but he claims that he himself changed his last name because he didn't want to be called "Frenchy"; in fact, Morton got his last name from his stepfather, Willie Morton, a porter.[24] And the name Morton itself is an anglicized version of Mouton.[25] Until recently, no one was sure of the exact spelling of La Menthe or of his birth date, which he himself changed to suit the needs of the moment. When Lomax asked the family about these details, they claimed ignorance. Morton's sister Amide replied, "I don't know for sure. . . . We tried to find out, but the old parish church had burnt with all the birth records."[26] More misinformation. The baptismal certificate turned up at another church, in another parish, the one where the Morton family had lived at the time of his birth. The document, discovered by Lawrence Gushee in the early 1980s, establishes that he was born on 20 October 1890 and baptized on 25 April 1891. The name is spelled Ferdinand Joseph Lemott, but even that spelling was corrected by Gushee to Lamothe.[27]

As for the misinformation, Gushee notes that "the church that did burn did not lose its records" and concludes, "Assuming that Lomax correctly recorded their thought, they [the family] were wrong or deliberately misleading. I find it difficult to believe that Uncle Henry [Monette] would have been ignorant of the facts of the matter."[28] Gushee's suspicions are well founded. Although his research indicates that Morton's recollections of his professional activities are remarkably accurate, he and his relatives were often "deliberately misleading" when it came to family matters. For instance, when Lomax asked Uncle Henry about whether Jelly's godmother, Eulalie Echo (probably spelled Hecaud), later known as Laura Hunter, was a voodoo practitioner, "old Henry hooted at the idea" and said, "No, she was nothing of the kind," even though many sources—including Morton himself—attest to the fact that she was.[29] Morton's sister, at one point in the interview, complains, "My people never told us children nothin'. . . . I barely know anything about my own father and mother."[30] The practice of lying or being "deliberately misleading" to both outsiders and family members about personal matters comes up again and again in this story.

The name "Jelly Roll" is even more significant than any of Morton's given names because it was a matter of conscious choice. According to his own version of the story, he adopted the nickname when he was working in vaudeville with Sandy Burns, "the blackface comedian and the first eccentric dancer in the United States":

> One night while working ad lib in the stage, doing comedy, Sandy said to me, "You don't know who you're talking to." I said, "I don't care." Right there we had a little argument and I finally asked him who was he? He said he was Sweet Papa Cream Puff, right out of the bakery shop.
>
> That seemed to produce a great big laugh and I was standing there mugging, and the thought came to me that I better say something about a bakery shop, so I said to him that he didn't know who *he* was talking to. He wanted to get acquainted, and I told him I was Sweet Papa Jelly Roll with stove pipes in my hips and all the women just dying to turn my damper down! From then on the name stuck to me.[31]

Anyone familiar with the African American blues tradition knows that the term *jelly roll* is sexual—both phallic (the shape of the pastry) and vaginal (as in "I'm going to put some jelly in your roll"—a standard blues line). According to *The Story of English* by McCrum, MacNeil, and Cran,

> In the African language Mandingo, *jeli* is a minstrel who gains popu-
> larity with women through skill in words and music. In the English
> Creole of the Caribbean, jelly refers to the meat of the coconut
> when it is still at a white, viscous state, and in a form closely resem-
> bling semen. . . . On the street, jelly roll had many associated mean-
> ings, from the respectable "lover," or "spouse," to the Harlem slang
> of the 1930's "a term for the vagina."[32]

Paul Oliver, in *Blues Fell This Morning*, cites a typical use in blues lyrics by Peg Leg Howell and His Gang:

> Jelly-roll, jelly-roll, ain't so hard to find.
> Ain't a baker shop in town bake 'em brown like mine.
> I got a sweet jelly roll,
> If you taste my jelly, it'll satisfy your worried soul.
> I never been to church and I never been to school,
> Come down to jelly I'm a jelly-rollin' fool.
> I got a sweet jelly to satisfy my worried soul
> I likes my jelly and I like to have my fun.[33]

In other words, *jelly roll* can be understood on four distinct levels: first, on the literal level, it is the pastry found in bakeries; second, as a meta-phor, it connotes the male and female sex organs; third, etymologically, it survives from the Mandingo *jeli;* fourth, as the phrase "bake 'em brown like mine" suggests, the term has racial connotations as well.

Morton's nickname amounts to sexual bragging, as does his other, lesser known, nickname, "Winding Boy," or "Winding Ball" (here too Lomax's transcription may be faulty—the Library of Congress record-ing itself suggests the latter spelling). Lomax reports that "winding" means "rotating the hips in dancing or in sexual intercourse" and quotes the banjoist Johnny St. Cyr to support that reading: "Winding Boy . . . means a fellow that makes good jazz [i.e., sex] with the women."[34] The refrain of the song includes a reference to Stavin Chain, a blues man notorious for the sexual content of his lyrics:

> I'm the Windin' Ball, don't deny my name. (Three times)
> Pick it up and shake it like sweet Stavin Chain
> Never b'lieve in havin' one woman at a time. (Three times)
> I always have six, seven, eight or nine.
> I had that gal, had her in the grass. (Three times)
> One day she got so scared a snake run up her big ass.
> Dime's worth of beefsteak, nickel's worth 'a lard. (Three times)
> I'm gonna salivate your pussy till my peter gets hard.[35]

That was the version that Morton sang—twice—for Lomax at the Library of Congress. But for the two commercial recordings, from 1939 and 1940, Morton eliminated the really "vulgar" lyrics and changed the title to "Winin' Boy." Oddly enough, in Lomax's book, Morton claims that the name came from his habit of mixing leftover wines at the end of a night's work at Hilma Burt's house in Storyville.[36] But on two of the Library of Congress versions he recorded for Alan Lomax, he explains that he took to singing "smutty" songs to avoid the stigma of effeminacy associated with male piano players in those days: "Of course, when a man played piano, the stamp was on him for life, the femininity stamp. And I didn't want that on, so of course when I did start to playin', the songs was kind of smutty, a bit—not so smutty, but something like this."[37] Perhaps Lomax distorted the material in an effort to "clean it up," just as Morton did for the commercial recording—or tried to do. Actually, he didn't alter the signature verse one iota, and there the sexual content lies barely hidden: "don't deny my name," he sings: "Pick it up and shake it like sweet Stavin Chain," as if his name has become a phallus that he has to *pick up*, suggesting something of its size and weight.

In *Mister Jelly Roll*, Mabel Morton confides something to Lomax that allows us to peek behind the persona of sexual braggadocio: "No, the truth about Mister Jelly Roll—the actual facts about Mister Jelly Roll was that he was not what you call a very high-sexed man. No, not a very high-sexed man. It was just once in a while with him. When that mood would strike him, yes, but otherwise he was too wrapped up in his *own* music. Often he told me he had no time for such foolishness; he had other things to think about. He used to go to bed thinking about music and get up whistling, dotting down those dots and poking those piano keys."[38] The "real" Morton, it seems, had very little use for jelly roll—an indication of the distance between the public role and the private person.

However little he valued sex privately, though, it certainly played a large part in his business and professional life. His experience with prostitution came early when, in his teens, he played piano in the sporting houses of Storyville, the notorious red-light district of New Orleans. He often admitted—boasted, really—that one of his specialties as a street hustler was pimping. In fact, until his 1917–23 stay on the West Coast, it seems that he was unsure of his focus—whether it was to be vaudeville, piano playing, pimping, or pool hustling, another of his sidelines. The entertainer and nightclub owner Ada "Bricktop" Smith remembers that "I really got to know Jelly Roll Morton at Murray's [the Cadillac Cafe in Los Angeles, circa 1917]. He was still there trying to figure out what to do with his life. He couldn't decide whether to be a pimp or a piano player. I told him to be both."[39]

On the other hand, critic William Russell views Morton's West Coast years as "Jelly's happiest and most prosperous," and adds: "He could have his big car, his diamond, and could keep his music as a sideline for special kicks while he made his real money from the Pacific Coast 'Line' [i.e., prostitution]. As one friend put it, 'You don't think Jelly got all those diamonds he wore on his garters with the $35 a week he made in music.' But whether Jelly was really 'one of the higher ups,' as he claimed, or just a procurer, is immaterial, for Jelly's real interest undeniably was music."[40] And evidently Morton was not alone among musicians in treating music as though it were a sideline. The jazz pianist Joe Sullivan once said, "Every hot piano player had a secret ambition to be a pimp or a pool shark or both."[41] And the bassist Pops Foster in his autobiography states emphatically, "All musicians back in New Orleans wanted to be pimps. . . . Pimping in those days was a lot of guys' head line and Jelly Roll was one of them. He only played piano as a sideline because you had to prove you were doing some kind of work or they'd put you in jail. Jelly was very good looking and had some good women."[42]

Nowadays, we think of Morton primarily as a pianist, composer, and bandleader, and his activities as a pool shark and pimp have receded into the background, if they are in the picture at all. In fact, though, from his early teens until he was about thirty-two, he used his music as a front for his hustling. For the next decade, however, his focus seldom wandered very far from music. What happened to effect such a dramatic turnabout? It could be mere coincidence that he became so sharply focused on music after 1923, but in this case the change is so dramatic that it amounts almost to a kind of conversion. Not that he was ever casual about his music; James P. Johnson heard him play in New York in 1911 and testifies that Morton was The Man on piano that early.[43] Some of his best and most famous compositions were written before 1917: "Wolverine Blues," "King Porter Stomp," "Jelly Roll Blues," and "Froggie Moore" (one of many variant spellings of this title), to name just a few. But the West Coast years do seem to have been fertile artistically: compositions like "The Pearls," "Kansas City Stomps," "Dead Man Blues," and "Mamanita," among others, date from that time. Lawrence Gushee concludes, "During this period, although Morton still on occasion functioned as a vaudeville performer, he seems to me to have pretty definitively cast his lot with piano playing, both as soloist and orchestra leader. It is my impression, also, that the majority of the compositions he recorded in Chicago between 1923 and 1928 stem from those West Coast years."[44] Gushee's view is supported by both the copyright list in Lomax's book and the "Chronology of Compositions" in Morton's *Ferdinand "Jelly Roll" Morton: The Collected Piano Music*, edited by James Dapogny.[45] His first copyrights for any of his compositions are 15 September 1915 for "Jelly Roll Blues" and 15 May 1918 for "Froggie Moore," published in Los Angeles by the Spikes brothers publishing company. His publishing career didn't really hit its stride, however, before 1923, even though much of the newly published work had been written years earlier—like the "King Porter Stomp," written around 1906 but published in 1924. In fact, Morton's version of why he left Los Angeles for Chicago has to do with a copyright dispute with the Spikes brothers over "Wolverine Blues," which he believed they planned to steal from him.[46] Quite suddenly, it seems, Morton's primary concern became publishing and recording his music.

We may never know exactly how Morton's "conversion" came about, but there is enough evidence to form at least some sort of hypothesis. Quite likely, more than one element came into play. Perhaps the most important of these is the woman who called herself Anita Gonzales. A light-skinned Creole, Anita got to know Morton in Biloxi, Mississippi, around 1902 (possibly earlier) through her brothers, Bill and Dink Johnson, musicians who often worked with Jelly Roll, and through his godmother, Laura Hunter, who maintained a summer place in Biloxi. As was the case with Jelly, Anita's name presents a mystery, though in her case an unsolved one. She was born Bessie Johnson, but no one knows when and why she changed it. One theory is that, as a proud Creole woman, she preferred not to be considered Negro or "colored," and that a Spanish name seemed more suitable—even though in the West there was as much or more prejudice against Mexicans as there was against African Americans. That prejudice, however, seems not to have been as strong in Nevada, where Anita ran a saloon business. The census lists for most of the state in 1910, about the time that she settled there, describe all people with Hispanic surnames as "white," so perhaps the change of names made it easier for her to do business and to own real estate—as we shall see, she was light-skinned enough to pass as a Latina. At any rate, in *Mister Jelly Roll* Anita recalls that "Jelly used to come over and see me [in Biloxi], making like it was to visit my brothers. I never gave him a second look because he wasn't decent. Used to play piano in a sporting-house."[47] When Morton arrived in Los Angeles, Anita had already been a saloon keeper in Las Vegas for several years, but they got together soon after—probably within a year of his arrival. She recalls, "When I met him again in California, I didn't know it was the same man. My brother, Dink Johnson, introduced us again and then we got together. For a while we were very happy."[48] Although both Jelly and Anita have been quoted as saying that she was the only woman he ever really loved, they separated in 1922 or 1923 for reasons that have never been made entirely clear.[49] In the Lomax interviews, Morton's feelings of regret over losing Anita are palpable: "I couldn't wish for a finer woman than Anita. In fact, I don't believe there was ever one born finer than Anita and I know I've missed an awful lot by leaving her. It was all a mistake, but nevertheless it happened."[50]

The depth of feeling that Morton betrays on the subject of Anita suggests that, whatever else happened to him on the West Coast, his encounter with her must have been at the center of his experience there, and that Anita played a major role in whatever change took place. Her influence may have been musical as well as personal; at least three of Morton's compositions are directly connected to her: "Mamanita" and "Sweet Anita Mine" both bear her name, and she wrote the lyrics (seldom performed) to "Dead Man Blues." And it seems quite likely that his return to Los Angeles at the end of his life had at least as much to do with Anita as with anything else. But more about that later.

Another likely impetus for Morton's change was the combined influence of his godmother, the voodoo priestess Eulalie Echo–Laura Hunter, and voodoo itself. According to Jelly Roll and his family, Laura was as responsible for raising him as his own natural mother, and it was apparently through Laura that he was first exposed to voodoo.[51] In *Mister Jelly Roll*, he remembers that he would often stay with her when he was about eleven and that "she used to monkey around with this spiritual business." He even speculated that "here, late years [the 1930s], I have often thought many of my troubles came from my being around during those seances when my godmother fooled around with that underground stuff."[52] According to her death certificate, she moved from New Orleans to Los Angeles in 1919, just after her godson arrived. Also, Laura's death in 1940 was the reason he gave to his wife, Mabel, for his return to Los Angeles: he was worried that someone would take advantage of his old, blind godfather and make off with Laura's jewelry.[53] There is good reason to believe he misled Mabel about this, but Laura's strong presence during three of the most crucial times in his life cannot be denied. The trouble is, we don't know much more about Laura than the facts I have just spelled out. However, we do know a good deal about voodoo practices in New Orleans and elsewhere, and that knowledge should help to fill out the picture at least a bit more.

There were social factors that came into play as well. From about 1910 to 1920, many of the heretofore legal red-light districts were shut down by the authorities in cities like New Orleans, Los Angeles, and San Francisco; then, Prohibition went into effect in 1919 and changed the conditions under which nightclubs and dance halls operated, as did the rise of organized crime that Prohibition brought about. And finally, the coming-of-age of the recording industry revolutionized the music business. The new medium allowed artists like Morton to advertise their work to an extent never before imagined, and eventually created a national rather than a purely local market. However, the effects of this development were not always positive ones: for one thing, the concentration of power in the hands of a few media giants meant that artists like Morton had less and less control over their work; for another, the constant demand for novelty that the new medium created meant that what was new yesterday would be obsolete tomorrow. Morton's case is typical: in about five years (circa 1925–30) he went from star to has-been.

2

In the interval between his departure from and his return to Los Angeles, Morton's life was an exact replica of the country's boom-and-bust cycle. During the Roaring Twenties, his career in music reached its peak. He and his Red Hot Peppers made some of the most popular and artistically satisfying records of the period, toured all over the East and the Midwest, and made piles of money. And he knew how to spend it. His wife, Mabel Bertrand Morton, whom he married in 1928, describes his high style of living:

> He was all diamonds, those days. He wore a ring with a diamond as big as a dime and a diamond horseshoe in his tie. He carried a locket with diamonds set all around it. His watch was circled in diamonds. His belt buckle was in gold and studded with diamonds. He even had sock-supporters of solid gold set with diamonds. Then you could see that big half-carat diamond sparkling in his tooth. That year [circa 1929–30] they called him the diamond king.
>
> Jelly used to dress so well that he used to pay fifteen and twenty dollars at Kaplan's for his pajamas and underwear. When I met him, he had about one-hundred-fifty suits, and overcoats of all kinds— some out of this "melton" material, one of beaver, one lined with muskrat and several more. He had fifteen or twenty pairs of shoes[,] too many shirts and ties to mention.
>
> Jelly liked the best. He would always tell me, "Never mind tomorrow. Tomorrow will take care of itself." [54]

During the 1920s, the world seemed full of people who lived by the motto "Never mind tomorrow. Tomorrow will take care of itself." Then suddenly, a dark tomorrow came and plunged that world into the Great Depression of the 1930s, and Morton's fortunes took a nosedive, just like everyone else's. Victor, the company that had issued all of his classic Red Hot Peppers recordings, was on the verge of financial collapse and let him go, though it continued issuing the existing recordings until 1934. From 9 October 1930 to 23 May 1938, when he began the Library of Congress interviews with Lomax, his only commercial recording date took place on 15 August 1934, when he was recorded as a sideman on a Wingy Manone session—and those recordings were not released until 1948.[55] In other words, after October 1930, Morton made no commercial recordings under his own name until a solo session in December 1938, in Washington, D.C., a hiatus of over eight years.

In August of 1938, near the end of that hiatus, Morton was stabbed in a brawl that took place in the Jungle Inn, the Washington dive that he had been managing for a woman named Cordelia. Mabel describes what happened:

> One night one of these riff-raff got to acting rowdy and Ferd called him. The fellow used some bad language. Ferd slapped him. Then he sat down at the piano and began to play and the fellow stabbed him the first time in the head, and, when Ferd turned, he stabbed him just above the heart. Then Ferd grabbed him and they went down.
>
> I was back of the bar mixing a Pink Lady when I heard the scuffle. When I came out from behind the bar I couldn't tell which was which, they were so covered with blood. The blood was just gushing out of Ferd like out of a stuck beef. I took a heavy glass ashtray and I struck this young man just as hard as I could in the head. Then we pulled Ferd away—Ferd was on top by then—and Ferd grabbed an iron pipe and was going to kill him, but Cordelia grabbed Ferd and the fellow got away.
>
> Some of these Polock [*sic*] cops they have in Washington came in and we took Ferd to the hospital. Took him in there and laid him right under an electric fan and put some ice-packs on the wound. Said that would clog the blood. I think right there was where he got his bad heart and the asthma—right there in that lousy Washington hospital.[56]

Morton never recovered his health; at the age of forty-eight he had already begun his three-year slide into the grave. Mabel convinced him to return to New York at the end of 1938, just after the solo recording session in December. He tried valiantly to resume playing and composing, but he just wasn't the same Jelly Roll Morton anymore. Lomax recalls meeting Morton by chance on a subway stair in New York: "He had to stop every few steps to get his breath; then, after a moment of cough-ing, he went on in a weak voice with his plans for suing ASCAP and breaking MCA. He was often tired, he told me. His composing had slowed down."[57] (See fig. 2, where Morton looks very thin and tired.)

By the 17th of April 1939, his condition had deteriorated to the point where he had to be hospitalized for three weeks and, as noted, doctors warned that he would live for another ten or fifteen years only if he stopped playing the piano. In spite of this warning, he was back in the recording studio within a month of his release from the hospital.[58] And in November of 1940, within a year of his release, he took it upon him-self to drive cross-country alone, through a series of snowstorms, to re-turn to Los Angeles.

Why, with his failing health, would he undertake such an exhausting journey at just that moment, at that time of year? Mabel says that Mor-ton left New York for California in November of 1940 because he learned of the death of his godmother, Laura Hunter. As already mentioned, he told Mabel he was worried about her jewels because his old godfather was blind and could be swindled easily.[59] Anita's account agrees with Mabel's story about the haste with which Morton traveled to California when he heard of his godmother's death. But she adds a new twist:

> The woman, Laura Hunter, who raised Jelly Roll, was a voodoo witch. Yes, I'm talking about his godmother who used to be called Eulalie Echo. She made a lot of money at voodoo. People were al-ways coming to her for some help and she was giving them beads and pieces of leather and all that. Well, everybody knows that before you can become a witch you have to sell the person you love the best to Satan as a sacrifice. . . . She loved Jelly better than Ed, her own husband. Jelly always knew she'd sold him to Satan and that, when she died, he'd die too—she would take him down with her.
>
> Laura taken sick in 1940 and here came Jelly Roll driving his Lin-coln all the way from New York. Laura died. And then Jelly, in spite that I had financed him a new start in the music business and he was beginning to feel himself again, he taken sick, too. A couple months

THE NEW YORK AMSTERDAM NEWS

Harlem After Dark

NITELIFE · · GOSSIP · · FEATURES

Crescendo Club Attends Premiere

Pictured here are members of
the Crescendo Club who turned
out for the premiere of All Negro Movie "Moon Over Harlem"
at the Regent Theatre last
Thursday. Seated, front row, left
to right: Miss Kay Parker, Eubie Blake, second row; Cecil Mc-
Pherson, Lucky Roberts, Chris
Smith, James P. Johnson, Porter
Granger, Claude Hopkins; third
row; Joe Jordan, Tim Brymn,
Wen Talbert, Henry Troy; standing in rear; Andy Razaf, J. C.
Johnson, president, Lawrence
Deas, Jelly-Roll Morton, Perry
Bradford, Edgar Sampson.

Figure 2.   The Crescendo Club in New York, evidently a social club for black musicians, at the 1939 premiere of the black gangster movie *Moon over Harlem*. Morton is standing in the back, fourth from left. Courtesy *New York Amsterdam News* and Historic New Orleans Collection.

later he died in my arms, begging me to keep anointing his lips with oil that had been blessed by a bishop in New York. He had oil running all over him when he gave up the ghost.[60]

That statement is an important one for many reasons and should be scrutinized in detail, especially for what Anita says about voodoo. For the moment, however, we should note only that Anita attributes two motives to Morton's seemingly sudden move from New York to Los Angeles: first, the voodoo curse; second, the desire to make "a new start in the music business." And—a curious touch—she implies that Laura Hunter was still alive when Morton left New York. In contrast, Mabel says nothing about a voodoo curse; in her version, the motives had to do with the godmother's death and the jewels. And she says nothing about a "new start" in music. Also, she clearly implies that the godmother died in November: "In November of 1940, the news came that his godmother had passed away. He got terribly restless."[61] The question of Morton's motives for the move to California is part of the story to come. But the truth is, her certificate of death states that Laura Hunter died on 14 February 1940—fully nine months before Morton was supposed to have been told—and the informant named on that document is none other than Anita Ford, the same Anita that Morton had left behind nearly twenty years earlier, now married to John F. Ford.

Why the delay? Jelly Roll's letters to Roy Carew show that Morton knew of Laura's death in February, and that fact suggests the strong possibility that he was in touch with Anita at least nine months before his departure for Los Angeles. Did he keep the news from Mabel until he needed to use it as an excuse for a seemingly sudden departure? If so, why wait until November, when he would have to drive cross-country in all kinds of bad weather?

Morton's own death certificate raises even more questions. After a feeble attempt to rehearse a band for his West Coast comeback, his heart finally gave out on 10 July 1941 at Los Angeles County General Hospital. The certificate of death identifies the cause as "Cardiac Decompen-

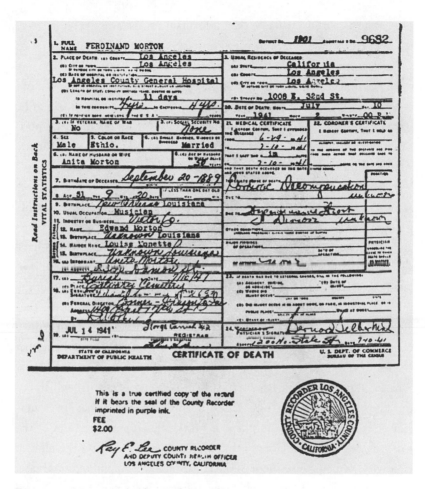

Figure 3. Morton's death certificate, 1941.

sation"—what we would call congestive heart failure these days—and indicates that he was buried in Calvary Cemetery, in east Los Angeles, on 16 July 1941.[62] (See fig. 3.) But the document also contains information that is either curious, questionable, or inaccurate. Under "Race or Color" it says "Ethio.," that is, Ethiopian; it says that he had been living in Los Angeles for four years, when he had moved from New York only nine months earlier; it names the informant as his wife, Anita *Morton*, when in fact Mabel, back in New York, was still his wife and, as far as anyone knows, he and Anita had never been legally married (and in any case, as noted above she was now Anita *Ford*). One more important piece of evidence should be cited here: Morton's deathbed will, in which he left everything—that is, all the future royalties from his many compositions—to his "beloved comforter, companion and help-meet for many years," Anita Gonzales.[63] To this day, the heirs of Anita's estate are collecting royalties from the music of Jelly Roll Morton.

The evidence is obviously incomplete and circumstantial, and it is difficult to make definitive answers to the questions raised by the discrepancies among various pieces of evidence. However, some writers have reached what seems to them the obvious conclusion, that Anita manipulated the situation to her own advantage, and that she is the villain of the piece. Harrison Smith, a promoter of jazz concerts and a sometime theater manager, implies as much in an interview with Bob Kumm. Smith claims that one of Morton's sisters, Frances Morton Oliver, told him that the family did not know of Morton's death until after the burial, and that "she could not reconcile herself to the authenticity of the will which bequeathed her 'the sum of one dollar'"; Smith concludes that "presentation of the will for probate purpose to [the] Surrogate's section of the Los Angeles Superior Court resulted in no-one protesting the alleged claim of Jelly being a resident of the City and State. Such being the case, acceptance was made of the claim as authentic information and the will was probated as valid."[64]

Clearly, Smith views the will as invalid, and his comments suggest that the misinformation on the death certificate was part of a deliberate ruse on Anita's part, intended to expedite the validation of the will. As we shall see, however, Smith had ulterior motives for questioning the validity of the will. Lomax's book ends with a brief passage that strongly implies a similar anti-Anita bias. After she describes Morton dying in her arms, "she . . . looked down at her diamond-studded hands at rest upon her silken lap. Then, with a quick smile, she did not forget to add. . . .

[*sic*] 'Be sure to mention my tourist camp in your book, Mr. Lomax. Our chicken dinners are recommended by Duncan Hines.'"[65] Promoting her chicken dinners just after describing the emotional deathbed scene certainly suggests crass commercial self-promotion at Morton's expense. Even worse, Lomax's mention of Anita's "diamond-studded hands upon her silken lap" implies, if only faintly, that she may have been the one who wound up with Laura Hunter's diamonds, which are mentioned twice in the closing pages of the book: once as the motive for Morton's hasty trip to Los Angeles, as noted above, and once in a letter from Morton in Los Angeles to Mabel in New York: "My godfather told me of many diamonds that my godmother left—all stolen and not one left. Some of their friends told me the same thing, too."[66]

The evidence is not conclusive, however. As valuable as Lomax's work is, it is curiously sketchy on the last year or so of Morton's life, especially on the last nine months in Los Angeles. The book becomes a real scissors-and-paste job at that point: a handful of letters from Morton to his wife, a copy of the obituary notice that appeared in *Down Beat* magazine, and Anita's description of the deathbed scene. Lomax makes little attempt to construct a narrative out of those elements, and he apparently made no attempt to examine the public documents that simultaneously shed light upon and raise questions about the events that took place between February 1940 and July 1941. Since the appearance of Lomax's book in 1950, however, more has come to light about that brief period, especially information included in Floyd Levin's excellent article "Untold Story of Jelly Roll Morton's Last Years." Also, many autobiographies of people that Morton knew and worked with have appeared since 1950, not to mention the oral history projects at places like the Rutgers University Institute of Jazz Studies and the Hogan Jazz Archive at Tulane University. None of those sources, though, have much to say about Anita. Until now, what was known about her came from Lomax—and most of that came from Morton's autobiographical narrative. Fortunately, I was able to get in touch with Anita's granddaughters, and they supplied me with information that has helped me to form a keener perception of what

Anita was all about and of what happened during the last year or two of Morton's life. Unfortunately, information about Laura Hunter is still conspicuously thin; however, the new evidence suggests a scenario that differs significantly from the conventional one first presented by Lomax, one that casts a kinder light on Anita's role in Jelly's last days. First, Morton's move to Los Angeles was not suddenly precipitated by his godmother's death—in fact, he had been thinking about it for some time; second, though he was hoping for some sort of miracle to keep him going, he knew he had not long to live and wanted to put his affairs in order; and finally, Anita was the only person he trusted to help him with that task. The other motives that have been suggested for the move may be partially valid, but it is precisely their status as half-truths that allowed Morton to use them as plausible explanations for his movements. His anxiety over Laura Hunter's diamonds may have been no more than a good job of acting for Mabel's benefit. And if Anita is right, some of his anxiety may have had more to do with voodoo than with jewelry. As for a "new start" for his career in music, one has to weigh that against the clear warning from the doctors in New York that he would not last another ten years if he continued to play piano. On three separate occasions, Morton made it clear that he intended to disregard the warning: first, in New York, on his way to a recording session just after his three-month stay in the hospital, he told Mabel, "Let me take my own chances" when she reminded him of what the doctors had said; and again, in a letter to Mabel from Los Angeles dated 20 November 1940, he wrote, "I will never be satisfied holding my hands doing nothing, because I like to make my own living." [67] And finally, there is the letter to Roy Carew, cited earlier, which expresses his decision to disregard the advice of his doctors. Clearly, Morton intended to continue playing until "the butcher cut him down," in the words of the old New Orleans funeral anthem "Didn't He Ramble?" Even though, as we shall see, he was literally praying for a miracle to keep him going, he was fully aware that any attempt to revive his career would only shorten his life.

At this point, an obvious question has to be asked: why bother with the sometimes petty, sometimes sordid details of Morton's last days? Until recently, it could be assumed that his best work was behind him; even the dozen or so new arrangements he brought with him to Los Angeles had supposedly been lost, and he was too weak to sustain a consistent effort to make gigs or recording dates. The final trip to Los Angeles would seem to be, literally, a dead end, a final chorus of the "Dead Man Blues." However, the new arrangements apparently have surfaced among the papers of the collector William Russell in the Historic New Orleans Collection. Reviews of a May 1998 performance of four of the arrangements indicate that Morton's declining health was all that prevented him from successfully making the stylistic transition to the swing era, as he had boasted he would—in fact, one piece, "Gan-Jam," is so advanced for its day that two recent observers have made comparisons between Jelly and the likes of Stan Kenton and Charles Mingus. And, if Lawrence Gushee is right—and I think he is—that the 1917–23 period on the West Coast was a crucial turning point in Morton's life, both artistically and personally, then a careful study of his activities and relationships on the Coast might help us to understand how Morton made the important transition from erstwhile pool hustler and pimp to full-time composer, bandleader, and pianist. And if, as I contend, his relationship with Anita Gonzales Ford was at or near the center of that transition, we need to know as much as possible about the nature of that relationship and about why he felt he had to return, after nearly twenty years of separation, to the person he called the only woman he ever really loved.

CHAPTER 2

Mamanita and the "Voodoo Witch"

1

Fans of Jelly Roll Morton, especially those weaned on Alan Lomax's *Mister Jelly Roll*, think of her as Anita Gonzales—not as Bessie Johnson or Anita Ford, but as Anita Gonzales, a Creole woman with a Spanish name and a temperament to match the stereotype: proud, passionate, willful, impulsive, the sweet and caring person to whom Morton dedicated "Mamanita" and "Sweet Anita Mine," yet at the same time possessed of a temper so explosive that it drove her to physical violence on at least one occasion during their relationship, when she broke a steak platter over Morton's head.[1] Yet Jelly describes her as the only woman he ever really loved and admits that she "managed" him—his own choice of words—as no other woman ever did.[2] Before Anita, the women he mentions are either nameless or faceless or both, like so many one-night stands; after Anita, there was Mabel—"Fussy Mabel"—but Morton totally dominated that relationship in a way that he never could with Anita.

Anita and Jelly were together for most of the five years he spent on the West Coast, though their relationship was a stormy one that suffered at least two temporary separations before the final split in 1923, when Morton left for Chicago. In Lomax's book, Jelly's version of the reason for the split differs from Anita's significantly in some details, but on one thing they both agree: he was supposed to send for her eventually but never did, for reasons that are never explained.

In fact, though she emerges as the dominant figure in Morton's life in the section of the book that deals with the West Coast years, there remains quite a bit about Anita that is never explained—above all, about the source or sources of her seemingly endless supply of cash. She first appears in *Mister Jelly Roll* as the financial backer of the Original Creole Band (another name for the Creole Band) around 1913 or 1914. After Morton arrives, she buys into and out of a series of businesses—the saloon in Las Vegas, the Anita Hotel in Los Angeles, a restaurant in Arizona (which she loses because of a mining stock investment that goes bad), the Jupiter in San Francisco, a boardinghouse in Tacoma, Washington. As soon as she abandons one enterprise, she has the cash to begin another, even though Morton himself admits to going broke on at least two occasions. Although he mentions each of her businesses in turn—some, like the Jupiter, he presents as a partnership between the two of them—he never says a word about the source of her finances.

Anita does not provide much help, either. Most of what we have in Lomax's book is Jelly's view of Anita. Although she was interviewed for the book, Anita's own words occupy only a handful of pages, in sharp contrast to Mabel's story, which provides Lomax with one entire chapter and part of another. Lomax says nothing about this curious imbalance, and we can only assume that Anita was not as willing or helpful a subject as Mabel, whatever the reason.

The story of Anita and Jelly during the years 1917–23 belongs to another chapter of this book. But to understand the Anita who lived those years with Morton, it will be helpful to place that story in the context of her life as a whole, insofar as that is possible. After all, despite her importance to the Morton saga, Anita was with Jelly for only four or five of her nearly seventy years. Her life apart from Morton's can provide a perspective other than the one that emerges in Lomax's book, one that perhaps can clarify what kind of person she was and why Morton was so drawn to her.

2

The death certificate of Anita Julia Ford, dated 24 April 1952, cites the cause of death as a "Coronary Occlusion" and notes the time of death as 7:30 A.M., two hours after the onset of the heart attack. (See fig. 4.) The certificate gives the motor court in Malibu as her permanent address and states that, for two weeks prior to the attack, she was staying at 1222 East Thirty-fifth Street, Los Angeles. The document also states that she had suffered from "Arteriosclerotic Hypertensive Heart Disease" for approximately ten to fifteen years—ironically, the same type of heart disease that brought Morton down. And then a second dose of irony: the onset of the condition in Anita coincided with about the time that Jelly returned to Los Angeles.

One can only assume that the medical facts are true as stated; as for the personal information on the document, however, most of it is "true" only in the sense that it truly reflects what Anita wanted people to think about her, a fiction that she had carefully created and lived for thirty years or more. Some of the misinformation is innocent enough. One point, in fact, is merely a matter of vanity: giving her birth date as 13 April 1892 instead of 1883, as it appears on the 1900 census. Also, the certificate gives her occupation as "House wife," when everyone who knew Anita has stated clearly that she was the real force behind the restaurant and hotel businesses she ran during the last fifteen or twenty years of her life. However, the rest of the misinformation is deliberate and reveals a consistent motive. Like Jelly, she created a public persona that was often at odds with the facts; unlike Jelly, who created his persona in response to his apprenticeship in vaudeville, Anita created hers for personal and business reasons. The informant named on the certificate is Jack Ford, listed as John F. Ford, Anita's husband, but the facts about Anita's life suggest that she and Jack collaborated as the source of the misinformation shown. Certainly, her marriage to Ford, an Irish-American, would seem to have provided sufficient motivation for her to pass as white during their life together, as she did. The death certificate names her race as "Cauc."—

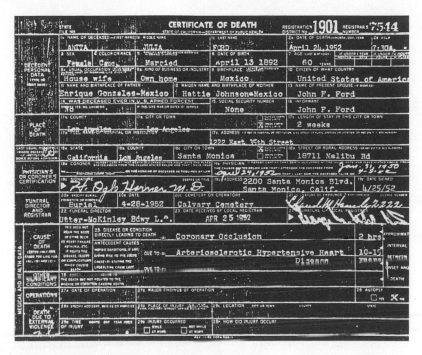

Figure 4. Anita Ford's death certificate, 1952.

Caucasian—mute testimony to at least part of a life spent "passing." For African Americans, that word alone summons up stories of light-skinned people who pass in the radical sense—that is, completely sever their relations to the African American side of the family to consistently maintain the fiction of their "whiteness." For those who make that choice, fear of discovery is complicated by a kind of absolute self-denial that can be very damaging. Others choose to lead double lives and have to devise ways to keep the two separate. That choice also involves the fear of discovery, but the self-denial is not absolute. Those who make that choice often have a practical motive for passing: to get into a particular school or university, to enter a certain profession, or to buy property in a whites-only area, for example. In her life with Jack, Anita chose the way of the double life, that much is certain. Though the choice is never an easy one, her Creole lineage must have helped ease the strain: her color and ethnicity would have given her some practice in straddling the line between white and black, in living the reality of being neither white nor black and having to live in both worlds to some extent. Perhaps for that reason, whatever fear of discovery she may have felt was not enough to force her to make the two worlds absolutely separate. Rose Mary Johns remembers working for her grandmother during summer vacations at the motel in Malibu, where she was under strict orders never to call her "Grandma" in public. There, they maintained the fiction that Rose Mary was the daughter of friends whom she was helping by providing summer employment—a very practical arrangement, one that allowed Anita to spend time with her granddaughter and at the same time provide Rose Mary with a job during summer vacations.

In many ways, that could not have been an easy fiction to maintain, either emotionally or practically. Rose Mary rarely talks directly about the stress she must have felt in the situation or over the fact that she was, as she calls herself, "the only black person in Malibu at that time." She does talk about being questioned once by a lodger at the motel, a woman who somehow suspected that Rose Mary and Anita were related. And Rose Mary remembers that there were two funerals when her grandmother died—one for the white side of the family and one for the black side. In another, more obvious way, the fiction must have been equally hard to maintain: in her photographs Anita does not really look white, in the strictest sense. Her features—broad nose, high cheekbones—look rather Native American, or Mexican, or both, with perhaps an admixture of white. By all accounts, she was of olive complexion and could have passed as a southern European. She must have had to deal with doubts and suspicions at times. Clearly, though, her color and features were ambiguous enough to allow her to pass. According to Rose Mary, a Greek man who had befriended the Fords in Malibu was shocked when told about her race at the time of her death.

As for when she began to pass, there is sufficient evidence to suggest that Anita was passing even before Jack Ford entered her life, that she began the practice when she left Biloxi, Mississippi, for a new life in Las Vegas, Nevada, and that it was interrupted—if, indeed, it ever was, entirely—only during her four or five years as Morton's wife.

Claims about Anita's "whiteness" would have to be supported by information about her parentage, as in fact it is on the death certificate: under "Father," the document names an Enrique Gonzales, born in Mexico; under "Mother," Hattie Johnson, born in Mexico; under Anita's birthplace, Mexico again. The ploy of creating some kind of Hispanic origin in order to pass for white—or at least for something other than black—was fairly common, especially among those blacks who were a bit too swarthy to pass convincingly as whites of the Anglo-German variety. A glance at the 1910 census for Clark County, Nevada, does not turn up the name Anita Gonzales (or any of her other names, for that matter), but it does shed some light on the issue of Mexican origins and race: outside of Las Vegas, anyone who has a Spanish surname is designated as white in the column for race; in Las Vegas, the original interviewer put "Sp." for "Spanish" to indicate the race of those with Spanish surnames but was overruled in every case by another hand, which wrote "OT" (evidently meaning "other") over "Sp." Even in Las Vegas, then, there was enough ambiguity about the racial identity of Hispanic people to accommodate someone like Anita, who simply wanted to avoid being characterized as black. This apparently was Anita's strategy in changing her name and inventing Mexican ancestry. And as we shall see, the motive behind the strategy was quite likely practical: her ambition to become a businesswoman.

The only "Enrique" of record in Anita's life is not her father, but one Enrique Villalapando. When he was quite young—no one is sure exactly how young—he and his siblings were orphaned within a year's time, first by the shooting of their father and then by the killing of their mother, who had taken up with another man in the mining town of Verde Valley, Arizona. No one is sure if Jack Ford and Anita had joined forces by that time or whether it was soon after, but Jack and perhaps Anita decided to adopt little Enrique, who then became Henry Ford.

Jeanne Ford told me this story about her late husband, and then produced two old, yellowed clippings from a newspaper called *Copper News*. The first, and by far the longer of the two, was about the father's death, the second about the mother's. Photos of Jack, Anita, and Henry taken in the 1930s graphically illustrate the racial dynamics of this family: Jack, the Irish American "rogue"—Jeanne Ford's term—looking very much like one of W. C. Fields's drinking buddies; Anita, the olive-skinned Creole passing for white or Mexican; and Henry, with straight, jet black hair and a very dark complexion, looking Mexican—perhaps another reason for Anita to claim Mexican ancestry.

The U.S. census of the Johnson family, enumerated on 27 June 1900, states that Hattie Johnson, listed as head of the household, was born in October of 1860 in Alabama, and lists her mother's birthplace as Tennessee and her father's as Virginia. The birthplace of all six offspring in the household, including Bessie, is given as Alabama, and their father's birthplace as Georgia. Under "Race," they are all listed as "B" for "black." The 1910 census changes that to "Mu"—that is, mulatto—but the effect is the same. They were light-skinned, but not Caucasian, not even Mexican.

When I first asked Rose Mary Johns if she had any idea when or why her grandmother changed her name, she said no. However, she later told me that, after some thought, she had come to the conclusion that the name change was part of Anita's plan to pass for white, although she still couldn't say when that had happened. As for why she would have wanted to pass, it is well-known that many western states and communities had restrictive covenants in real estate contracts or laws that prohibited sale of real estate to all but whites. The problem is, the prohibition often included Mexicans as well—this was true in California, for example. Perhaps those restrictions were enforced less strictly in Nevada, especially in Las Vegas: in the years between 1905, when the town was founded, and roughly 1915 or 1920, Las Vegas was eager to attract settlers, especially women, who were usually a tiny minority in pioneer settlements.

Although there is no clear evidence that allows us to pin down a date or even a year for the change, there are enough bits and pieces to allow an educated guess. The change of name and identity would have offered obvious practical benefits to a woman like Anita, if she came west with the idea of going into business for herself and owning or managing property, so the change probably coincided with the move. Even the date of the move is impossible to pin down with any precision, however. The last verifiable trace of Bessie Johnson in Biloxi shows up in the 1905 city directory, which lists her as Bessie Seymour, living with her husband, Fred Seymour. The 1910 census has Fred Seymour still living in Hattie Johnson's household, at 735 Croesus Street, along with Hattie Seymour, Anita's daughter and the elder Hattie's granddaughter, who was five years old at the time. There is no mention of Bessie. In the Library of Congress interviews, Jelly Roll states that, when he arrived on the West Coast in 1917, Anita had been running for some time a saloon in Las Vegas called the Arcade.³ Also, Lomax, who deleted the name of the saloon from his version of the interview, records Morton's claim that Anita, already on the West Coast, helped to finance the Creole Band in Los Angeles sometime in 1913.⁴ The only surviving photo of the band, taken around 1914, shows both of Anita's brothers, Bill and Dink (Ollie) Johnson, as members — Bill, in fact, was a founding member of the group. In an interview for the Hogan Jazz Archive at Tulane University, Dink says he left New Orleans to help his sister in Las Vegas when he was about nineteen years old, which would have been roughly 1911 or 1912. The 1913 city directory for Biloxi lists Martin and Ollie Johnson, but no other Johnsons or Seymours, at 735 Croesus Street, the address listed as Hattie's household in the 1910 census. Given all the information about Dink, it appears that, by the time the 1913 directory was published, he had already moved west.

Although the above evidence is fragmentary and inconclusive, it does suggest a rough chronology. Anita may have moved to Las Vegas by 1908 or 1909, perhaps even earlier. She may even have moved to Los

Angeles first and gotten wind there of the land sales and commercial buildup of Las Vegas. Stanley W. Paher's very useful *Las Vegas: As It Began, as It Grew* shows that both the Las Vegas Townsite Company and the Las Vegas Land and Water Company were operating out of Los Angeles; the flyers reproduced in Paher's book offer prospective settlers bargain prices for lots in the newly formed city of Las Vegas.[5] In any case, Anita was certainly no longer with her husband and child in Biloxi when the 1910 census was taken; she was well established on the West Coast by 1913, and her practice of passing for white probably coincided with that date.

As for Anita's motives for making the move, they were no doubt similar to those of so many people who migrated west at the time: expanding opportunities for work, housing, and land ownership, especially for minorities and women. For the independent spirit that emerges from the pages of *Mister Jelly Roll*, the possibility of beginning a new life, one in which she could own her own land, open her own business, and be a new kind of family matriarch, must have been appealing. The choice of Las Vegas, which in the 1910 census had barely nine hundred inhabitants, may seem strange, but a brief summary of the town's development between 1905 and 1915 should shed some light on exactly what the advantages were.

The site that officially was to become known as the city of Las Vegas on 15 May 1905 already had a long history as a watering hole in the middle of a vast stretch of desert. Even before the official founding and naming, it was often referred to as *las vegas*, or simply *vegas*. In Spanish, the word means "fertile plain or valley." The name stuck to the area because of the abundant supply of underground water that was the source of a stream that ran steadily through the area and, eventually, of the artesian wells that supplied the town with water. As far back as 1831, it was a watering stop on the Old Spanish Trail, which ran from Santa Fe to Los Angeles and was used by Mexican traders to transport woven blankets to trade for mules and cattle in California. Briefly a Mormon religious mission, it was settled by Octavius D. Gass and came to be known as Las Vegas Ranch, which prospered from about 1865 through the end of the century. Shortly after the turn of the century, officials of the San Pedro, Los Angeles, and Salt Lake Railroad company decided to take advantage of the water supply there by buying the land, dividing it into smaller parcels to sell to settlers, and establishing the spot as a railroad town, station and all. The date 15 May 1905 marks not only the founding of the city but also the first day that the newly surveyed parcels of land went up for sale at auction—starting at one hundred dollars a lot.[6]

The fact that Anita's name appears (as Bessie Seymour) in the 1905 Biloxi city directory does not entirely rule out the possibility that she was in Las Vegas as early as 1905, though a photo taken that year showing the saloon she ran there seems to indicate that she arrived there sometime after the picture was taken. The Arcade was located on what is usually referred to as the "infamous" block 16, bounded by First Street to the north, Second Street to the south, and by Ogden and Stewart Streets to the east and west. (See figs. 5 and 6.) In the photo of the east side of First, at the end of the street—beyond the saloons known as the Gem, Arizona Club, and Red Onion Club—stands the Arcade itself. The street looks like the Hollywood set for a cowboy movie: the dust, the palpably bright, hot desert sun, the men in cowboy hats lounging on the shaded porch of the Arizona Club. The picture tells us emphatically that the Las Vegas Anita knew was virtually a frontier town. Under the name of the Arcade, at the far right of the photo, appears a barely legible name, apparently that of the proprietor: Jim Fegan or Regan or Megan. Apparently Anita was not the original owner but instead bought or leased what was an ongoing business establishment sometime after the photo was taken.[7]

On 5 September 1905, a fire that destroyed much of the newly built town spared block 16. According to Paher,

> Thereafter, riotous block 16 was the only seat of pleasure. Nearly every night, including Christmas, it ran full blast. The Gem, the Red Onion, the Turf, the Favorite, the Double-O, the Star, the

Figure 5. "Block 16" in Las Vegas, Nevada, with the Arcade saloon at far right, 1906. Courtesy of University of Nevada, Las Vegas.

Figure 6.   Detail of the Arcade saloon, eventually
owned by Anita Gonzales. Courtesy of University
of Nevada, Las Vegas.

Arcade saloons and the Arizona Club were continually crowded with
sharp-eyed dealers and boosters and men standing around trying to
solve the mysteries of gambling. . . .

Outside the saloons but conveniently nearby, small establish-
ments sported prostitutes. At the dance halls, these "beautiful" ladies
waited to bestow their affections for a consideration. That part of
Las Vegas looked like a rip-roaring. whiskey-drinking, gun-toting,
gambling town, while the rest of the town was conservative and
business-like.[8]

Here, the connection between the saloons and the prostitutes is por-
trayed as rather loose and unofficial. According to another source, how-

ever, "this infamous block served as Wild West Central," where "the Double-O, Red Onion, Arcade and others served ten-cent shots, featured faro, roulette and poker, and sported cribs out back for customers with the 'Urge.'"[9] Both sources note that the Arizona Club eventually built a second story "for the convenience of the ladies of the night and their gentlemen," thus formalizing what to that point may have been an informal relationship between saloons and prostitutes.[10]

Given the nature of the town and the kind of business she ran, it is certainly easy to understand why even as courageous and enterprising a woman as Anita would want brother Dink Johnson in residence, and one suspects that she probably called for his assistance soon after she bought into the business. In the interview for the Hogan Jazz Archive, Dink says that he tended bar during the day and played piano at night. His presence in the saloon must have been as reassuring for his sister as it was constant. When Morton showed up on the West Coast in 1917 and Anita joined him in his odyssey, she "turned [the saloon] over to Dink" (Lomax has Jelly say "Bill," but on the Library of Congress recording, he clearly says "Dink").[11] It seems that there may have been another of the Johnson brothers involved in the business at that time: the 1918 military draft records for Clark County, Nevada, list a Martin Johnson in Las Vegas. His date of birth is given as 28 January 1890—which coincides exactly with that of the Martin Johnson, age twenty, listed in the 1910 census as part of Hattie Johnson's household in Biloxi—and his race as black. At any rate, the Arcade must have been quite a lucrative business, for, soon after Anita turned it over to Dink, she and Jelly saw him riding in a McFarlan, a fairly expensive car at that time. Morton's wording ("she turned it over") implies that Anita may have remained the owner and perhaps continued to draw an income from the business even while she was with Jelly. At any rate, by 1917 or 1918 she had been running the saloon for five or six years and would have had ample opportunity to save quite a bit of money. In either case the Arcade was quite likely the primary source of her seemingly endless supply of capital when she was with Morton. All of her surviving relatives, on both the black and the white sides of the family, unanimously praise her as a shrewd businesswoman, and the saloon in Las Vegas appears to have been the first of her successes.

The Arcade also provides some evidence that Anita seems to have had at least a nodding acquaintance with prostitution. Even if the Arcade did not have its own "cribs," as the small, ground-level rooms, each with its own entrance, were called, the stock-in-trade of the saloons of block 16 was alcohol, gambling, and prostitutes, and Anita would have had to come to something like an indirect arrangement with the prostitutes who worked on the block. If there is any substance to the rumors that Morton's main source of income on the West Coast was pimping for his "Pacific Coast 'Line,'" Anita's relationship with Jelly certainly would have extended her nodding acquaintance, especially because they were business partners on at least two occasions—at the Anita Hotel in Los Angeles and the Jupiter nightclub in San Francisco. However, as she herself describes the relationship to Lomax in *Mister Jelly Roll*, Morton was so fiercely jealous and protective of her, it is hard to imagine him allowing her to have anything directly to do with prostitution: "I bought a hotel [the Anita] here in Los Angeles, but Jelly was very jealous and made things tough for me. Whenever the front bell would ring, I would have to go to my room so nobody could see me. He wouldn't let me walk in the hallways or make up beds or wait on customers. So we had to hire a chambermaid and a clerk. That didn't pay and we sold out." [12] She goes on to say that she accompanied Morton on every job, where "he made me sit right by the piano and not move or tap my feet or nothing," and that he was "so jealous he wouldn't have anybody around us, he wouldn't even have a man up for dinner." [13]

It is not clear exactly when Anita gave up the Arcade or when she met and married Jack Ford, so there is a gap in the story of her life from the time she and Morton split up. As near as anyone in the family can recollect, Anita and Jack opened the restaurant known as Ford's in Canyonville, Oregon, sometime in the mid-1930s, and soon after, around 1940, they were also running the Topanga Beach Auto Court in Malibu, California. (See fig. 7.) Their reason for wanting to run two businesses at

Figure 7. Anita Ford, Jack Ford, an unidentified friend, and Henry Villala-pando Ford, Anita and Jack's adopted son, in front of Ford's, late 1930s. Courtesy Henry Villalapando Ford Collection.

such a distance from one another is uncertain, but one thing is absolutely clear: Ford's was a highly successful and respectable business. When she says to Lomax, "Be sure to mention my tourist camp in your book. . . . Our chicken dinners are recommended by Duncan Hines," she is referring to the listing of Ford's in Hines's yearly handbook of approved restaurants, *Adventures in Good Eating*.[14] The citation of Ford's in the 1946 edition recommends more than just the chicken dinners: "*Open all year, 8 A.M. to 10 P.M.* Known for their pan-fried chicken, special cut steer steak, baked ham, also fried young turkey, May 1 to Nov. 1. If you're in this neighborhood, better join the long list of enthusiastic boosters for the food at Ford's. Phone ahead, if possible. Tel. 145. D. $1.50 and $2."[15] Along with the verbal blessing came a highly coveted placard—"Recommended by Duncan Hines"—that the restaurant could display as evidence of its culinary excellence. (At that time, some barrooms made up a mock placard that read, "Recommended by Drunken Hines"—a kind of backhanded acknowledgment of Hines's prestige.)

In other words, during the last decade or more of her life, as she approached the age of seventy, Anita, along with Jack, ran two successful businesses: the restaurant in Canyonville, begun in the early to mid-1930s and canonized by Duncan Hines, and, some eight hundred miles away, the motel in Malibu, begun in the early to mid-1940s. Today, in the freeway age, the trip takes roughly twelve to thirteen hours by car traveling virtually nonstop; it must have taken at least twice that amount of time in Anita's day. (Coincidentally, it was the construction of the I-5 freeway that forced Henry Ford to move the business to Portland, where it thrives to this day.) It must have been a tremendous strain on Anita, in her sixties, heart condition and all, to maintain two businesses so distant from one another. Why did she do it? Perhaps it had something to do with her leading a double life and maintaining ties to her black family in Southern California. Not only were all her business ventures family businesses, but Rose Mary Johns stated emphatically on several occasions that Anita was generous in her financial support of her daughter, Hattie, and of her grandchildren. In any case, her ability to keep two successful businesses going under such conditions can mean only one thing: as her family has repeatedly stated, she was a born entrepreneur. Perhaps that alone explains the strenuous life she led to the very end.

And perhaps it helps to explain a curious incident that occurred toward the end of her life—in 1950, two years before her death. Floyd Levin spells out the details in a justifiably well-known article published in 1991, "Untold Story of Jelly Roll Morton's Last Years." After narrating the events of 1940–41 in Jelly's life, Levin moves ahead to 1950, when the fledgling Southern California Hot Jazz Society (SCHJS) discovered that no marker had been placed on Morton's grave, even though almost ten years had passed since his burial. The SCHJS decided to organize a benefit to raise the money for a gravestone and began preparations in earnest: the musicians' union was contacted to waive the usual minimum wage requirement; musicians like Zutty Singleton, Albert Nicholas, Joe Sullivan, Conrad Janis, and others agreed to perform; arrangements were made to show Bessie Smith's short film, *Saint Louis Blues;* and so forth. However, when Levin and Bob Kirstein announced the benefit concert on their weekly radio program, the station got an irate phone call from a woman calling herself Morton's wife—Anita, in fact—demanding to know why the Society had taken it upon itself to honor her husband's grave with a marker and demanding that the activity stop. When one of the men spoke to Anita on the phone she insisted that in no way would she allow the Society to proceed with its plans. Levin and Kirstein asked if they could visit her personally to talk about the issue; she agreed and invited them to the Topanga Beach Auto Court.

When they got there, she was most gracious and lovely in her welcome. She even started frying them some chicken and brought them some cold beers as she fondly reminisced about her years with Morton. But when Levin finally brought up the matter of the grave, "her mood changed. She became quite adamant. 'I cannot allow strangers to buy the marker for my beloved. Tomorrow I plan to purchase the plaque. I'll have it no other way!' From the tone of her voice, it was evident that she was determined to halt the project we had worked so hard to complete."[16] They asked if they could hand the proceeds over to her to help buy the plaque, but she insisted that she would not accept the money. She finally agreed to allow the Society to mount a second marker, its own, along with hers, but Calvary Cemetery declared that that was against their policy and that Anita was the only person who would be allowed to place any marker. Levin and Kirstein wined her and dined her and again asked if they could donate the proceeds of the concert for the gravestone: "'I ordered it yesterday,' she snapped. 'And it will be placed on the grave next week!'"[17] The Society went ahead with the benefit anyway and placed the money in a bank account called "The Jelly Roll Morton Fund"—and there it sat until 1966, when the New Orleans guitarist-banjoist Johnny St. Cyr died, at which time the SCHJS donated the fund to pay for his marker.[18]

Levin says that he was often tempted to ask why, if the issue was so important to Anita, she had not bothered to place a gravestone years earlier. But he diplomatically refrained, sensing that it would only harden her resolve. Had she simply put off the task until the years had slipped quickly by? How could she do that if Jelly were truly her "beloved"? Was she so ruthless that, once she had what she wanted out of Morton, she simply put the grave out of her mind? But then why all the emotion, why all the fuss about being the only one to do it, if all she really cared about was her claim to his royalties?

It seems that the word "enigmatic" was invented for people like Anita —a person whose personality embraced extreme opposites. Her tenderness and concern for Jelly seem genuine; at the same time, she was an entrepreneur, and the idea that she could benefit financially by backing the revival of his career must have been attractive, even if it was a gamble. Those two aspects of her involvement with Jelly may seem logically incompatible, but in fact they are emotionally quite plausible. Anita was a businesswoman, and any businessperson has to have at least a touch of ruthlessness to succeed. That does not mean she was necessarily unmoved by love, eros, and all the fundamental human emotions. Certainly, Floyd Levin's tale of Anita reveals a woman full of enigma and contradiction. (See fig. 8.)

3

There is yet another death certificate to consider, this time because it affords us a glimpse of Anita's relationship with a woman who seems to have been as important to Anita as she was to Jelly: Laura Hunter. (See fig. 9.) The document sets the date of Laura's death at 14 February 1940 and names Anita Ford as the informant. Unlike in the case of Morton's certificate, however, she seems not to have had much information, or misinformation, to supply. The word "Unknown" appears five times, but whatever information Anita did supply is verified by the 1920 census in Los Angeles. As with Morton, Anita described Laura's "Color or Race" as "Ethio."; in both instances, she consistently avoided the more obvious "colored" or "Negro," even though Morton himself described Laura as "a very dark woman."[19] Laura's occupation is described as "Housewife," and the certificate names Edward Hunter as her hus-

Figure 8. The "enigmatic" Anita and an unidentified friend, probably in the late 1920s. Courtesy
Henry Villalapando Ford Collection.

band. Her date of birth is given as 20 June 1869, a difference of two years
from the date implied on the 1920 census: there, her age is listed as fifty-
three, which would make the year of her birth 1867. Anita's memory may
simply be off a bit here, or it is quite possible that Laura herself may not
have been sure of the exact year. In 1867—in fact, well into the twentieth century—government bureaucracies on all levels did not place much
importance on recording the vital statistics of African Americans.

Anita did not supply much information about Laura's parents, but the

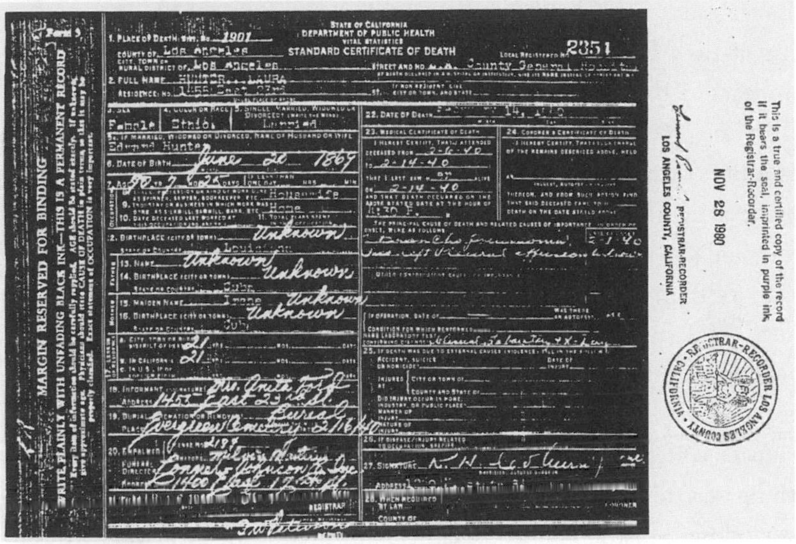
STATE OF CALIFORNIA
DEPARTMENT OF PUBLIC HEALTH
VITAL STATISTICS
STANDARD CERTIFICATE OF DEATH

MARGIN RESERVED FOR BINDING
WRITE PLAINLY WITH UNFADING BLACK INK—THIS IS A PERMANENT RECORD

This is a true and certified copy of the record if it bears the seal, imprinted in purple ink, of the Registrar-Recorder.

NOV 28 1980

REGISTRAR-RECORDER
LOS ANGELES COUNTY, CALIFORNIA

Figure 9. Laura Hunter's death certificate, 1940.

bits she did provide are quite suggestive. The father's name and the city or town of his birth are unknown, but under "State or Country" the word "Cuba" appears. As for Laura's mother, all Anita could remember was the first name, Irene, and her birthplace, again Cuba. The 1920 census corroborates all of the above, except for the father's birthplace, listed there as Louisiana. The census names Cuba as the birthplace of Ed Hunter's mother.

Laura's death certificate supplies two more pieces of information to consider. First, the length of Laura's residence, both in the "City, Town or Rural District" of Los Angeles and in the state of California, is stated as twenty-one years. If that is accurate, the Hunters moved west in 1919. According to the 1920 census, taken in January of that year, the Hunters were living at 537 Lark Street in the city of Watts in the county of Los Angeles (Watts was not incorporated into the city of Los Angeles until the late 1920s). In other words, Morton's godparents arrived in the Los Angeles area just two years after he did. The second has to do with

Laura's address at the time of her death. By 1940, the Hunters were living at 1455 East Twenty-third Street in Los Angeles, the address that appears by their names in the city directories of 1932, 1936, and 1939. The one piece of deliberate misinformation on the subject of addresses is Anita's own, listed as 1455 East Twenty-third Street, Los Angeles, the same as Laura's. Anita was living in Canyonville, Oregon, at that time— why did she not give her correct address? The most innocent explanation for the address may very well be that Anita was claiming to be some sort of relative of Laura's in order to make things like funeral arrangements easier to manage expeditiously. Of course, those who see Anita as exploiting the situation for her own benefit will be inclined to draw a more sinister conclusion. We will probably never know for certain, but one thing that the document clearly suggests is that Anita's ties to Laura were very close. Morton's blind godfather, still alive at the time, evidently entrusted Anita with the task of making the final arrangements for Laura.

But the death certificate is not the only testimony to those ties; there is no overabundance of it, and some of it is circumstantial, but all of it together points to a long-term relationship between the two women.

The trail begins in Biloxi, Mississippi. As we have seen, both the census list of 1900 and the city directory of 1905 place Anita and the entire Johnson family in that city. In *Mister Jelly Roll*, Morton refers to his godmother as Eulalie Echo, the name that she later shed for the less exotic Laura Hunter. (The last name came from a previous marriage to one "Paul Echo," according to what the family told Lomax, and she took the name "Hunter" with her second marriage.[20] In the interview, there is no discussion at all of the change from Eulalie to Laura.) Morton tells Lomax, "I was about eleven years old at the time [circa 1901] and used to stay with my godmother, Eulalie Echo, who spoiled me and gave me a little freedom. When school closed, she permitted me to go pick berries at the strawberry farm."[21] Later, he identifies the location as "Biloxi, where my godmother had her country place in the summer."[22] It was probably during those trips to his godmother's farm that he got to know Anita, in spite of what she tells Lomax in the *Mister Jelly Roll* interview:

"Most everybody . . . thinks I met Jelly out here in California, but the truth is I knew him from New Orleans."[23] Although she says "New Orleans," she must mean something like "back home," for, as we have seen, her addresses around 1900 to 1905 are all in Biloxi. In other words, Anita probably knew both Jelly and his godmother, Laura, as early as 1900 or 1901, perhaps even earlier. The subsequent statement that she "never gave him a second look because he wasn't decent" does not make much sense, considering that in 1901, when Jelly began to visit the strawberry farm regularly, he was only eleven years old to Anita's eighteen. By 1905, Jelly would have been fifteen and Anita twenty-two, a more likely time for a budding romance, but by then she was married to Fred Seymour and was nursing a baby. Whenever Jelly's infatuation with Anita began, however, the three-sided relationship between Anita, Laura, and Jelly must have begun during this period.

The well-known photograph of Jelly performing in blackface presents another clue to the Laura-Anita connection. On the back of the photo, Morton wrote a dedication to Laura: "To my beloved godmother, from Ferd Morton." I first noticed the inscription when I met Floyd Levin and he gave me access to his collection, which includes the original photo. When I asked Floyd how he obtained it, he told me that Anita gave it to him when he met her, around 1950. Anita, then, got it from Laura at some point—perhaps indirectly, after Laura's death, but perhaps as far back as 1919, after Laura's arrival and during the time when Anita and Morton were living together as husband and wife.

When I first asked Rose Mary Johns if she had any recollection of Ed and Laura Hunter, she said no unhesitatingly. However, in a later conversation, when I happened to mention Jelly's godparents, Rose Mary said, "Oh yes, that's Nan-nan and Parrain. I remember them." She then explained that the words were French for godmother and godfather (Creole French, no doubt, since the correct term in Parisian French is *marrain*; my spelling of *nan-nan* is speculative). Evidently, the entire family addressed them as Godmother and Godfather, and Rose Mary knew them only by those names. Whether Laura had actually baptized any of the family, including Anita, Rose Mary could not say. In the African American community, the title "godmother" or "godfather" often has no specific connection to the ritual of baptism. It is often bestowed upon a close friend, with the idea that the friend will take a special interest in the child's welfare. As I spoke to Rose Mary, I recalled the telegram that Anita in Los Angeles sent to Jelly in Denver: as Lomax cites the message, it reads, "NAN AND DAD BOTH AT POINT OF DEATH. MUST UNDERGO OPERATION IMMEDIATELY. COME HOME. ANITA."[24] When I repeated the message to Rose Mary and asked her about the "nan," she said that it was short for *nan-nan* and that the message was about Jelly's godparents. That insight explains the utter panic of Jelly's reaction: as we shall see, Jelly dropped everything and left immediately for Los Angeles, even though he was so broke he had to "ride the blinds"—that is, ride a freight train illegally, as a hobo. In the Library of Congress interviews, Morton says that Anita's mother was living with them in Los Angeles; but the "nan" of the telegram is not Hattie Johnson, though Lomax's presentation of the material allows for that confusion. Whoever Anita's father was, he was out of the picture in the 1900 and 1910 census lists, where Hattie is listed as the single head of the household, and Jelly's statement to Lomax makes no mention of anyone but Anita's mother living with them. "Anita loved her mother very much," Morton says, "and I thought an awful lot of the old lady myself."[25] That rather lukewarm statement of affection hardly explains the panic that seized Jelly when he received the telegram.

All evidence indicates that Jelly's ties to his godmother were very close, indeed. In *Mister Jelly Roll*, he tells Lomax that when he was a baby she used to pass him off as her own.[26] Both Morton and Amide, Jelly's sister, tell Lomax that it was Laura who paid for whatever formal musical training he had.[27] His natural father had abandoned the family when Morton was just an infant, and Amide says that, after their mother died, when Morton was about fourteen years old, "Ferd stayed most of the time with his godmother, Eulalie Echo. Used to *love* to stay uptown with her. Lalee, he called her."[28] Even his taste for diamonds and fancy clothes seems to have been inspired by his godmother, as he himself suggests:

"She kept boxes of jewels in the house and I always had some kind of diamond on. Through her I came to be considered the best dresser."[29] When his mother died, she left him in the care of his uncle, but that relationship was not a happy one and the arrangement lasted no more than a year. At age fifteen, he was disowned by his great-grandmother for playing piano in the bordellos of Storyville, a traumatic event that left him emotionally devastated; he turned quite naturally to his godmother, the only member of his otherwise respectable Creole family who would have anything to do with him: "The first night after my great-grandmother told me to go, I attended the Grand Theatre and saw a play in which they sang a very sweet song, entitled *Give Me Back My Dead Daughter's Child.* I thought about how my mother had died and left me a motherless child out in this wide world to mourn, and I began to cry. Fact of the business, I was just fifteen and so dumb I didn't even know how to rent a room. So I walked the streets till morning and then caught a train for Biloxi, where my godmother had her country place in the summer. I knew she would take me in, no matter what happened."[30] From that point until her death, Laura became the center of whatever Jelly could call family.

But there may have been yet another reason for his panic at reading that Laura was at death's door. If Anita's version of Jelly's end has any truth to it, his response to the telegram may have been motivated by fear as much as by love. I have cited most of the following statement by Anita before, but it is worth repeating here:

> Jelly was a very devout Catholic. . . . But voodoo, which is an entirely different religion, had hold of him, too. . . .
>
> The woman, Laura Hunter, who raised Jelly Roll, was a voodoo witch. Yes, I'm talking about his godmother who used to be called Eulalie Echo. She made a lot of money at voodoo. People were always coming to her for some help and she was giving them beads and pieces of leather and all that. Well, everybody knows that before you can become a witch you have to sell the person you love the best to Satan as a sacrifice. Laura loved Jelly best. She loved Jelly better than Ed, her own husband. Jelly always knew she'd sold him to Satan

and that, when she died, he'd die, too—she would take him down
with her.

Laura taken sick in 1940 and here came Jelly Roll driving his Lincoln all the way from New York.[31]

As we have already seen, Anita's version of the story is tailor-made to
corroborate Morton's lie to Mabel that his sudden move to California
in November of 1940 was motivated by concern over his godmother's
death; it is quite possible, in other words, that Anita's statement is just a
fiction, and that it should simply be dismissed as such. Certainly, her
wording repeats some of the popular stereotypes about the nature of
voodoo, and one wonders how someone who had known Laura for so
long could be so far off target.

The most obviously false note has to be Anita's assertion that the
haste of Morton's final trip west was inspired by his knowledge that he
had been sold to Satan and that he was therefore fated to die soon after
his godmother. Morton knew he was a dying man well before he got the
news about his godmother's final illness. Also, the phrase "voodoo witch"
and the idea that Laura had made a pact with Satan suggest that Laura
was involved in what has been called black magic, a practice that has a
problematic relation to voodoo. Serious scholars—Albert Metraux, for
instance—acknowledge that black magic does have a place in voodoo
(zombies, evil spells, poisons, and the like) but warn that it is possible to
overemphasize that aspect, as has occurred in most Hollywood movies
on the subject. Most scholars point out that most voodoo practices fall
into the category of white magic—that is, rituals, talismans, prayers,
and so forth that are intended to be helpful rather than harmful: to cause
someone to succeed in love or finance, for example, or to bring good luck
or cure an illness. Jim Haskins, in his book *Voodoo and Hoodoo*, even warns
against imposing the "arbitrary moral judgements" of the terms "good"
and "bad" on voodoo: "In love, for example, if a woman uses conjure to
keep her husband from going out at night, she can be said to be practicing malign conjure against him. But such conjure is at the same time be-

nign from her standpoint. . . . Similarly, with regard to the law, if a man
employs some supernatural method to win a court suit, the method can
be classified as benign from the viewpoint of the man himself and malign
from the standpoint of society."[32] Elsewhere in the book, however, Haskins does allow that there are unambiguously evil voodoo conjuring practices, though nothing he describes even vaguely resembles what Anita
says about Laura. Morton himself describes his godmother as a woman
who was "very intelligent, had a pleasant personality and plenty money."
As noted earlier, he also observes that "she used to monkey around with
this spiritual business. There were glasses of water around her house and
voices would come out of those glasses. Very prominent people would
consult my godmother and she would give them stuff like uncooked
turtle heart—*cowein*—she'd have them swallow that, *and, afterwards, they
had good luck and no one could harm them.*"[33] He adds that his recent bad
luck may have come about "during those seances when my godmother
fooled with that underground stuff," but that could be no more than an
expression of the belief, common in voodoo, that approaching the religion with the wrong attitude, or neglecting to pay a priest or priestess
for services rendered, could have serious consequences, even years later.
Morton's main emphasis is on the good luck and the prophylactic intent
of Laura's practice.

The historian Al Rose, in his book *Storyville, New Orleans*, offers some
corroboration of the idea that Laura practiced white magic: "Eulalie
Echo, whose real name was Laura Hunter, was closely associated with
the sporting women of the tenderloin until about 1905. Widely known
as a 'good' voodoo woman, she was constantly being consulted by madams, barkeeps and strumpets on vital matters. Her solutions required the
use of quantities of gris-gris, turtle hearts, black cat bones, and other such
esoteric stock."[34] Unfortunately, Rose does not name his source. However, his statement offers some points of comparison with the other two
descriptions of Laura's work. Morton's "very prominent people" become "madams, barkeeps and strumpets" in Rose's words. Jelly does tell
a story about how, when he was six months old, his godmother loaned

him "to one of her acquaintances, some type of sporting-woman."[35] So perhaps Rose's version spells out more candidly what made Morton's "people" so very prominent, though the well-known fact of the hold voodoo had on people of all classes in New Orleans makes it altogether possible that Laura's clientele included "respectable" people as well. All three versions either state or imply that Laura was fairly successful at what she did—Anita and Jelly both talk about her making a lot of money, and Rose discusses her among the most prominent people in the tenderloin. Rose, however, does not clarify the significance of the date 1905; if he means to imply that Laura gave up her voodoo practice after that date, neither Jelly nor Anita make any such indication. Both Morton and Rose mention turtle heart, but that item, along with gris-gris and black-cat bones, has always been used in voodoo. The use of the word *consult* in both Morton's and Rose's statements raises the possibility that Laura was actually what Haskins would call a "conjurer" rather than a priestess—that she trafficked in voodoo-based amulets and spells but did not formally lead a congregation or conduct regular and elaborate communal rituals and ceremonies. Anita, too, says that people came to Laura for help and that she would give them "beads and pieces of leather and all that."[36] Haskins's book, *Voodoo and Hoodoo*, maintains that the term *hoodoo*, normally a simple variant or synonym for *voodoo*, should be restricted to the conjurers who deal exclusively in voodoo magic and folk medicine.

In *Mister Jelly Roll*, Morton tells of two critical episodes in his life when he turned to voodoo practitioners, and there too we find the same pattern emerging: he turned to them only when he sought "cures" for specific instances of ill health, bad luck, or both. He does not ever appear to have been a regular member of a particular voodoo cult. The first episode occurred soon after he was expelled from his family by his great-grandmother because he was playing piano in Storyville. After a short stay with his godmother in Biloxi, he returned to New Orleans only to have a "run of bad luck"—"I felt sick and bad," he says. "Something seemed to be wrong with my hands."[37] He was approached by one Papa Sona, described by Morton as one of those "operators" who "did some kind of workmanship with frog legs and boa-constrictor tongues to make someone fall in love with you."[38] He even uses the same phrase he applied earlier in his description of his godmother's activities—"underground stuff," he calls it, instead of "voodoo."[39] Papa Sona "cured" Morton of his malady by putting him through a series of three ritual baths, and Jelly ruefully notes that, in spite of the cure, "I never thought of paying Papa for what he did, because I never really believed he helped me. I should have realized that he used some very powerful ingredients. I should have been more appreciative, for I have lived to regret this ungrateful action."[40] The last statement seems an acknowledgment that Morton sees the "ungrateful action" as the reason for the voodoo-based curse that he believed had been put on him in the 1930s, when again he consulted a practitioner, this time in New York: a Madame Elise, who, like Papa Sona, prescribed a ritual bath, among other things.[41]

Of the three descriptions of Laura's practice, only Anita's evokes black magic imagery. Since there is none in Morton's or Rose's statements, it is possible that the imagery is Anita's invention. Considering the length of time the two women knew each other, however, it is hard to imagine that Anita could be so misinformed about the nature of Laura's voodoo practice or about the religion itself. In fact, their lives parallel each other so closely it is hard to resist the temptation to speculate about whether Anita herself may have been involved in the practice, though there is virtually no evidence to support that possibility. The title of "Mamanita," Morton's "Spanish tinge" piece dedicated to her, is suggestive: voodoo worshipers commonly use the prefix "Mama" when they address a priestess, or *mambo*. The title of Karen McCarthy Brown's excellent book *Mama Lola: A Vodou Priestess in Brooklyn*, suggests how common the practice is. Also, Anita's lyrics to Morton's "Dead Man Blues," her only direct contribution to his musical opus, clearly evoke the blues as a kind of spell cast upon an unfaithful lover:

I want to tell you
About the dead man blues.

They are awful
They are fearful
REFRAIN: Blues, blues, blues, blues.
They'll set you crazy
Those dang'rous dead man blues
Were you ever blue?
Mean and hateful too?
They'll make you curse your maw
And slap your paw in the jaw.
Oh those dead man, those dead man
Blues, blues, blues, blues.
Last night, I had a dream
It was the meanest thing I ever seen
About the dead man, oh those dead man
Blues, blues, blues, blues.
I dreamed my friend Sal
found my man with another gal.
Oh those dead man, oh those dead man
Blues, blues, blues, blues.
When I heard him
Right from the start
I formed a killing
Right in my heart.
Oh those dead man, oh those dead man
Blues, blues, blues, blues.

On the surface, the lyrics seem to express the conventional lament of a jilted lover—a common enough theme in the blues repertoire. On closer inspection, however, they make no mention of actual infidelity, but of a dream in which the singer's friend discovers her man "with another gal." The onset of the "dead man blues" seems motiveless and unprovoked, an "awful, . . . fearful" spell that will "set you crazy." That the mere dream of a betrayal inspires the final, sinister curse—"I formed a killing / right in my heart"—only intensifies the sense of irrationality that permeates the wording and the imagery of the lyrics. This is not the conventional "jilted lover" type of blues lyrics, but one that involves dreams, spells, and curses—voodoo lyrics, in effect. As we shall see, though, the "voodoo blues" subgenre is quite old and quite conventional stuff itself, so Anita's use of it should not be taken as an entirely personal statement; the lyrics may be regarded as evidence of Anita's variation on an old theme. But the fact that she chose *that* theme for her only recorded musical effort may hold some significance.

Another part of her statement needs to be qualified: where Anita says that voodoo is "an entirely different religion" in relation to Roman Catholicism.[42] While a few scholars have denied that Roman Catholicism had any significant influence on voodoo, by far the majority view voodoo as a syncretic religion, developed in Haiti, that fused West African religions with Catholicism, along with perhaps some Native American forms and imagery. A similar fusion appeared wherever African slaves came in contact with Catholicism—*santería* in Cuba and *candomblé* in Brazil, for example, are widely regarded by scholars as parallel phenomena, parallel to each other and to voodoo. In his foreword to *Voodoo in Haiti*, Metraux answers his own rhetorical question ("In fact—what is Voodoo?") by explaining, "Nothing more than a conglomeration of beliefs and rites of African origin, which, having been closely mixed with Catholic practice, has come to be the religion of the greater part of the peasants and the urban proletariat of the black republic of Haiti. Its devotees ask of it what men have always asked of religion: remedy for ills, satisfaction for needs and the hope of survival."[43] In all of the Spanish, French, and Portuguese colonies, the mixture was brought about by two factors: first, the forcible baptism and conversion to Catholicism of the slaves and, second, the lack of any consistent or thorough indoctrination of the slaves into Church dogma. The first African Americans filled the gap with whatever they could remember of their native religions. Because they saw St. Patrick depicted as mastering the snakes in Ireland, they used his image to represent the serpent divinity Danbala;

when they saw chromoliths of St. Isidore dressed in peasant garb, they connected him to Papa Zaka, patron of agriculture; they saw images of Ezili Danto, fiercely protective mother holding a child on her knee, which they easily fused with those of the Virgin Mary holding Jesus. The correspondences between Christian saints and West African deities have been enumerated many times in studies of voodoo as well as *santería* and *candomblé*. The syncretic nature of those religions extended to ritual, as well: for example, many writers have noted that the importance of water spirits in West African religions gave a special significance to the sacrament of baptism in voodoo, especially in New Orleans, where Saint John the Baptist was the patron saint of the cult, and Saint John's Eve the most important day on the calendar.[44]

The theme of ritual cleansing by immersion in water dominates the two incidents described above when Morton consulted Papa Sona and Madame Elise, and it seems also to have played an important role in Jelly's return to Roman Catholicism at the end of his life. The scrapbook material in the Ford Collection includes two newspaper articles about the miracle cures at Lourdes, in France. Both are dated 1939, so Morton took the trouble to save them for a year or more and to bring them along when he moved west. One is just a clipping of a woman supposedly cured of her blindness by her trip to Lourdes. The other is quite substantial—two whole pages on one sheet of paper, containing two articles that appeared in the *American Weekly* sometime in 1939. The first is mostly a lecture delivered by Dr. Smiley Blanton, an "American psychiatrist," before the American Psychiatric Association. Dr. Blanton focuses for the most part on the allegedly miraculous cure of a Charles McDonald from tuberculosis. Most relevant to Jelly's story is the description of McDonald and other pilgrims undergoing a series of ritual immersions in the waters of the grotto where the Virgin Mary supposedly appeared to Bernadette, a peasant girl eventually canonized as a saint because of the cures and other miracles that took place. The allegedly curative power of ritual baths was obviously not a new idea to Morton, who had experienced the process at least twice through voodoo practitioners. It seems that Morton turned, or re-turned, to the Catholic Church for the very same reasons that he had turned to voodoo earlier: 1939 was the year of Jelly's heart attack and the warning from his doctors that he should stop playing music. As we have seen, Jelly first considered following the doctors' prescription and then changed his mind, writing to Roy Carew that "we have a much greater power that has something to say about those things—that's the Supreme Power above."[45] Simply put, Morton was hoping for a miracle, and, although he turned to the Church rather than to voodoo this time, he did so in terms that are entirely compatible with his earlier experience of voodoo.

Anita had living proof of the connection between Catholicism and voodoo in the person of Laura Hunter, who was Jelly's godmother in more than name only: his baptismal certificate lists her as godmother officially, which means that she would have had to be in good standing with the Church, at least when the ceremony was performed. And, as we have seen, Anita's family also knew her as godmother, though perhaps in a less official sense. Why, then, does Anita call Laura a "voodoo witch" and insist that voodoo is a religion entirely different from Catholicism?

There are three possible explanations. The most likely is that Anita may simply have given Lomax what she thought he wanted or expected to hear on the subject of voodoo. People who are interviewed for oral histories often respond in such a way, for a variety of reasons, especially on a topic like voodoo. In his interview of the Morton family, for instance, Lomax notes a reluctance on Morton's uncle Henry Monette's part to speak candidly on the subject and explains, "In the south you have to know people mighty well before they will talk about voodoo[,] and old Henry hooted at the idea that Lalee had been a practitioner. Yet it seemed to me that perhaps old Henry was suspiciously overemphatic in his protests that voodoo was just humbug."[46] By the time of Lomax's encounter with Anita, a number of popular books and movies had instilled in the public mind some lurid stereotypes on the subject, ones that persist to this day: voodoo priests sticking pins in dolls, zombies walking at night, and the like. Perhaps Anita was merely sensationalizing an already sensational story by dressing it up in a Hollywood wardrobe of stereotypes. If Anita embellished her tale of Jelly's end because she suspected that Lomax was susceptible to that kind of sensationalism, she judged her man correctly. In the preface added to the 1993 edition of *Mister Jelly Roll*, Lomax even embellishes Anita's embellishments: "When Jelly was a boy, his loving godmother sold his soul to the devil in return for a gift of boundless musical talent. For him, I believe, this bargain with Satan became quite real. In spite of his outcaste origins, he fulfilled all of his ambitions. . . . When he lost all that he had gained, he attributed his misfortune to sinister unseen influences. And on his deathbed, so his mistress said, he was calling for holy oil to cheat the devil of his godmother's bargain."[47]

According to Anita, Laura sold Jelly's soul to the devil so that she herself could become a "voodoo witch," not "in return for a gift of boundless musical talent" for her godson, as Lomax has it in his version. What follows in the new preface clarifies his motive for the exaggeration: Lomax wants to emphasize the Faustian aspect of Morton's story in order to establish parallels between that and other legends about bluesmen like Robert Johnson and Peetie Wheatstraw, who allegedly sold their souls so that they could become "masters of their instruments."[48] Obviously, Lomax was a very receptive audience for the tale Anita told. It may be that the ground had been prepared by Lomax's contact with Zora Neale Hurston, whose book *Mules and Men* deals primarily with conjuring practices and prescriptions of what she calls "hoodoo" in New Orleans, rather than voodoo as a communal, ritualistic religion. In her second appendix, she gives a number of prescriptions addressed to particular purposes: "TO KILL AND HARM," "TO MAKE PEOPLE LOVE YOU," "TO BREAK UP A LOVE AFFAIR," and so forth.[49] The distinction that Haskins attempts to maintain between the terms *voodoo* and *hoodoo* derives at least in part from Hurston's work, which he cites approvingly on the assumption that "being black she had a greater understanding of the practice of voodoo among black people."[50] The deference that Lomax pays to Anita's statement may have been based on a similar assumption.

But there are two other possible explanations. First, in her old age, Anita may simply have moved toward the conventional, conservative response of Christianity to voodoo. In Haiti, the Roman Catholic view moved in cycles between a grudging tolerance of the cult to outright persecution. In North America, Protestants tended rather uniformly to reject voodoo as paganism or heresy. Laennec Hurbon, in "American Fantasy and Haitian Voodoo," an excellent article on the perpetuation of voodoo stereotypes in print and in film, notes that the Baptists, in particular, held that "Vodou [a variant spelling of *voodoo*] maintains the empire of the devil."[51] It is a widely known fact, attested to by many, that black Baptists and Pentecostals often referred to the blues and to jazz as "the devil's music." Austin Sonnier Jr., in his *Guide to the Blues*, lists a number of blues titles that refer directly to voodoo terminology, including Lightnin' Hopkins's "Black Cat Blues," Junior Wells's "Hoodoo Man," and Muddy Waters's "Got My Mojo Working," among many others.[52] The only direct reference to voodoo in Morton's recorded work occurs in the Library of Congress interview, in his monologue on Aaron Harris, which ends with a twelve-bar blues ballad that was evidently a popular expression of Harris's legend as "a bad, bad man, / Baddest man ever lived in the land." The ballad concludes, "He got out of jail every time he would make his kill, / He had a hoodoo woman, all he had to do was pay the bill."[53] Of his own compositions, only a few imply or evoke a voodoo context: "Bugaboo," a title that denotes a kind of nameless fear; "Ponchatrain" [*sic*], a reference to a lake in the New Orleans area that served as the center of the cult of the voodoo queen Marie Laveau; and possibly "Jungle Blues," which sets the same kind of exotic, misterioso mood as the other two. That same mood informs most of Morton's "Spanish tinge" compositions ("The Crave," "Mamanita," "Creepy Feeling"), and we should remember here that most of the popular Latin dance rhythms are in fact African in origin and derive from religious ritual (Desi Arnaz's most popular hit, "Babaloo," was originally a *santería* hymn, for example). The fact that a good part of Morton's repertoire consisted of the blues, and that he often played in honky-tonks and whorehouses, would have made it easy to associate him with the devil and voodoo.

Finally, there may actually be some truth to what Anita says. The term "voodoo" covers a very broad spectrum of religious activity and experience. Metraux warns that "Voodoo is a religion which is practiced by autonomous cult groups[,] of which each often has its own particular custom and tradition. Whatever anyone may say to the contrary, there is no Voodoo liturgy and doctrine to which priests and priestesses are obliged to conform. Such an idea is a widespread illusion which we must avoid."[54] Sidney Mintz and Michel-Rolf Trouillot are even more emphatic: "Vodou was created by individuals drawn from many different cultures. It took on its characteristic shape over the course of several centuries. It has never been codified in writing, never possessed a national institutional structure—a priesthood, a national church, an orthodoxy, a seminary, a hymnal, a hierarchy, or a charter. . . . It is widely dispersed nationally [in Haiti], in the form of what appear to be local cult groups. It has no geographical center or mother church. *Its practice seems to be highly variable locally*."[55] If voodoo was so "variable" in Haiti, the land of its birth, we should expect an even wider variety of practices to have developed when it moved to New Orleans, a city predominantly Creole and Catholic but also floating in a sea of black Baptists. If there is any truth at all to Anita's statement, it may reflect practices and ideas peculiar to Laura Hunter.

A review of voodoo in New Orleans would be helpful here, but nearly all scholarly work on the religion has been focused on Haiti, not New Orleans. For the most part, books and articles of any substance on New Orleans voodoo are for popular consumption, which means that documentation is spotty where it exists at all. However, accounts of New Orleans voodoo all agree on one thing: that the priestess known as Marie

Laveau, who dominated the field from about 1830 to the 1870s, shaped and defined the practice of voodoo in that city as no one else before or since. She was a legendary, almost mythic figure whose influence was said to have been pervasive on all levels of the city's life; in fact, there was a direct connection between Laveau and Morton's family.

The most extensive treatment of Laveau and her work can be found in the book *Voodoo in New Orleans*, by Robert Tallant. Tallant is sometimes uncritical in the ways in which he mixes fact and folklore, but he does at least provide the outlines of a preliminary chronology, and he does provide a theory about the nature of Laveau's impact on voodoo in the Crescent City, though his theory is more folklore than fact. Tallant sketches a chronology of her life: Laveau was born about 1795 in New Orleans, and died there on 24 June 1881 at approximately eighty-five years of age. She married Jacques Paris, a Creole quadroon, on 4 August 1819. Though the marriage failed within about a year or two, and soon after that she became involved in a long-standing common-law marriage with a Christophe Galpion, with whom she had fifteen children, she was known as "the widow Paris" (Paris died shortly after their separation) for the remainder of her life.[56] She became the "queen" of New Orleans voodoo by about 1830, and maintained that position of prominence until approximately 1871–72, by which time she had become too old and infirm to carry on.[57] She was succeeded by her daughter, also named Marie Laveau, born to Laveau and Galpion on 2 February 1827, though exactly when the shift occurred is not certain.[58] Tallant cites a *New Orleans Times* story of 21 March 1869 that supposedly describes the moment when "she reigned as queen over a Voodoo conclave for the last time." And then Tallant declares, "Two months later, on June 7, 1869, the cult held a meeting and reached a decision that since Marie Laveau was now past seventy she should be retired," though he offers no source for the latter statement. He does offer a source, the *Daily Picayune*, for a story about what must have been one of her last public appearances, a charity visit to the cells of two condemned prisoners in the Parish

Prison.[59] Such visits had become a regular part of her ministry since the 1850s, and Tallant earlier cites a number of those visits without offering any documentation.

Tallant also offers several rather lurid tales that purport to describe the goings-on at Laveau's voodoo rituals. Tallant, like Lomax, seems susceptible to the sensationalist elements of the subject. Much of it is fairly standard stuff—drums, dancing at nocturnal campfire meetings, ritual slaughter of animals, drinking of blood, and the like—all culminating, supposedly, in a sexual orgy. He even repeats, as fact, claims that some of the rituals were staged (with even more sex in the mix) for the benefit, or titillation, of whites attracted to the "exotic" beauty of black women, and that Marie Laveau often acted as a procuress. Tallant does not document any of this except for the citation of interviews with people who claim either to be eyewitnesses or to repeat eyewitness accounts. However, Tallant himself frequently asserts that it is virtually impossible for anyone alive in 1945, when his book was first published, to have participated in any of Laveau's "orgies"; and, of course, secondhand accounts are notoriously unreliable.

One documented firsthand account, a story in the *New Orleans Times* about Laveau's last performance at a "Voodoo conclave," says little explicitly about sex acts. It describes the participants moving with a steadily increasing tempo in a circle: "As the motion gained in intensity the flowers and other ornaments disappeared from their hair, and their dresses were torn open, and each one conducted herself like a bacchante. Everyone was becoming drunk and intoxicated with the prevailing madness and excitement."[60] The torn-open dresses are the only evidence here of anything sexually suggestive. Another account, about two pages of fine print that forms the centerpiece of Tallant's evidence, describes a ritual event that took place at Lake Pontchartrain on Saint John's Day in 1872. The story appeared in the *New Orleans Times* on 28 June of that year, and describes a ceremony that proceeds along the same lines as the one cited above, except that at one point Laveau orders the participants to undress, after which they take turns putting various ingredients into the communal pot: salt, pepper, various herbs, a snake, a black cat, a black rooster, and so forth. After a ritual bath in the lake, Laveau tells the participants, "I give you all half an hour recreation," and the narrator tells us that they all "scattered promiscuously," whatever that means. When the time is up, Laveau calls them back to finish the ceremony.[61]

The source of the story and some of its details raise serious questions about its accuracy, however. First, we are told that the congregants consisted of "about two hundred persons of mixed colors—white, black, and mulattoes"; then, at the end of the long citation, Tallant notes that the "scene seems to have been fairly representative of the spectacles the white people who sought to view a Voodoo gathering were permitted to attend."[62] In other words, the story describes not an authentic ritual performed and attended by initiates only, but instead a sort of tourist spectacle put on for the entertainment of white folks. Tallant also tells us that the Marie Laveau who conducted the ceremony was probably not the original but her daughter, whom he refers to as Marie II and who, as he says elsewhere, increased the sexual content of the rituals. Finally, the author of the tale begins by describing the source as "an obliging correspondent who was fortunate enough to reach the scene of the voudous [*sic*] incantation some hours before our reporter."[63] The story turns out to be the secondhand transmission of an anonymous source.

Paradoxically, Tallant's theory about Laveau's main contribution to voodoo is that she Christianized it—a seemingly odd idea, given all the sexual stuff, but an idea that Tallant gives a predictably moralistic turn: "Marie never lessened in any way the mysticism and sensuality of the frantic Zombi worshippers—all the orthodox trappings of the spectacle were retained: the snake, the black cat, the roosters, the blood-drinking and the finale of fornication—but she added some new tricks, both borrowed and original, principally Roman Catholic statues of saints, prayers, incense and holy water. The Voodoos had been devil-worshippers originally. Marie renounced this and always insisted that her people were

Christians. She offered Voodoo to God. Castellanos, in *New Orleans As It Was*, wrote: 'To idolatry she added blasphemy.'"[64] Tallant appears to have done much of his research in movie theaters—he packs so many of the sensationalist, wrongheaded Hollywood stereotypes into a single short paragraph. The "Zombi" phenomenon is a minor one, condemned even by many in the religion, but Hollywood, in films like *White Zombie* (1932) and *I Walked with a Zombie* (1943), magnified it so that it became central to popular ideas about voodoo. Marie Laveau most emphatically did not add Roman Catholic elements to the religion; they were there from the very beginning. And no serious student of the subject would ever subscribe to the notion that "the Voodoos had been devil-worshippers originally." But the black-magic imagery in Anita's statement surely bears a close family resemblance to Tallant's. Again, one wonders whether Anita was confirming what she figured would be most white people's prejudices about voodoo.

At least one member of Jelly Roll Morton's family was at one time directly connected to Marie Laveau herself. Of special relevance to his family history is a document involving Laveau that was uncovered by historian Lawrence Gushee in the Orleans Parish, Louisiana Second District Court, Succession Records 1846–1880. The document, dated 11 May 1872, involves a legal dispute concerning the estate of Pierre Monette, Morton's maternal great-grandfather. Pierre's son, Julian (or Julien) Joseph Monette, claimed that he was the sole heir to his father's estate because his half brother, Edouard, was illegitimate. Gushee paraphrases the relevant information:

> The court summoned Marie Laveau. The dossier contains the deposition of Marie Laveau, widow Paris, about 70 years of age, 152 St. Ann St, who has lived in New Orleans since her birth. She is too sick to leave her room and cannot walk. She deposed that she had known Pierre Monette and was intimately acquainted with him since they were both about 20 years of age, also, Louise Boulin, from around 40 to 50 years ago. Louise Boulin lived in concubinage for many years with Pierre and they had 2 kids, a daughter who died

young, and a son, Julian. Edouard's mother was a woman known as
Zabelle, now dead, who sold calas (a kind of rice cake) on the levee.[65]

The court concluded that, as Pierre Monette and Louise Boulin had
named both Julian and Edouard as their sons in their marriage contract,
dated 2 November 1867, they had thereby recognized both as legitimate.

There is no evidence that Morton knew of this important family connection, though it is hard to imagine that he had never heard of it at all,
considering the stature of Marie Laveau. However, the document certainly attests to her influence in New Orleans, both public and private,
and it suggests the possibility that Morton's family was involved with
voodoo long before Laura Hunter. In his "Preliminary Chronology" of
Morton's early years, Gushee establishes that Pierre Monette was born
in what is today called Cap Haitien in Haiti and that Jelly's paternal line
of descent "quite probably goes back to Port-au-Prince."[66] In addition,
Gushee notes that the Hecaud family, into which Laura-Eulalie first
married, were also Haitian. The status of voodoo as the unofficial national religion of Haiti establishes a high degree of probability that Morton's family, Haitian on both the maternal and paternal sides, had a
long-standing relationship to the cult. And this, in turn, raises questions
about the possibility that Laura may have been a family relation as well
as a godmother to Jelly, either directly or through her first marriage to
Paul Hecaud. In Catholic tradition, parents often do choose a godparent
from within the family, but that is not necessary—after the baptism, the
godparent becomes a member of the family, often in more than a merely
symbolic fashion. But at present no documentation has come to light to
provide even a clue.

4

If anything, Jelly Roll Morton's statement that Anita Gonzales was the
only woman he ever loved grossly understates the length and depth of
their relationship and the extent of their ties to one another. The story

of their five or six years together on the West Coast, so movingly told by Morton himself in his Library of Congress reminiscences, is certainly a passionate one, full of highs and lows, of angry breakups and tender reconciliations, of joy and sorrow, of bright promise and darkest regrets. But the complete story of their relationship spans at least forty years, from roughly 1901 to 1941. If Anita was right, his romantic attachment to her began early, when he was still in puberty or in his early teens and she was eighteen to twenty years old. They probably met in Biloxi, the location of both the Johnson family residence and the strawberry farm of his godmother, where he spent his summers starting in 1901. From the beginning to the end of their relationship, whenever Jelly and Anita were together, Laura was somewhere in the picture, even in her death a little over a year before Jelly died. Anita's family also addressed Laura as godmother, and Anita was well aware of Laura's voodoo practice, though it is hard to tell from the scant evidence whether or to what extent she herself was involved in it. As for Jelly, despite his statement that he "didn't half believe" in voodoo, he was in fact deeply affected by his godmother's practice in his childhood and himself consulted practitioners on at least two significant occasions. He also knew and on occasion worked with Anita's brothers, the musicians Dink and Bill Johnson, founding members of the Original Creole Band in Los Angeles, for which, according to Jelly, Anita provided the financial backing. There is no evidence of whether or when Jelly and Anita were ever legally married, but he consistently referred to her as his wife and to her brothers, Dink and Bill, as his brothers-in-law. He obviously regarded the time he spent with Anita on the West Coast as one of the best periods of his life, and it also appears to have been one of the most fertile musically, as we shall see. Although he was supposed to send for her when he left for Chicago in 1923, he never did, and both of them eventually married other people. The extent to which he may have stayed in touch with her during the 1930s will be covered in another chapter, but at the very least she must have contacted him when Laura fell ill and eventually died. She apparently followed him to Los Angeles on his last trip west and probably provided some financial support as well. His last will and testament, signed on the 28th of June 1941, names Anita as the heir to the bulk of his estate, and, according to her, she was with him at the very end.

In short, theirs was not just a love story; Anita's relationship to Jelly touched virtually every aspect of his life.

CHAPTER 3

L.A. Jelly, 1917-1923

1

He wanted to leave Chicago. Given his chronic wanderlust, there was nothing surprising in that. Beginning in New Orleans, Morton traveled to Pensacola (1907), Biloxi and St. Louis (1909), and briefly back to New Orleans. Then it was on to Chicago, Mobile, and Jacksonville, Florida (1910); and then Memphis and New York (1911). On to Houston, next, then to Oxnard, California; and back once again to New Orleans (1912–13). He made a brief return to Chicago (1913), but during his "Texas years" (1912–14) Houston and San Antonio served as his base of operations as he worked the Midwest—Oklahoma City, St. Louis, Indianapolis—which he followed with an extended stay in Chicago (1914–16). Finally, after a brief road tour that included Detroit, and an even briefer return to Chicago, he moved on to the West Coast in the summer of 1917.[1]

Lawrence Gushee correctly describes Morton's 1914–16 stay in Chicago as "probably the longest period [Jelly] spent in any one place since leaving New Orleans around 1907–8," so the move from Chicago was, if anything, overdue.[2] In *Mister Jelly Roll*, Morton offers two explanations for ending his stay in Chicago, though they should perhaps be regarded as rationalizations for his naturally itchy feet: the first was competition—the trumpeter Freddie Keppard and the Creole Band "certainly finished *me* at the Elite [in Chicago]. Business went to the bad, and, as I did not wish to stay on and not satisfy everybody, I hit the road again." Second was the fact that, when he returned briefly to Chicago (1917), he found to his dismay a "different class of people invading the city at the time."[3] The latter is a clear reference to what historians call the Great Migration of 1915–1929, when southern blacks moved in huge numbers north, east, and west—primarily to Chicago and New York, but actually to all urban centers in the United States, including Los Angeles. The already established black communities in those cities often regarded the newcomers as too "countrified," crude and illiterate, even though that was not always a fair judgment.[4] Morton's response to that "invasion" was thus fairly typical of those blacks who considered themselves "a different class" than the new immigrants, for whatever reason, even though, ironically, the diaspora of New Orleans music and musicians can itself be seen as a part of that Great Migration.

Why Los Angeles? During a short, earlier visit somewhere around 1908–10, Morton had found that not much was happening musically in California, except in Oxnard, which he called "a very fast-stepping town"; but in 1917 he went in response to the concrete offer of a gig, whereas the previous trip seems to have been a spur-of-the-moment affair.[5] In any case, he was not the kind of person to stay in one place for very long. His West Coast years were themselves an odyssey within an odyssey, which began in Los Angeles (1917–18). Next he lived and worked in San Francisco and Oakland for part of 1919, before moving to the Seattle-Tacoma-Vancouver area (1919–20). He worked the winter of 1920–21 in Denver and then returned to Los Angeles (1921), which he used as home base while he worked in the Southern California area, including San Diego, and in Tijuana, Mexico. Many of his last gigs on the West Coast were at the Wayside Park–Leak's Lake amusement park built by Reb Spikes and later taken over by Morton and William "Pops" Woodman.[6]

The story of Jelly's odyssey set against the historical backdrop of the

Great Migration does indeed take on epic proportions at times, in the sense that it is the embodiment of the story of the African American people at that time, moving restlessly from place to place, trying to make a new life—trying to find a voice for a tradition that began on the shores of West Africa with the slave trade and arrived in the twentieth century with a migration that was itself an odyssey. Morton resembles no epic hero so much as Odysseus: braggart, trickster hero, and vagabond, shuffling identities like a card shark, famous and popular one minute, Noman the next, here a sharply dressed pool hustler and pimp, there a shuffling, raggedy blackface clown. Of all the various aspects of Morton's persona, this one lies closest to his heart; he was, as they say, "made for the part"—the vagabond minstrel, the man of many wiles and talents who never fails to come up with a way to get the next meal, the next gig, the next train ticket, and who has learned to exploit the role of Stranger in Town to the full. Which Jelly Roll would show up—pimp, pool hustler, card shark, piano player, vaudevillian, minstrel—depended on the town and the circumstances, just as Odysseus modulated himself, from lover to supplicant to warlord to beggar. And, like Odysseus among the Phaeacians, Jelly got a chance to tell his own story.

2

The gig in Los Angeles in the summer of 1917 did not get off to a very promising start. He expected his clothes, which he had sent ahead in trunks, to be waiting for him when he arrived, but for some reason they were delayed three to four days. Meanwhile, Morton had only the one blue serge suit he was wearing, which, though brand new when he left Chicago, became covered with dust during the long ride through the desert in a railroad tourist car. When he got off the train at the Southern Pacific Railroad terminal, he was "almost as dusty as a boll weevil," as he recalls.[7] To make matters worse, the Cadillac Cafe, the site of his gig, was located across the street from the station, and when he arrived he was greeted by a brass band. The gig was set to begin the very night of his arrival, so until his trunks showed up he was stuck with his brand new, but very dirty, blue serge suit. Locals were understandably puzzled and even angry at Mister Jelly Roll, the man with the hotshot reputation, showing up in such sorry shape. In spite of this inauspicious entrance, Morton claims the opening night was such a huge success that the police had to be called out "to stop the crowd (I guess it [was] pretty well advertised)."[8] There are no ads in the *California Eagle*—the Los Angeles–based black newspaper that served all of California—for Jelly's appearance and no reports of police being called out, but possibly his reputation alone could have packed the house. For the next few days, until the trunks arrived, he took some heavy criticism about his clothes; after that, "I turned the town out. They thought I was one of the movie stars, I had so many clothes."[9]

Morton is not very specific about his fellow performers at the Cadillac. Though he says there were "about ten" in the company, the only ones he names are those in the well-known group photo with Jelly taken in front of the Cadillac: Albertine Pickens, Ross and Rucker ("Common Sense" Ross and Eddie Rucker, a singer-comedian team), and the eventually famous Ada "Bricktop" Smith, who appears in Lomax's book as "Bright Red."[10] Morton says nothing about Mabel Watts, also in the photo. (See fig. 10.) In an interview with William Russell, Shep Allen, who knew Jelly in Chicago, describes going to Los Angeles around 1917–18 with a singing group, the Panama Trio, which included Cora Green, Carolyn Williams, and Florence Mills; according to Allen, Morton accompanied the trio at the Cadillac. Like all early jazz musicians, Jelly did not simply get on the bandstand and play music. Instead, he was often responsible for staging a floor show with dancers, singers, comedians, and the like. Among his 1926–28 Red Hot Peppers recordings, those with spoken comedic dialogue—like "Dead Man Blues" and "Sidewalk Blues"—probably give a more accurate idea of a typical Jelly Roll Morton performance than the purely musical takes, though many listeners

Figure 10. "Common Sense" Ross, Albertine Pickens, Jelly Roll Morton, Ada "Bricktop" Smith, Eddie Rucker, and Mabel Watts at the Cadillac Cafe in Los Angeles, circa 1917–18. Courtesy of Floyd Levin.

are uncomfortable or embarrassed by the Stepin Fetchit overtones of the comedy.

Jelly mentions the Black and Tan Orchestra as also having played at the Cadillac, but he leaves unclear whether they actually accompanied him or merely preceded him: "Previously [they] had a band playin there when I went to the Cadillac. This band was named the Black and Tan Band—that's the name [they] had taken. They had no fame at all—juss a band consisting of four pieces: trumpet n trombone n drums n piano. But they didn have a regla piano player, they picked up anybody that could halfway [do it]."[11] He then adds that he "was . . . takin the job away from these boys," but he might very well have meant that he took charge of the job and relegated them to the status of house band. Morton makes no mention of a reed player, though by 1917 the tenor saxophonist and clarinetist Paul Howard was a regular member of the Black and Tan Orchestra. In an interview, Howard once remembered playing with Morton "at the station." [12] Could he mean the Cadillac, since it was so close to the Southern Pacific terminal? Unfortunately, no one involved in the interview follows up on that clue. At any rate, Jelly seldom had anything flattering to say about most other musicians, and he certainly does not spare the Black and Tan, who were one of the most popular bands in Los Angeles at the time and must have been one of his chief competitors when they were not sharing the bandstand with him. The band originated in Texas and moved to Los Angeles around 1914–15, when ads for their performances began to appear in the *California Eagle*. The trombonist Harry Southard, the leader, remained active in Los Angeles well into the 1940s, when he was Horace Tapscott's first music teacher. The cornetist Ernest Coycault was a New Orleans Creole who had moved to Los Angeles in 1908 with the first version of the group that eventually became known as the Creole Band, which originally included Dink and Bill Johnson, Anita's brothers. In spite of Morton's disparaging words, they were an able group of musicians, certainly able enough to back him up.

Morton's way of life often forced him either to "front" an established band or to assemble a pickup group of available talent, especially when he traveled alone to areas far from the centers of the jazz world, like Los Angeles. The few times he imported New Orleans musicians to give the West Coast a taste of "the real thing," the taste lasted only until the musicians got homesick, and there were very few black or Creole musicians in Los Angeles who were familiar with the New Orleans style. The 1920 census for the city records that, of a total of 1,146 musicians, only 48 were black—and not all of them were jazz players. [13] The years 1917–25 saw a notable increase in New Orleans musicians on the West Coast; of the 52 listed, 41 relocated during those years, most of them to Los Angeles. Many of those musicians had been major figures in New Orleans, like Kid Ory, who moved west in 1919 and sent for Papa Mutt Carey to form Kid Ory's Creole Jazz Band, which played at the Cadillac for almost a year. It must be said, though, that those numbers are rather small, especially considering that the popular success of the Original Dixieland Jazz Band's 1917 recording of "Livery Stable Blues" created a market for any group that could call itself a jazz orchestra.

At about this time the Black and Tan Orchestra added the word "jazz" to its name in *California Eagle* ads. A look at the *California Eagle* of the period shows that the musical tastes of black Los Angeles, at least of the professional and business classes, were decidedly conservative: the feature articles are invariably about classical recitals and church music; the only evidence of any budding jazz scene is an occasional ad for a nightclub or a dance. Jelly's later practice of writing out arrangements and even solos was no doubt forced on him, in the beginning at least, by his travels to areas where he had access to a small group of musicians who could be described as "hot" players and to a larger group who could not play "hot" or improvise but who could at least read music. Also, since local musicians in places like Los Angeles were not familiar with the New Orleans repertoire, Morton often was restricted to the popular tunes of the day in many of his West Coast gigs; he tells Lomax that he would call tunes like "The Russian Rag," "Maple Leaf Rag," "My Melancholy Baby," "Li'l Liza Jane," "Daddy Dear," and "When the Midnight Choo-Choo Leaves for Alabam," among others.[14]

Arna Bontemps's description of one of Jelly's bands refers to one of the last gigs he played in Los Angeles, at Leak's Lake, but reflects what must have been a fairly typical group from the very first, beginning with the Cadillac: "In Los Angeles his fortunes flourished. He rode in an impressive automobile, dressed like a mad prince. . . . The small combination with which he played was made up partly of neighborhood musicians, including Ben Albans, Jr., a high school student. Jelly patiently taught the young cornetist, as well as the other musicians he had found in the community, the style of playing he required. He brought two or three of his regular men with him. The results were most satisfactory.

Crowds of Jelly's admirers filled the place [Leak's Lake] regularly. Many of them had known him in New Orleans and Chicago, and he seemed happy to be among them."[15] The pianist Buster Wilson also attests to Morton's acceptance of a mentor's role to young musicians in the city: Jelly not only coached the twenty-year-old musician on his instrument but also allowed him to sit in on the piano when King Oliver came to town.[16] It was evidently a role that Morton played with some relish, even near the end of his life, in New York, where he took the young guitarist Lawrence Lucie under his wing: "Jelly would play on the piano and show me his material and we used to exchange ideas about music and rehearse together."[17] As for the crowds, the fact that so many people in the black community had known Jelly previously explains how he could have done so well at the Cadillac without press coverage. Of a total population of 576,673 in the city, only 15,579 were black (2.71 percent), most of whom were forced by restrictive housing covenants to live in a narrow corridor that occupied both sides of Central Avenue, roughly from First to Vernon.[18] Word of mouth, with the help of flyers and posters, easily could have been enough to pack the house.

Further on in the monologue about the Cadillac, Morton says the house stayed packed, and "then the movie-star trade began, and we didn't have anything but movie stars at the Cadillac Cafe as long as I stayed there."[19] He mentions no names, and Lomax makes no attempt to pin him down, but the Hollywood connection was quite genuine and existed on many levels. Many of the stars of the budding movie industry were fans of what was to them a new form of popular music called jazz. In fact, Fatty Arbuckle, whose fame at the time rivaled that of Charlie Chaplin, had worked in vaudeville with Reb Spikes in Oklahoma around 1910, and when Reb and his brother, Johnny, moved back to Los Angeles in 1919, their music store on the corner of Twelfth and Central became the nerve center for jazz and black music. Reb served informally as a kind of booking agent when directors and producers needed black extras, bands, or background music to set the mood for the actors in the studio;

with some amusement, Spikes even notes that the stars would send their chauffeurs to the store to pick up the latest "dirty records," as they called them.[20] Even though in 1917 Spikes had not yet permanently returned to the city, his reminiscences provide valuable clues to the identity of the movie stars Morton talks about. In addition to Arbuckle, Spikes mentions that Charlie Chaplin, Mary Pickford, Mary's brother Jack, and Blanche Sweet used to frequent a nightclub called Baron Long's in Watts, where nightclubs and dance halls could stay open all night—unlike those in Los Angeles, which had to close at midnight. (Rudolph Valentino was one of the featured attractions at Baron Long's, dancing the tango there just before he got his break in the movies.)[21] In Tom Stoddard's *Jazz on the Barbary Coast*, the San Francisco musician Sid LeProtti remembers that when he and his So Different Orchestra, a San Francisco–based group, were playing in Los Angeles, Morton's composition "The Crave," a tango, had become wildly popular among the Hollywood set, "especially Jack Pickford, . . . Fatty Arbuckle, and Max Scherman, and they broadcasted it all over Los Angeles."[22]

"The Crave" sparked a controversy between the two musicians that almost ended their relationship. Morton gave LeProtti manuscript copies of some of his tunes, "The Crave" among them, when LeProtti's band was playing in Los Angeles. Then LeProtti heard Jelly playing the tune, but in a different arrangement: "He was pretty cagey; he'd play it one way, then he'd change it and play it again. One day I caught him playin' it and heard him say to a fella, 'Well, this is the way I play it when I'm playin' ad lib.'"[23] The existence of two versions is confirmed by the recorded evidence. In Morton's only commercial recording of the piece, recorded by General on 14 December 1939, he follows the thematic pattern AABCC, with a standard modulation to the key of the subdominant in the C section. In the Library of Congress recording, the format is AABBACC. Morton's performance on this version is not as spirited or precise as on the former, but the repetition of B and the return to A afterward allow him to improvise more freely. Perhaps that is what Jelly means by "this is the way I play it when I'm playin' ad lib," although the shorter General version may have been necessary because of the three-minute limitation imposed by ten-inch 78 rpm recordings; the Library of Congress version runs four minutes and thirty-seven seconds. LeProtti made his own arrangement of it based on the ad lib version; he claims that it was his band's performances of the tune that made it so popular with the Hollywood crowd:

> People would walk in every night and say, "They tell me you play a number called 'The Crave,'" and we'd play it for them.
>
> After we got done playin' our regular job, we'd come down to Murray's Cafe—which was the leading Negro cafe, in fact the only one in Los Angeles in 1916—and play. We was down there playin' "The Crave" and Jelly walked in. You could've cooked an egg on his head, he was so hot. The next day he jumped me.
>
> He said, "What do you mean to do? God, man lend you a number and you try to steal his stuff. You're a heck of a guy; that's all I hear, "The Crave," "The Crave," my stuff!
>
> That was a great word for your own numbers, if you had them, in those days, my stuff.
>
> I said, "What do you mean, stealin' your stuff?"
>
> He said, "When I lent you that tune, I didn't want you broadcastin' it all over. The next thing I know, you'll be tryin' to publish it."
>
> I said, "Jelly, I got the brains enough not to publish your tune. When you gave it to us, you gave it to a mighty fine band. Not me, but the rest of the band, the horns; them's the boys that put it over."
>
> He said, "If I'd known that, I would've [*sic*] given it to you. Have you got it here?"
>
> I said, "No, I haven't got it now, but I'll get it and give it to you tomorrow."
>
> So I brought it to him. I met him on the corner of Fifth and Main streets and I gave it to him, and, you know, that character, when I handed it to him, he took it and tore it up and threw it in the

trashcan on the street. He walked away and said, "I'll be seein' you later on."[24]

Some of the details of the anecdote are off at least a bit. Most obviously, it could not have happened in 1916 because Morton did not arrive in Los Angeles until the summer of 1917; 1918 is more likely closer to the truth. Also, it is unlikely that LeProtti and his band would play anywhere in the city proper after their regular gig, given the midnight curfew that Reb Spikes mentions. And Murray's Cafe was in fact the Cadillac, often referred to as "Murray's" after the owner's name, Nolie B. Murray.[25] It must be said here that "The Crave" is a fine piece of music, one of Morton's best, especially among those in the "Spanish tinge" mode. In this case, the rhythmic feel is pure tango, and the various strains are rich, even luxurious; one can understand its popularity with the Hollywood crowd. The seventeen-piece big-band version arranged by Dick Hyman and recorded in 1973 gives some idea of what an orchestral version sounds like, though LeProtti's So Different Orchestra was much smaller—usually about six pieces. The performance by Hyman and the big band, issued on *Jelly and James* (a tribute to Morton and James P. Johnson), is one of the highlights of the album. It's a brilliant orchestration, and the band's dazzling performance captures the piece's rhythmic vitality and melodic lushness. It is extremely odd that Morton waited until 1939 to record the composition commercially, especially considering the popularity of the tango during the 1920s.

In spite of the minor glitches in LeProtti's story, it rings true, not only because it is so vividly recalled, but, even more important, because of Jelly's possessiveness about his "stuff." It is well known that most of Jelly's generation of musicians were initially wary of writing or recording their music, because that would allow other musicians to steal their "stuff." The story most often told about that attitude has to do with why, allegedly, the Creole Band was not the first jazz orchestra to record. According to Johnny St. Cyr, they were given the opportunity, but the trumpeter and leader Freddie Keppard vetoed the idea: "Freddie plain refused, said he wasn't gonna let the other fellows hear his records and catch his stuff. That way they missed out being the first jazz band to record and the chance came to a white band—the Original Dixieland [Jazz Band]."[26] Some historians have cast a shadow of doubt over the authenticity of that story, but Morton, in his early years, obviously shared Keppard's suspicions. Jelly says as much to Lomax in the recorded interviews and adds that musicians were paid rather poorly by music publishers—in a single night's work they could get many times the amount of money a publisher would pay for a song, so why bother?[27] By 1917, the only composition by Morton that had been published and copyrighted was "Jelly Roll Blues," in 1915, by Will Rossiter in Chicago, even though he had already written at least a dozen compositions, many of which became among his most popular. Then in 1918, in Los Angeles, Morton deposited a handwritten copy of "Froggie Moore Rag" for copyright, though it was not published until 1923, by the Spikes brothers. It is not clear why Jelly felt he needed to copyright that particular tune at that moment, but it does seem that his experience on the West Coast and developments in the music business forced him to rethink his attitude toward publishing and protecting his compositions, and toward recording as well. In *Mister Jelly Roll* he tells Lomax that he made his first recording in 1918, the same year he copyrighted "Froggie Moore" (using the "Frog-i-more Rag" variant of the name), in Los Angeles: "Reb Spikes, Mutt Carey, Wade Whaley, Kid Ory and I recorded *The Wolverines* and *King Porter*, but we never heard from those records. I don't know why."[28] The recordings have never come to light, and Reb Spikes said on a few occasions that he did not remember such a session.

Morton's relationship with the Spikes brothers seems to have been a combination of friendly rivalry and business partnership: I have already alluded to the controversy over the authorship of "Someday, Sweetheart"; also, in the Library of Congress interviews Jelly tells Lomax that he left Los Angeles for Chicago to stop the Spikes brothers from stealing his "stuff"—in this case, "Wolverine Blues."[29] It seems that the West Coast years mark Jelly's gradual coming to grips with the realities of the modern music business—his awareness that he could not afford to ignore those realities, that if he did ignore them someone else would get the credit and the profit from his "stuff." Some of his nervousness on that score must have been exacerbated by the Spikes brothers, who gave him no credit for his contribution to "Someday, Sweetheart," and who on two other occasions ("Wolverine Blues" and "Froggie Moore") wrote lyrics to Morton compositions and then claimed composer credit alongside of Jelly. And one can easily imagine that Anita, the entrepreneur extraordinaire, would have given Jelly quite an earful about his carelessness, not to say his naïveté, in protecting himself from exploitation.

3

Bricktop sabotaged Morton's first engagement at the Cadillac Cafe. At least, that's the claim he makes in the Library of Congress monologue:

> Bricktop, I've known [h]er since she was a kid, born and raised in
> Chicago, and much younger than myself, but she had learned the art
> [of] the average entertainer. That was when she got a big bill to
> switch it and put a smaller bill in its place. And I had my eyes on her.
> . . . In those days I never looked at the keys, I never turned around; I
> always looked at the entertainers. . . . Their every move they'd make
> I had em. Whether they were singin or whether they were stealin, I
> had em both ways.
>   So . . . Bricktop went South in [h]er stockin with a ten-dollar
> bill.[30]

Obviously, the entertainers at the Cadillac had what amounts to a fairly common arrangement, then as now: all tips went into a common kitty and then were divided, sometimes in equal shares, sometimes in portions that reflected the hierarchy of stars, costars, and underlings of various kinds. When Morton told the boss what he had seen Bricktop do, Murray offered to make up the difference out of his own pocket. But Morton would have none of it: "You payin it will only encourage her to steal further," he said.[31] Even though Jelly says the boss did not follow up on his complaint, when Bricktop got wind of it she was not pleased and, without saying anything to Morton, somehow managed to get the pianist Bill Hegamin to come from New York to Los Angeles to take over the job—at least, as Morton tells the story. Jelly found out about the arrangement by surprise one day when he went to the Cadillac to get his meal—a fringe benefit, evidently—and found Hegamin warming up at the piano. The two knew each other, so Morton asked Hegamin what he was doing there; when Hegamin replied that he was working there, Jelly repeated the question in surprise and got the same answer. Then Jelly said, "Tha-, that's strange. I been workin here all the time and they didn tell me a thing about it. . . . So he was sorry to know he had taken my job. Of course, I knew nothing about it. . . . The boss happen to be there. . . . So, he said 'Well', I was 'hard to get along with,' not realizin the fack that I was right n the party was wrong in stealin the money, and he 'juss went and got somebody juss as good as you.' I told him okay, but I would close the joint in two weeks."[32]

Bricktop says nothing about all this in her autobiography. In fact, she makes only one reference to her relations with Morton, which I quoted earlier: "I really got to know Jelly Roll Morton at Murray's. He was still there trying to figure out what to do with his life. He couldn't decide whether to be a pimp or a piano player. I told him to be both."[33] One would think that she would make some reference to the incident, if it really were the big issue that Morton makes of it. Perhaps she regarded it as a minor squabble—so minor that she may even have forgotten it. In *Mister Jelly Roll*, Lomax has Morton call her Bright Red, so even if she knew the book, she is not explicitly identified as the culprit.[34] Jelly's story does seem somewhat inconsistent: if he were the star of the show, and Bricktop merely one of the supporting cast, how did she get the authority to send for Hegamin all the way from New York and to release Jelly? Even in his own story, Morton says that Murray was releasing him because he was "hard to get along with," and there is plenty of testimony by those who knew him to substantiate that impression—Sid LeProtti among them. Most likely, Murray and others at the cafe had found Morton's manner abrasive, and the Bricktop incident may have been only one in a number of instances when Jelly tried to tell someone, in this case Murray, how to run his business.

Still, it is odd that Bricktop makes no further mention of Jelly in her autobiography. The gig at the Cadillac is one of the few they worked together, at least on record, but they knew each other a long time, as Morton acknowledges, and the itinerary of their careers on the West Coast is nearly identical. They both left Chicago for Los Angeles in 1917 and worked there through 1918; both moved to San Francisco and were working in the Barbary Coast district when Prohibition took effect in the summer of 1919; they then moved north to the Seattle-Vancouver area to work—sometimes in the same clubs, but evidently not always at the same time—from 1920 to 1921; both returned to Los Angeles in 1921 to work in Southern California and then left in 1923 to return to Chicago. It is not likely that they planned their itineraries to coincide so neatly, but the similarities may not be entirely coincidental, either. Reb Spikes's travels on the West Coast during the same period roughly parallel those of Morton and Bricktop, so I suspect that the pattern reflects something about the dynamics of the music business on the Coast at the time.

Jelly claims he made good on his promise to "close" the Cadillac: "There was a roadhouse out in a little place called Watts, about nine or ten miles from Los Angeles. The colored owner, George Brown, wasn't doing any good, so, when I offered to come out there, he immediately accepted. I told him I didn't want to open until he notified Hollywood that I'd be working there. We had invitations printed and, my opening night, all Hollywood was there. That ended the Cadillac. They kept going down and down until they had to close."[35]

Jelly's move may have affected business adversely at the Cadillac, but it is almost certain that he is exaggerating when he says he closed it. The Cadillac may have closed briefly for some reason, but later in the same monologue Morton says that he returned for a second gig—and this time he clearly identifies the Black and Tan as the group he fronted.[36]

But the entrance of George Brown at this point in the story is note-
worthy. Reb Spikes describes Brown as "a big politician—a fixer, you
know. Anything [*sic*] you got in jail or anything, he could fix it for you."
And he describes his place in Watts as "a little dump" just a few blocks
from Baron Long's, where Spikes used to play for Valentino; Spikes
clearly says that the stars he mentions came to Baron Long's rather than
to Brown's "dump."[37] Meanwhile, the events that led up to Morton's return to the Cadillac made an enemy of Brown, and though he is a minor
character with regard to the space he actually occupies in the story of
the West Coast years, in Morton's view Brown's influence on his life in
Los Angeles grew more and more sinister, until at the end Jelly claims
that Brown was one of the reasons he left for Chicago. Jelly, like Reb
Spikes, calls Brown "a big politician." According to Jelly, Brown came to
Morton once with a proposition: "'If you'll put up $600 and your part-
ner $600, I'll kick in the same amount and we'll control this campaign
and run this town to suit ourselves.' I told him that I wasn't interested in
running the town as in making some money, and that caused him to
deepen in his anger toward me."[38]

Morton's version of what followed is at least a bit self-serving: He invited Willie Tyler to join his band at George Brown's club, and Tyler,
whom Jelly praises highly as a violinist, somehow managed to convince
Brown to let him take over the orchestra. Tyler then invited Hegamin
to occupy the piano chair, which left Jelly out of the picture. At that
point, Murray called Jelly to invite him back to the Cadillac, and when
the movie star trade followed Morton to the Cadillac, Brown had to close
down his place in Watts. Brown then opened a club half a block from the
Cadillac, hired an eight-piece band, and "did fairly well from the over-
flow trade."[39] Morton maintains that his popularity with the Hollywood
crowd doomed Brown's efforts, and the house band had to be cut back
repeatedly, until all that was left of the octet was Hegamin playing solo
piano; eventually Brown was forced to close the place: "That left me
with George Brown as a real enemy from then on," Morton concludes.[40]
From then until 1922, Brown's appearances in the Morton saga are brief,

but ominous; Jelly came to regard him as a kind of nemesis, his own personal Professor Moriarty, elusive, almost invisible, but relentlessly poisonous in his intentions.

At about this time, Jelly sent to New Orleans for the trumpeter Buddy Petit, the trombonist Frankie Dusen, and the clarinetist Wade Whaley, each already a legendary figure on his instrument. The music must have been memorable, but the gig occupies the space it does in Morton's recollections not only for the music but also for the comedy. Morton says that he and Dink Johnson brought them into town secretly because they were sure to wear "the antiquated dress habitual to New Orleans musicians"—"those boxback coats and those trousers, so tight you couldn't button the top button."[41] Even the way they carried their horns was rather homespun: Petit's cornet in his suitcase, Dusen's trombone wrapped in newspaper, Whaley's clarinet in his back pocket. The plan was to get them some decent clothes for the gig so they wouldn't look like country bumpkins and make the band look bad as well, since as horn players they would be standing in front of the orchestra. The new clothes were purchased over the complaints of the three musicians: "Man, they wanted to kill us for making them change their suits, which they thought was very, very much in the mode." The band played extremely well and they made good money,

> but those guys couldn't get used to all that money. They used to bring their food on the job, just like they was used to doing in the lowdown honky-tonks along Perdido Street. Here they'd come every night to this Wayside Park with a bucket of red beans and rice and cook it on the job. (Man, I wish I had some of that stuff right now. The best food in the world!)
>
> So anyhow, Dink and me got to kidding the boys about this, because, as a matter of fact, this cooking on the job made us look kind of foolish. And Buddy and Frankie blew up, threatened to kill us. Next day, they left town, without notice, and went back to New Orleans. Which shows you never fool with a New Orleans musician, as he is noted for his hot temper.[42]

Morton calls it a "very, very funny incident," and it is, but his recollection of it poses a problem: it could not have happened in Wayside Park, at least not in 1918. Lomax's footnote to the incident quotes Reb Spikes correctly saying, "I built up Leek's [*sic*] Lake, out in Watts. Made a pile of money, too. They call it Wayside Park today, but it's still Leek's Lake to me."[43] In the Rutgers University interview, Pat Willard is deceived by the sequence of events described in Lomax's book when she cites the passage to Spikes: "But when Jelly Roll left the Cadillac, he went to the Wayside Inn [*sic*]—he went to your place. Right?" Spikes replies, "No. No, it wasn't built then. He . . . I built the Wayside Inn in about '22 but what he's talkin' about is uh . . . uh, around '15 or '17, ain't he?"[44] The source of the confusion is Morton himself: in what must be one of his most glaring lapses of memory, he places his connection to Wayside Park just after the sequence that begins with his reunion with Anita, her decision to leave Las Vegas, and her purchase of the Anita Hotel. A gig with "Buddy Petit et al." has been confirmed in Gushee's chronology: according to the *Chicago Defender*, Jelly played with the "Creole Jazz Band" in San Diego on 23 February 1918. According to Gushee's article, "New Orleans–Area Musicians on the West Coast, 1908–1925," Wade Whaley never left the West Coast, and both Buddy Petit and Frankie Dusen returned to Los Angeles from New Orleans in 1922, so it is possible that the appearance at Wayside Park could have happened then;[45] but if the group played in Los Angeles in 1918, as apparently it did, it could not have been at Wayside Park.

4

By late 1918 or early 1919, Morton left Los Angeles for a short stay in San Francisco and then moved on for a longer stay in the Seattle-Vancouver area. The most significant events of the 1918–19 period are his reunions, first with Anita and then with Reb Spikes, in that order. The exact dates of the reunions are uncertain, but Anita and Jelly were no doubt together by the end of 1917 or early 1918, and Spikes and Morton played a gig together in Oakland in 1919. Jelly's reunion with Spikes was short this time around; Morton spent about a year and a half in the Seattle area after leaving San Francisco, while Spikes went to Los Angeles to open his music store. But when Jelly returned to Los Angeles, the two men made some important business arrangements.

Jelly and Anita had been together for about a year by the time they moved north to the Bay Area and opened the Jupiter nightclub in the Barbary Coast district of San Francisco. In his monologue on Anita, Morton says that he was unable to contact her immediately upon his arrival in Los Angeles, primarily because her brother, Dink Johnson, for whatever reason, would not tell Jelly where she was: "I would constantly ask [Dink] where Anita was. . . . He wouldn never tell me. So . . . finally I ran up on the old lady [Anita's mother]. . . . I found out where the old lady was stayin . . . and she says, 'Oh, my, how Anita would like to see you.' And she got me in touch with Anita. At that time Anita was down in Nevada. . . . So anyway, somehow . . . her mutha [had] notified her I was in Los Angeles n she got in touch with me, she came up to Los Angeles to see me, and we went back togetha." [46] (See fig. 11.) Especially notable is the wording of that last phrase—"and we went back togetha"—which implies that the two had either lived together, or had been married, or both, at some previous time. No clue has surfaced to give even a hint as to when that might have been. Morton often referred to her as his wife and to Bill and Dink Johnson as his brothers-in-law, but no evidence has come to light that they were ever legally married. But the fact that Anita and Jelly "got together" so quickly after being reintroduced certainly does imply a previous relationship of some intimacy.

Both Jelly's and Anita's statements about their life in Los Angeles suggest that they may have been together for a while before they moved north. Morton says that Anita was willing to let the saloon in Las Vegas go unless he wanted to move there, and that he gave it a try: "So I tried Las Vegas a while, but it was too doggone cold in the winter and too hot in the summer." [47] It is unlikely that he went for an entire summer and winter, and even more unlikely that he would have considered, even for

Figure 11. Anita Gonzales and Jelly Roll Morton
in Los Angeles, circa 1917.

a moment, the Las Vegas of 1918 a promising place to work. Rolling
stone that he was, he no doubt gave the place a quick look. Anita then
opened a hotel in Los Angeles—called, logically enough, the Anita—
but the venture did not last very long, at least not long enough to war-
rant a listing in the Los Angeles city directories of the period. The only
listing of an Anita Hotel is in the directory for 1920, when Anita was
running a boardinghouse in Tacoma; besides, the address of that hotel
does not correspond to the location of Anita's as described by Morton—
"on a corner of Central near Twelfth."[48] Finally, after a brief falling-out
between the two, Anita opened up a restaurant in Teroma, Arizona—a
venture that must have been even more short-lived than the Anita. Lomax's book and the notes in the Library of Congress from interviews
that were not transcribed are at odds about the details of this restaurant

business, especially as to whether Jelly accompanied her or stayed in Los Angeles, with Lomax indicating that Jelly accompanied her to Arizona before the move to San Francisco.[49] Exactly how much time all of that activity took is anyone's guess, but assuming that it took Morton at least a month or two to get in touch with Anita after he arrived in Los Angeles in the summer of 1917, and that they were in San Francisco by the end of 1918 or, more likely, the beginning of 1919, they managed to do it all in about a year.

Jelly and Anita could not have been in the Bay Area very long. In Tom Stoddard's *Jazz on the Barbary Coast*, Reb Spikes says he played with Jelly in Oakland, but that seems to have been toward the end of Morton's stay there. The earliest document that attests to his presence comes from the Ford Collection: the receipt for a postal money order for $35, postmarked 5 February 1919 in San Francisco and addressed simply to Twelfth and Main Streets in Los Angeles. Gushee's chronology cites a *Chicago Defender* note, dated 22 February 1919, about Jelly "in San Francisco with his 12-cyl. touring car."[50] On 21 May, Jelly sent a postal money order for $35 from San Francisco to a V. J. Pye at the Bank of Italy in Los Angeles. A postal money order dated 5 August 1919 in Morton's hand and postmarked Tacoma, Washington, and an article in the *Defender* that places Jelly with an eight-piece band in Vancouver on 9 September both indicate that Jelly and Anita had moved north by the end of the summer.[51]

Most of their activities in San Francisco were centered on the Jupiter nightclub, located on Columbus Avenue between Pacific and Jackson. According to the Library of Congress notes, the place served mostly whites, which means it served blacks, too—it was what they called a "black and tan" club in those days. In fact, when Jelly describes to Lomax the police harassment they suffered at the club, he says, "I guess what worried them was that my place was black and tan—for colored and white alike."[52] A *San Francisco News* article of 1934 cited by Stoddard identifies the Jupiter, along with the Neptune Palace and the Cave, as one of "three choice resorts" that flourished on "the outer fringes" of the Barbary Coast as early as 1906.[53] As Anita had done with the Arcade in Las Vegas, she and Jelly apparently took over an established business and rented or managed the place; considering the short span of time they were in the city, it is highly unlikely that they owned the place.

As Jelly describes the Jupiter, it could not have been small: Morton led a ten-piece band and ten entertainers, while Anita handled the bar and ten waitresses.[54] Of course, the 1906 version of the Jupiter may not have been the same as the one in 1919, but Barbary Coast nightspots—quite a few of them, at least—had a track record for longevity, especially Purcell's and the Hippodrome, both of which are cited in the 1934 article.

In *Jazz on the Barbary Coast*, Sid LeProtti remembers when Jelly first arrived in San Francisco. His first words to LeProtti were "I'm gonn'a open a joint right over there. I'm gonn'a close you up, you and Mapp [Lester Mapp, a nightclub owner]"; as LeProtti describes the Jupiter, it may not have been as large as Morton portrays it: "The place he had was right on Columbus Avenue, downstairs in a cellar; you went downstairs to get in it. Well, he had a bad spot because everything was on Pacific Street. We had moved and was on the corner of Columbus Avenue and Jackson Street, and we were downstairs but we carried the name Purcell's with us. So Jelly went on over there and got him a little band there, and he started out pretty good. My boys used to slip over there at night to hear them. Jelly started with three pieces; he had clarinet and cornet."[55] When their paths crossed on the street one day, Jelly asked LeProtti how much he paid his men. Naturally, LeProtti was curious about why Jelly wanted to know, and Jelly said, "Because I'm gonna give them fifty dollars a week. I'm gonna take all your men." It was not meant to be an idle threat, and LeProtti's narration of Morton's attempt to carry it out bears witness to how Jelly was regarded by some fellow musicians:

> He had no right to tell me he was gonn'a take my band, but sure
> enough the boys came back to me and said Jelly had offered them
> fifty dollars a week to go over there and play. One of the boys said,
> "I wouldn't work for that character for anything."
>   I said, "What's the matter?"

He said, "There'd be a fight right there!"

Then he told me how they worked over there. Jelly would be playin', then they'd play a chorus together, and Jelly would say, "All right, lay down there and let me have it." Then he'd play a solo—of course, he could play; there was no gettin' away from it. Then the clarinet would be playin' a solo—and didn't play to suit Jelly—and he'd holler for him to quit, and he'd take it. If you didn't play according to Jelly's idea, he was just liable to bawl you out right there.[56]

Jelly's prickly personality must have caused at least some of the problems he and Anita faced at the Jupiter. However, true to form, Morton attributed official harassment of the Jupiter to sinister forces working against them. Admittedly, some of those forces were real. Racism was certainly a factor, as we have seen: since the Jupiter was black and tan, and official San Francisco frowned on interracial dancing (in some cities, it was illegal), Jelly and Anita had trouble getting a dancing license. Jelly laid the blame on Earl Dancer, manager of a rival nightclub across the street, whom he described as "the boss politician" behind the trouble over the license—the George Brown of San Francisco, one is tempted to add.[57] In fact, Jelly's problems were endemic to the area before 1919. The Barbary Coast was the San Francisco version of the red-light districts that had been legalized, either in fact or in practice, around the turn of the twentieth century and were eventually abolished. The real trouble began in 1913. Goaded by William Randolph Hearst's *San Francisco Examiner*, which vowed to destroy "the open marketplace for commercial vice" and replace it with "wholesome fun," the city enacted a series of laws that prohibited dancing and barred women from patronizing or working in any "cafe, restaurant, or saloon where liquor is sold" in the district.[58] The Forces of Vice regularly made comebacks, during which the laws were enforced unevenly, if at all, making selective enforcement against places like the Jupiter not only possible but inevitable. With Prohibition, the Forces of Good were given fresh and pow-

erful ammunition in their crusade. As Morton recalls, "The night prohibition came in, the police told me it was the penitentiary for me if I
sold liquor. From then on the police would hang around the door of the
Jupiter and annoy the patrons with uncalled-for remarks—'Why do you
come here? What's your name? Don't you know this place is likely to be
raided any time?'"[59] They even paid one of the Jupiter's waiters, Frenchy,
"to plant a bottle of whiskey in the slop barrel, but that fool went and
got drunk at a bar owned by a friend, told this friend I was going to be
raided, and the friend tipped Anita off." Anita hid the whiskey, and when
the police arrived, the captain said,

> "You're under arrest, because you're breaking the law."
> Now I was getting so hot that I was just about ready to shoot
> somebody with that left handed wheeler of mine and I told the po-
> lice captain, "Who said so?"
> "I said so."
> "Well, your word's no prayer book," I said and began to feel for
> my gun, because I had decided to go down fighting. Just then Anita
> kicked me under the table.
> I hollered, "Why are you kicking me under the table?"
> Anita began to laugh and I began to laugh and that policeman
> must have thought we were both crazy. He said, "Boy, they're going
> to find you in a ditch dead some day," and he dashed to the place
> where he thought the liquor was hidden and, when he didn't find it,
> he began to raise hell.[60]

But the problem with Morton's recollection of the chronological sequence of events is that Prohibition did not begin officially until January of 1920, and by then he had been in Tacoma for at least five months.
The story he tells hinges so specifically on the planting of a bottle of whiskey that it's not likely he is confusing that confrontation with others having to do with trying to get a dancing license for the Jupiter. Perhaps the
police, emboldened by the local—and national—enthusiasm for the im-
pending enforcement of Prohibition, decided to enforce the 1913 city

ordinance barring women from places that sold alcohol. Anita's presence in the Jupiter would certainly have given the police all the pretext they needed to anticipate the official beginning of Prohibition by five or six months. Jelly's memory may simply have tricked him into thinking that the event coincided with the official enforcement of Prohibition. Whatever the cause of the confusion, Jelly and Anita left the city just in time to miss hearing the last gasps of the Barbary Coast after a series of brutal raids in 1921 finished it off for good.[61]

Dink Johnson's account of what happened at the Jupiter is worth noting here, even though it contradicts Morton's on a number of points. According to William Russell's summary of the interview:

> Anita had invested heavily to fix up "an old barn" into a fancy club, with over a dozen girls—a real elaborate place. On opening night, an old-fashioned cop came walking into the place twirling and bouncing his nightstick. . . . Jelly came over to the cop and said, "You'll have to take your hat off if you come in here; everybody that comes in here has to take their hat off."
>
> The cop just grunted, "Oh, is that so?" and walked out. Two minutes later he was back again with half a dozen other police and really talked tough. He told Anita that he knew she'd spent a lot of money on the joint and he was going to give her a break and let her remain open. However, if they ever caught Jelly in the place again, they'd close it up instantly. He said it would be OK for Jelly to come around when the place wasn't open to the public. Well, Jelly stayed away for about a week or ten days and then went in one night when he didn't know the place was being watched. It was too bad then; Anita lost all the money she'd sunk into the Jupiter.[62]

If Morton's version is pure fiction, it is certainly an elaborate one. The two stories have only one thing in common: they both agree that trouble with the police eventually closed the place. Johnson told his story to Russell in 1947, almost thirty years later, so perhaps his memory had dimmed somewhat. Also, according to Morton, Dink was supposed to be manag-

ing the Arcade in Las Vegas at the time. Perhaps he got the story secondhand from Anita, but he quite possibly could have made a trip to San
Francisco to be at the Jupiter for the opening. At any rate, Anita and Morton were not in the city for very long, so the club must have opened and
closed quickly.

Anita left first. After trying unsuccessfully to convince Morton that
he should give up on the Jupiter, she took off for Seattle without warning
and then wired him a note threatening to cross the border into Canada
and disappear completely, perhaps as far as Alaska.[63] Jelly says ruefully,
"Anita managed me, the way she always did"—and left immediately for
Seattle, after Jelly "wired her that her mother was sick and to wait."[64] According to Lomax, Jelly "left the Jupiter just as it was and caught the next
train to the state of Washington," but it is doubtful that there was any life
left in the club at that point.[65] An ad for the Dixie Hotel Bar and Cafe in
the 5 April 1919 issue of the *California Eagle* announces "Entertainment
Every Evening by the Great Jelly Roll and his Jazz Band"; obviously,
Morton could not have been spending much time at the Jupiter. And the
Dixie was not an isolated example of Morton's extracurricular activities
at that time: just before he left for Seattle, he was also working in Oakland with Reb Spikes, who remembers that Morton got the telegram
from Anita "about eight o'clock, and by twelve o'clock, he was on the
train. Got right up and quit—quit us right in the middle of the night."[66]

5

Although Morton spent almost as much time in the Pacific Northwest—
about two years—as he did in Southern and Central California, less is
known about that period than about the rest of his five years on the West
Coast. Gushee's "Preliminary Chronology" lists five dates that attest to
his presence in the Pacific Northwest, and one of these is a vague reminiscence by a Jerome Pasquall, who told the discographer Laurie Wright
that Morton was in Seattle in June of 1920.[67] Two of the remaining dates
are closely connected: at the end of 1920 Morton paid his dues to Local

145, the Vancouver branch of the American Federation of Musicians, and then quickly withdrew them in January of 1921.[68] Only two of the five dates have to do with gigs: the first, from a letter to the *Chicago Defender*, places Jelly with an eight-piece band at Will Bowman's cabaret, the Patricia Cafe in Vancouver, on 9 September 1919; the second, from the same newspaper, this time in Ragtime Billy Tucker's regular column, "Coast Dope," places "Kid Jelly Roll" and singer Ralph Love in Portland on 31 July 1920, on their way to the Entertainer's Club in Seattle.[69]

As for Lomax, he seems to have worked primarily from the transcribed Library of Congress notes, as none of the recorded interviews cover the period—and it is very difficult to extract a coherent chronology from the notes; Lomax attempts to do so in *Mister Jelly Roll* but manages only to distort the sequence of events in a few spots in his attempts to impose some kind of coherence onto the material. One of the distortions comes directly from the Library of Congress notes, according to which Jelly went directly from Will Bowman's Patricia Cafe to Patty Sullivan's Regent in Vancouver.[70] In fact, the gig at the Patricia took place in September of 1919, and the engagement at the Regent did not happen until the end of 1920 or the beginning of 1921.

Even more difficult to place chronologically is the three-month summer vacation that Jelly and Anita took in Alaska. Since Lomax places that event after the Regent gig, that would mean the vacation took place in the summer of 1921, which is impossible on two counts: first, Jelly spent the last part of the winter of 1920–21 in Casper, Wyoming, and Denver, Colorado, after he and Anita had temporarily split up, and their reunion, in Los Angeles, where Anita had returned, happened in the summer of 1921; second, Gushee's "Preliminary Chronology" cites three newspaper items, two from the *Chicago Defender* and one from the *California Eagle*, that place Morton at gigs in Los Angeles in June, July, and August of 1921.[71] The summer of 1919 is even less likely—Jelly clearly states that they took the vacation because Anita had been running the rooming house for a while and was "feeling restless"; however, they had just arrived in Tacoma that summer.[72] That leaves the summer of 1920, but even that presents problems: the note from the *Chicago Defender* cited above places Jelly in Portland on 31 July 1920, to which can be added Pasquall's vague recollection of Jelly in Seattle in June. If we grant that Pasquall's memory could have been off by at least a month, there remains enough of a gap in the chronology to allow for a three-month summer vacation in May, June, and most of July.

Fortunately, the receipts for money orders in the Ford Collection help to fill in some of the gaps in the record. The last of the receipts from San Francisco is dated 21 May 1919 and the first from Tacoma 5 August, so the move north occurred in that time frame. The gig at the Patricia Cafe, as documented in the *Chicago Defender* of 9 September and cited above, could not have lasted more than a month or two, since the next money order receipt is postmarked 10 October in Tacoma. From that date, the sequence, all postmarked Tacoma, is: 23 October and 15 December 1919; and 2 January followed by 16, 19, and 21 April 1920. The last receipt reinforces the possibility that the Alaska vacation happened sometime between 21 April and 31 July 1920, the only verifiable gap of roughly three months that could qualify as a "summer" vacation.

The receipts also suggest that most of Morton's first eight or nine months in the Pacific Northwest were spent in Tacoma. The fact that the only documented gig during that period was at Will Bowman's Patricia Cafe does not rule out the possibility of other, undocumented engagements, but most of the verifiable information about Jelly's activity in the music business comes from 31 July 1920 and after. One thing is certain: no matter how many undocumented engagements Morton had, Tacoma was home base for most of his first year in the area. There are no money order receipts from Portland, Seattle, or Vancouver, though he worked in all three cities at one time or another; Anita's rooming house was in Tacoma, although there is no evidence that he played any gigs in that city. Seattle, the closest of the major urban centers in the area, is some forty miles from Tacoma; Portland is 140 miles away, Vancouver 180. The choice of Tacoma as home base seems to have been dictated primarily by the location of Anita's rooming house.

All of the above raises a question or two: given that Anita forced the move north, and given Jelly's apparently limited activity in the music scene during his first year in the area, is it possible that the rumors that Morton supported himself primarily through his "Pacific Coast Line"— that is, prostitution—during his stay in the Pacific Northwest may have been true? An affirmative answer to that question would certainly make it more likely that the "rooming house" was a front for the "Pacific Coast Line." The Pacific Northwest was entirely new territory for Jelly, and that alone may have forced him to rely more heavily on his "side-lines"—not just prostitution but also gambling, as well as bootlegging and prizefight promotion by the time he got to Denver in early 1921.[73] Although Lomax allots only two and a half pages to a period that spanned two years of Jelly's life on the West Coast, almost half of that space is devoted to his gambling. No sooner had Morton arrived in Seattle than he ran into Ed Montgomery, "an old New Orleans sporting-life friend" who was "now a big-time gambling man."[74] Montgomery introduced Jelly to the gambling crowd in Seattle, and soon Morton was down to his last dime, about to be bailed out by the call from Will Bowman for the gig at the Patricia Cafe. But the focus of his gambling activity seems to have been Patty Sullivan, owner of the Regent, one of Morton's few verifiable gigs in the area, which means that Jelly's relation to Sullivan and the Regent may have had as much to do with gambling as with music. In fact, Morton himself says that Sullivan, a "big-time gambler . . . used to take me along on his trips as a front man—I guess you might say he used me as a decoy the way I used my piano in my pool-playing days."[75] Morton remembers that one of those trips was long enough to force him to leave his clarinetist, Horace Eubanks, in charge of the band, and recounts a particularly harrowing session with some high-octane gamblers:

> One night through my boss, Patty, I got hooked up in a game with some of the biggest gamblers in the country—Nigger Nate, Chinese Smoke, Guy Harte, Russell Walton, and Blackie Williams. The smallest bet on the table was $100. I lost $2000 before I knew what

happened. They broke me and I was sitting there wondering what to do when Bricktop came in. I asked for a loan and Bricktop said, "All I've got is $10 and I wouldn't loan it to my mother."

Finally Patty gave me $5 and let me ride on his money. He hit eighteen straight licks and I stayed with him till I had my $2000 again, when I began to bet for myself. At the end of the game I had $11,000. A little guy named Jimmy had cleaned everybody else completely out—and that meant he had to pack his winnings off in a suitcase; those guys carried their money in bales.[76]

It is tempting to write off Morton's claim that the game involved "some of the biggest gamblers in the country" as one of his exaggerations, but a story that Bricktop tells in her autobiography verifies the claim in regard to at least one of the company, Nigger Nate. She describes him as "a white man, a friend of gambler Arnold Rothstein," who "got his name because of his tight, curly hair."[77] She remembers meeting him in Vancouver, "a whole lifetime away from New York during World War II"; at that time, some twenty years after meeting Nigger Nate, the mere fact of her acquaintance with him cost her a job at Tony's, a nightclub next to the Three Deuces on Fifty-second Street in New York City:

> One of the partners came in and asked[,] "Is your name Bricktop?" When I told him it was, he turned to the manager and said[,] "She can't work here."
>
> "Why not?" he protested.
>
> The partner completely ignored the manager and turned to me.
>
> "Ain't you a friend of Nigger Nate Richmond?" he demanded.
>
> "Why, of course," I said. "What's that got to do with it?"
>
> "No friend of Nigger Nate works here," he said, and just walked away.[78]

She was never able to find out the source of that partner's hatred, but only a powerful man can make such powerful enemies.

Another of Morton's problems in finding work in music was the relative scarcity of "hot" musicians in the Pacific Northwest, even compared to Los Angeles; and, as in Los Angeles, those who could lay claim to that label had migrated to the area from elsewhere. Of the musicians and entertainers linked to the Patricia Cafe in Vancouver, for example, only one, Leo Bailey, came from as nearby as Seattle; Oscar Holden, in spite of the fact that Morton says he was "no hot man," was from Nashville and Chicago; Bricktop was from Chicago; and Lillian Rose from New York.[79] Morton claims that he sent to Oakland for the trombonist Padio (variously spelled Pattio, Padeo, etc.), originally from Biloxi, who, "if he heard a tune, would just start making all kind of snakes around it nobody ever heard before"—obviously a "hot" player.[80] Morton's claim may be valid, though reports in the *Defender* indicate that Holden, not Jelly, was the leader during that engagement—which in turn suggests that Jelly's notorious temperament may have cost him some work in the area; Morton was on the Patricia gig for only a month or two, as we have seen, but Holden was still there a year later.[81] Even the trio that Jelly later brought to the Regent were outsiders: "Doc Hutchinson out of Baltimore on drums and Horace Eubanks, a beautiful hot clarinet from East St. Louis, who had learned from New Orleans men."[82] Further evidence of Morton's regard for Eubanks appears in a 1923 recording session in Chicago, where the clarinetist is featured on "Someday, Sweetheart" and "London Blues." As for Ralph Love, the singer mentioned by Ragtime Billy Tucker in his column, his origins are unknown.

In *Mister Jelly Roll* Morton himself says something that hints at another possible reason for the scarcity of work, at least in Vancouver. Sticking stubbornly to his claim to be the leader at the Patricia gig, he says, "I had good men, but somehow that cabaret didn't do so good. Folks there didn't understand American-style cabarets."[83] Bricktop is far more explicit: "Bowman's biggest customers—and I do mean big— were Swedish lumberjacks who came into Vancouver on their time off. Tall, strapping fellows, they could make a bottle of whiskey disappear in no time. Pretty soon they'd be drunk and ready to fight."[84] Considering the size of the place—it held three hundred people—it comes as no surprise when Bricktop describes what she calls "the fight to end all fights" on New Year's Eve in 1920, when she wound up with a broken leg.[85] Of course, Jelly had been working in honky-tonks all his life, so he was no stranger to the rough-and-tumble atmosphere that Bricktop describes. Perhaps the back-stabbing rivalry that had begun between the two at the Cadillac in Los Angeles carried over to Vancouver. In her autobiography, Bricktop claims that "around 1920, a fellow entertainer and I went up to Vancouver with some musicians to work for Billy [Will] Bowman. I'd known him in Chicago, and he wanted me to open up his new place."[86] But according to what Morton told Lomax, "Will Bowman asked me to bring a band into his cabaret in Vancouver, Canada."[87] It is quite likely that the gig at the Patricia became the sequel to the one at the Cadillac, and with the same result: Bricktop in, Jelly out. Oscar Holden, the nominal leader according to reports in the *Defender*, must have had his hands full.

By the time Morton returned to Vancouver at the end of 1920 for the gig at Patty Sullivan's Regent, his relationship to Anita must have become somewhat frayed, to put it mildly. When he first arrived in Seattle, his gambling had already wiped him out at least once. His association with Sullivan meant a renewal of his gambling and at least one other wipeout, as we have seen. And in *Mister Jelly Roll*, Anita recounts an anecdote from the period that must have been particularly embarrassing, if not humiliating: "In my day I was a good ragtime singer and I was always wanting to sing with the band. One night, playing for Patty Sullivan's Club [*sic*] in Vancouver, the girl singer got sick and, before Jelly could stop me, I went up and started singing and dancing. Right there Jelly quit playing and, because he was the leader, the rest of the band stopped playing, too, but I kept straight on with my song. When I finished, there was a stack of money on the floor. Jelly was furious. He dragged me outside and made me swear to never sing or dance again, but don't think he hit me. Jelly was a perfect gentleman."[88] The gig at Patty Sullivan's could not have lasted much longer than the one at Will Bowman's Patricia Cafe, about a month or two: soon after Jelly, Horace Eubanks, and Doc Hutchinson paid their dues for the first quarter of 1921, Jelly withdrew from the local.

Back in Tacoma, Anita gave vent to her frustrations over their relationship. As Jelly describes it, "One night in Tacoma she drank some Worcestershire Sauce with a little whiskey as a chaser and all of a sudden picked up a great steak platter and busted it over my head. It took several strong men to keep her away from me. I got the feeling she was mad enough to kill me. Next day she was all right, and said she couldn't remember a thing about what she'd done. We decided to split up for a while."[89] Anita returned to Los Angeles, and Jelly went on to Casper, Wyoming, and Denver, Colorado, during late winter on through the spring of 1921. Little is known about his activities at that time, except that he played some gigs and again lost a lot of money gambling—"by May I had lost my $20,000 and all my diamonds."[90] Also, according to the notes from the Library of Congress interview, in Denver he was involved with Gus West, a prizefight manager, and the boxer Kid Lee in both bootlegging and prizefight promotion. Jelly claims he made a lot of money at both activities before he gambled it away.[91] Then, the telegram from Anita, already cited, arrived: "NAN AND DAD BOTH AT POINT OF DEATH. MUST UNDERGO OPERATION IMMEDIATELY. COME HOME. ANITA." Jelly remembered that she also stated, "And the baby's blind," referring to one of her brother's children, according to the typed summary included in the Library of Congress notes. At the time, Morton was broke, but he was ashamed to ask for money; he managed to have his clothes sent ahead by train and left Denver "on the blinds"—riding illegally between the first and second cars.[92] When he finally reached Los Angeles, everyone was well; the telegram was evidently a ruse, and he did not take it lightly: "I was so mad I raved and hollered and left the house."[93] His return to California had been prompted by a summons, an ultimatum from Anita, just as his departure had been. He must have been thinking, just as he had before: "Anita managed me, the way she always did."

Once his anger subsided, they resumed their relationship, even though by now it was apparently strained beyond repair. We do not hear much about Anita until just before the final split in 1923, when Jelly left for Chicago. Anita's success in "managing" Jelly must have taken its toll by this point, but it must be said that he himself did his own share of managing. With both Anita and Mabel, Morton was pathologically insecure and jealous. As we have seen, the Anita Hotel in Los Angeles failed largely because Jelly would not let her deal directly with the public and they had to hire too much extra help to do the work. Anita's life on the road with Jelly must have put tremendous stress on her: "I went on every job with him. He made me sit right by the piano and not move or tap my feet or nothing. And he wouldn't let me dance with anybody. I didn't want to dance because I loved him very much."[91] Mabel tells exactly the same story: "You see, I was right with him on the bandstand at every date. He was very jealous, didn't like anybody to speak to me—in fact, he would get mad at his best friends if they so much as pass [*sic*] the time of day with me, but he wanted me there, dressed my best, so everybody could see me. Sometimes the boys in the band would ask him to let me sing, but he would never allow that. He used to tell me, 'After all, I'm the big thing here, it would be bad for me if I shared with you my popularity.' To tell the truth, he was a little too jealous in that way, because after a while I began to want to go on with my professional career."[95] Although Mabel chafed under Jelly's control, she never actually rebelled as Anita did that night in Vancouver when the vocalist fell ill and she took it upon herself to act as substitute. Acceding to Jelly's wishes on the surface seems partly to have been another way in which Anita "managed" him. Underneath it all, she remained in control, as she would remind him when she did things like leaving suddenly for Seattle. On both occasions, Morton simply caved in.

A pattern clearly emerges from his relationships with both Anita and Mabel: the need to display each of them as a trophy on his bandstands, to have them simply sit there like statues and look pretty, speaks of a man with a deep-seated need to prove his masculinity. And Jelly Roll Morton, the pimp, whose very name is a form of sexual bragging, in private showed little interest in sex, according to Mabel. We will never know if he was the same way with Anita, but we do know that, as a child, he avoided playing the piano at first because he feared "the femininity stamp" would be placed on him. And, on the Library of Congress recordings, he tells Lomax that whenever he would enter a club where the pianist Tony Jackson, an openly declared homosexual, was playing, Jackson would slyly alter the lyrics of his famous song "Pretty Baby" so that they addressed Mr. Jelly Roll himself. Is it possible that Morton was a latent or "closet" homosexual, and that he spent his entire life denying or concealing his sexual orientation? In these days of pop psychology, an attempt to answer that question would seem to be in order; but posthumous psychoanalysis is a risky business. One thing is clear: when it came to sex and his relations with women, Morton was a deeply troubled man. Perhaps the problems began in his midteens or earlier, when he began playing piano in the whorehouses of Storyville. In *Mister Jelly Roll*, he remembers Emma Johnson's Circus House, "where the guests got everything from soup to nuts. They did a lot of uncultured things there that probably couldn't be mentioned, and the irony part of it, they always picked the youngest and most beautiful girls to do them right before the eyes of everybody. . . . People are cruel, aren't they? A screen was put up between me and the tricks they were doing for the guests, but I cut a slit in the screen, as I had become a sport now, myself, and wanted to see what everyone else was seeing."[96] The poignancy of that statement suggests something about the extent to which his later attitudes toward sex and women were shaped by witnessing, in his adolescence, practices that probably included masochism and bestiality. His humane aside on the cruelty of people is offset by his statement that he slit the screen so that he too could witness the spectacle and validate his newly acquired status as a "sport." The conflict between revulsion and fascination, between compassion for the victims and his own complicity in their exploitation as a voyeur, must have been troubling, to say the least, to an adolescent

Morton coming to terms with his own sexuality in the midst of such spectacle.

All speculation aside, I raise the question of his sexuality only to indicate that, whatever the source of his troubles, playing the part of Jelly Roll Morton's wife must have been very stressful, and in more ways than one.

6

Ads and notices in newspapers speak only of engagements that can be verified for a given period of Jelly's career; they say nothing about those that either were not advertised or went unnoticed. And there is always the possibility that an advertised performance might not have come off as planned. Nevertheless, Lawrence Gushee's "Preliminary Chronology" lists eight advertised performances for Morton during the period 25 June 1921 to 23 September 1922. Add yet another, not listed in Gushee's chronology but advertised in the *California Eagle* on 1 July 1922, and the grand total becomes nine,[97] exactly the number of engagements listed for the entire period of 10 November 1917 to February 1921. Also, four of them seem to have lasted at least a month or more, and one of the three involved him as owner and manager. Moreover, at least two of his most celebrated compositions were penned during that time ("The Pearls" and "Kansas City Stomps"). Morton's last stay in Southern California (1921–23) seems to have been a period of intense musical activity, especially compared to the time he spent in the Pacific Northwest.

An examination of sources that provide verifiable, exact dates, or at least something close to this, yields an itinerary for Jelly during this period. Ads and articles in the *Defender* and the *Eagle* on 25 June, 16 July, and 6 August 1921 place Morton, with a band, at the Paradise Gardens in Los Angeles.[98] On 7 October, Morton obtained a visa to work in Mexico; a note in the *Defender* places Jelly at the Kansas City Bar in Tijuana on 15 October.[99] And although Morton supplies no exact dates for his involvement with horse racing, this probably happened during the time he spent in the San Diego–Tijuana area, since the Tijuana Race Track, newly opened in 1916 just south of the border, was the only track in the Southwest at the time—gambling on horse races was legal in Mexico, whereas it was banned north of the border, as was alcohol. In November of 1921, he wrote the *Defender* from 542 Sixth Street in San Diego, saying he "would like to hear from the Pensacola Kid," a world-class pool player Jelly had known when he fancied himself a championship player of the game; an item in the 28 January 1922 issue of the *Defender* says that Jelly is "still there" in Los Angeles; and according to the 22 April issue of the *Defender*, Jelly, as manager of Wayside Park, "introduces King Oliver" to Los Angeles.[100] The 1 July 1922 issue of the *California Eagle*, cited above, has an ad announcing "Music by Mr. Jelly Roll's Incomparable Jazz Orchestra" at the Fourth of July celebration at Wayside Park (i.e., Leak's Lake). The 15 July issue of the *Defender* has Jelly "and band" at Leak's Lake; on 23 September 1922, the *Defender* has Jelly's "Incomparables on tour with Mantan Morland."[101] Morton's name last appeared in Ragtime Billy Tucker's column on 24 February and 17 March 1923, in connection with a political controversy over a black man who was being tried for murder in Tijuana. Morton and other black performers, including Sonny Clay, Eddie Rucker, and Mantan Morland, staged a benefit concert in Los Angeles for a defense fund. The 17 March column is the last record of Morton's presence on the West Coast in 1923.[102] By the spring of that year, Morton was in Chicago to begin his recording career; the exact date of his departure from Los Angeles is uncertain.

Some of the dates on the itinerary are nothing more than useful signposts that fix a time and place along the way but have little or no narrative content. The first three, for example, determine fairly accurately when Jelly returned to Los Angeles from up north and suggest that he was playing at the Paradise Gardens for the entire summer of 1921, but he says nothing about the gig in the transcribed Library of Congress notes or in the Library of Congress recordings. Similarly, the letter to the Pensacola Kid via the *Defender* in November of 1921 places him in San Diego but says nothing about why, at that particular moment, he wanted to hear from his old friend. Two clusters of dates do carry with them significant narrative content: his activities in the San Diego–Tijuana area especially, because at least two of his major compositions came out of that short period; and the 28 January to 15 July 1922 period, during which Morton renewed contact with Reb Spikes, worked for him at Leak's Lake, and eventually, for a short period, became owner and manager of the place. In addition, the primary sources contain a significant amount of narrative that cannot be dated with any precision, especially the matter having to do with his own personal Dr. Moriarty, George Brown, who reentered, stage left—"with a vengeance," one might say. Finally—most important of all—the composition of two of his indisputable classics during this busy time raises questions about what else in the Morton canon may be attributed to his West Coast years.

In *Mister Jelly Roll* Morton tells Lomax that, after his return to Los Angeles, he "fooled around and organized a band[,] and we played dates in the Imperial Valley as far south as San Diego."[103] If the Paradise Gardens gig lasted from June to August of 1921, his travels south of Los Angeles probably began in late August or early September. The one engagement he does mention by name took place at the U.S. Grant Hotel in San Diego, where he and the band "had a nice set-up, . . . at least I thought it was okay until I heard their white band was paid double what my boys were getting. Then I pulled my band out of that joint with no notice!"[104] In a January 1938 interview in *Down Beat*, Morton says that the gig at the hotel was five nights a week, three hours a night, which would have made it difficult to work in Los Angeles at the same time.[105] According to the Library of Congress notes, however, it was an old friend, Bob Rowe, who lured Jelly south: "Rowe asked[,] 'Whyn't you come down to San Diego? Nobody's hanging around here now.'"[106] In his reminiscences of the tenderloin in New Orleans, Morton describes Rowe as one of the "sports" of Storyville and says that he was "the kingpin of the district" before he left for California.[107]

It's hard to tell which came first, the gig at the hotel or Bob Rowe's invitation, but it is also possible that a man of Rowe's resources could have pulled a few strings and landed the job at the U.S. Grant to entice Jelly to move southward. Whatever the case, the job would certainly have been attractive, even flattering, to Morton: built in 1908, the hotel was, and remains to this day, one of the premier hostelries in central San Diego. Morton's comments to Lomax imply that the engagement was short-lived, but it may have lasted through the month of September. His note regarding the Pensacola Kid in the *Defender* places him in San Diego in November of 1921, but since that city seems to have been Rowe's base of operations for his horse-racing activities, Jelly's presence there at that time may simply be testimony to his own involvement with the horses—or with one particular horse, Red Cloud. That involvement renewed Jelly's passion for gambling, and, predictably, he "went broke" once again.[108] As usual, he took his losses with great equanimity; he tells the story of his ownership of Red Cloud with at least a touch of sardonic humor: "My old friend Bob Rowe put me onto the horses. Before I knew it, I owned one, a nag named Red Cloud. The owner told me, 'Red Cloud is the fastest race horse in the world. You can blindfold him and he can outrun anything on the tracks, by feeling his way along.' Truth was that horse couldn't outrun me; he wasn't even a good mule and the officials wouldn't permit him on the track because they claimed I wasn't feeding him. So I had to forget old Red Cloud and the former owners had to forget the $400 dollars they wanted me to pay."[109]

Because the only racetrack in the Southwest was located near Tijuana, Morton's contact with Rowe and the horses inevitably drew him south of the border. As he tells Lomax, "The horses had taken me to a little place called Tia Juana [*sic*] on the borders of Mexico, where I got a job in a place called the Kansas City Bar." There he was reunited with another old friend, Jack Lanes, the owner of the bar, whom he describes as a light-skinned Negro millionaire that he knew from Muskogee, Oklahoma.[110] The job must have been the reason Jelly obtained the visa, dated 7 October 1921, allowing him to work in Mexico—he would not have needed a visa simply to cross the border. (See fig. 12.) While Mor-

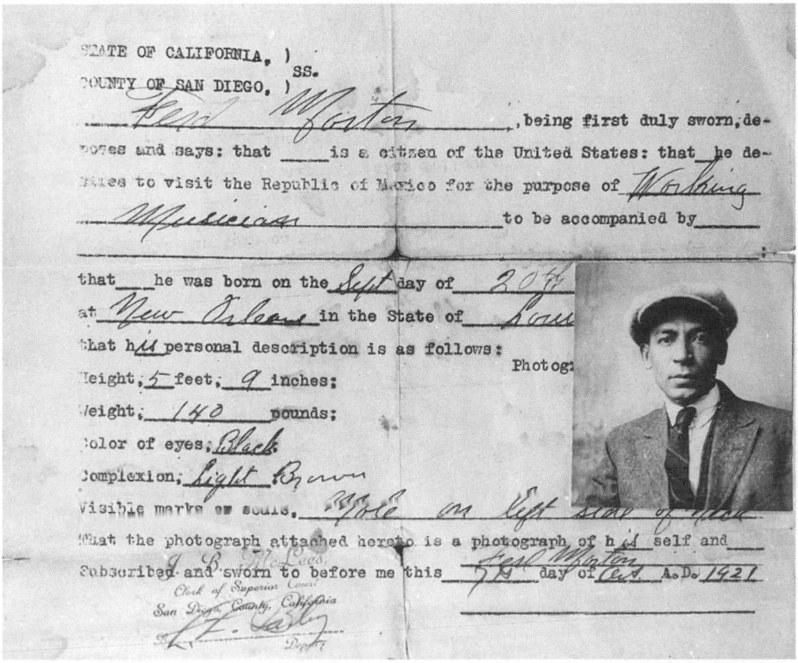
STATE OF CALIFORNIA,)
SS.
COUNTY OF SAN DIEGO,)
Ferd Morton, being first duly sworn, deposes and says: that ___ is a citizen of the United States: that he desires to visit the Republic of Mexico for the purpose of Working Musician to be accompanied by ___

that ___ he was born on the Sept day of 20th
at New Orleans in the State of Lou
that his personal description is as follows:
Photog
Height, 5 feet, 9 inches;
Weight, 140 pounds;
Color of eyes, Black
Complexion, Light Brown
Visible marks or scars, Mole on left side of face
That the photograph attached hereto is a photograph of his self and ___
Ferd Morton
Subscribed and sworn to before me this 7th day of Oct A.D. 1921
J. B. McLees
Clerk of Superior Court
San Diego County, California
By ___ Deputy

Figure 12. The visa Morton obtained in 1921 in order to work in Mexico. Courtesy Historic New Orleans Collection.

ton was working at the Kansas City, though, Lanes and his wife, Queen Anne, had to leave town in a hurry, so the gig could not have lasted very long: it seems that Lanes had come to Tijuana as a fugitive because he had murdered a man in Oklahoma, and Sylvester Stewart, a partner of his in the Newport Bar in Muskogee, had tipped off the police. As Morton tells the story, Lanes and his wife took off for the interior of Mexico, but American officials caught up with him and had him deported; he was convicted and sentenced to twenty years in jail.[111] Seventeen years later, Lanes would still have been in jail as Morton recounted the story for Lomax. Queen Anne reopened the Kansas City Bar, and Jelly "kept going back in the summer to Tia Juana [*sic*]."[112] That would have been

1922—the date of the work visa precludes any possibility that it might have been the summer of 1921.

The job in Tijuana allows us to put an approximate date on two of his most important compositions, the "Kansas City Stomps," named after the bar, and "The Pearls." About the former, Morton says little except that it was named after the place where he was working; however, he is much more specific about his inspiration for the latter: "There was a very pretty little waitress at the Kansas City Bar and I dedicated a composition to her. This was *The Pearls*, consisting of several sections, each one matching the other and contributing to the total effect of a beautiful pearl necklace. There are very, very few pianists, if any, that can play *The Pearls*, it being the most difficult piece of jazz piano ever written, except for my *Fingerbuster*."[113] The last comment has puzzled many commentators, since "The Pearls" is not particularly difficult in terms of technique—certainly nowhere near as difficult as "Fingerbuster." James Dapogny has come as close as anyone to finding a solution to the puzzle: "Like many of Morton's other pieces, *The Pearls* is built upon contrast, rather than upon interrelationship, its form dependent upon the balance of its parts. In identifying *The Pearls* in particular as more difficult to play than many other pieces requiring greater technical facility and stamina, Morton shows the depth of his musical judgement: he is referring not to 'mere' technical difficulty, but to the artistic task of drawing together the piece's diverse elements into a coherent whole."[114] Whatever the reasons for Jelly's comments, one thing is certain: "The Pearls" is one of Morton's most beautiful and dynamic compositions, and one that has always been a favorite among musicians, critics, and fans. Perhaps the most eloquent tribute of all is the 1938 recording of the piece by the pianist Mary Lou Williams: she captures the essence of "The Pearls" even though she does not render a slavishly faithful note-for-note version of it as written or played by Morton himself. Morton never commented on her version, but it is played entirely in the spirit with which he himself approached "The Pearls" in his 1926 solo version, which could quite accurately be titled "Variations on the Themes of 'The Pearls.'"

As for the pretty young barmaid Morton had his eye on when he wrote "The Pearls," her anonymous but indelible fingerprint on the piece remains a small but poignant part of the Jelly Roll legend—as no doubt he intended when he made the comment. All he admits to is writing a song for the woman; but he seems to be saying it with a wink. A man as intent as Jelly to prove his masculinity would have been at least a flirt, if not an out-and-out philanderer, and would possibly even have exaggerated the number and nature of his conquests, if not downright lied about them. At the very beginning of his renewed relationship with Anita, during his first year in Los Angeles, she had already suspected him of being unfaithful: "The police were making trouble about the license for Anita's hotel, and I couldn't help her because she was accusing me of another woman. She wouldn't even talk to me."[115] Even if those incidents were no more than flirtations intended to bolster his ego, they must have contributed to the tensions that led to their eventual breakup, especially considering that his activities with the "Pacific Coast Line" brought him into close and frequent contact with "fast" women. Indeed, there seem to have been times in Los Angeles when he and Anita were not living together. In a 1969 interview with William Russell, William Woodman Sr. remembers that "Jelly Roll lived with his godparents on 111th Street in Watts. You know, a lot of times Jelly didn't have a girl friend and he'd go down there and live with the Hunters." In another part of the interview, Woodman makes it clear that he is referring to the period just after Morton returned to Los Angeles in 1921.[116]

The San Diego–Tijuana interlude could not have lasted much more than three months, roughly from early October through December of 1921. An item in the *Defender* on 28 January 1922 places Morton once more in Los Angeles, which became the primary focus of his activities through most of 1922. During that time, Morton seems to have played often at Reb Spikes's Leak's Lake dance hall. Three of the dates have been verified by then-contemporary newspaper ads: 22 April, when he featured King Oliver; a Fourth of July celebration with his own "Incomparables"; and 15 July, when he again appeared with his own band.[117] Those were certainly not the only dates that Morton played there, however. According to Spikes himself, Jelly led the house band at Leak's Lake for a while. In the Rutgers interview, when Pat Willard asks, "And who worked it? Did you have a band in there, or what band worked in there?" Spikes replies, "No, I had Jelly Roll in there for awhile, and then different bands after that. Jelly Roll went away."[118] Spikes clearly implies that Morton worked at the club from the time that it opened, or shortly thereafter, until he left Los Angeles to head back east. The story of Morton's last year seems inextricably bound to the story of Leak's Lake in its early days.

Spikes himself is not clear about the exact date he opened Leak's Lake. In the interview, he says that it opened six months after he closed the Dreamland Cafe in Los Angeles—the time it took to build the structure and move the furniture from the Dreamland to the new dance hall in Watts—and that he had opened the former in 1921. When asked if it is true that Morton presented King Oliver at Leak's Lake in 1922, Spikes hesitates: "No, because I ... I ... I don't think it's '22. I ... I ... I didn't build it till '22—'21 or '22. '22, I think, when I built it."[119] However, the ad cited above fixes the exact date of Oliver's appearance as 22 April 1922, and two ads in the *California Eagle* testify that Leak's Lake was open by the summer of 1921. The first, dated 24 June 1921, looks like the kind of ad that is trying to drum up business for a new establishment: "Leak's Lake/Open Saturdays, Sundays, Mondays/Call or Write/Church Picnics/Lodges or Private Parties/Can Be Rented for [*sic*]/Spikes Bros. & Carter Music House/1203 Central Avenue."[120] The second, dated 5 August 1921, advertises the "Fourteenth Annual Picnic Barbecue" of the Hod Carriers and Building Laborers Union.[121]

Even the exact name of the place changes according to the person doing the talking and what stage of the club's development is under discussion. In the interview, Spikes first says, "I built a place in Watts was called the Watts Country Club," and he identifies it as the place where Morton worked for him.[122] Later, when Willard brings up Wayside Park, he says, "Yeah, well, that's my place," to which Willard responds:

[WILLARD]:   You said Watts Country Club. Is that another . . .

MR SPIKES: Well, I said . . . was in Watts. When I first opened it, I
              called . . . And when I uh . . . uh . . . sold it, I sold it to Jelly
              Roll and the band.[123]

Some of the ellipses seem to indicate inaudible portions of the tape,
and others express his hesitation. The problem is that Bricktop, in her
autobiography, remembers a place called the Watts Country Club, run
by a George Henderson, as the site of her first job in Los Angeles when
she arrived in 1917.[124] Perhaps Spikes's memory or his tongue was playing tricks on him when he first called the place the Watts Country Club,
but even so, he says unequivocally that Morton's was the first band he
hired and so identifies it as Leak's Lake. And his statement, mentioned
earlier, that "they call it Wayside Park today, but it's still Leek's [sic]
Lake to me," suggests a possible explanation for those two names. All of
the earlier newspaper ads cited above call the place "Leak's Lake," except for the one advertising the Fourth of July party, where it becomes
"Wayside Park." Possibly Morton and the other musicians who bought
Leak's Lake from Spikes decided to change the name to Wayside Park.
Whatever the case, an ad in the *California Eagle* on 23 September 1923
calls it "Leakes [sic] Lake" once again.[125]

The 24 June 1921 ad in the *California Eagle* shows that Spikes thought
of Leak's Lake as a hall for rent as well as a regular dance hall and jazz
club: it encourages those needing a location for "Church Picnics/Lodges
or Private Parties" to call for bookings. And in fact the second ad, also
cited above, announces a Labor Day picnic sponsored by a labor union.
Spikes's original plan was to construct a family-oriented amusement park
around the dance hall, which he built facing the lake. When Pat Willard
asks him whether it was a dance hall, he replies, "A big dance hall, yeah. . . .
I had a merry-go-round out there for the kids, and I had concessions—
drinks and souvenirs and things on the outside that a couple of fellows
rented for—you know, they sold souvenirs and things on the outside—

was going to have a regular little park out there but it didn't pan out so good." Willard prods him a bit: "Daytime and nightime [*sic*] operation," to which he responds, "Mostly holidays daytime—afternoon—but the rest of it was generally Saturday nights, Sunday nights."[126] The July 1922 ad for the Fourth of July party featuring "Music by Mr. Jelly Roll's Incomparable Jazz Orchestra" at Wayside Park emphasizes the "family fun" aspect of the place: "Base Ball, Merry-Go-Round, Bathing, Boating, and many other interesting features." So it was an amusement park with a dance hall attached that, during the day, could be used for private parties and, on Saturday and Sunday nights, was strictly a dance hall. According to the vocalist Jimmy Rushing, he met Morton in Los Angeles around 1921, and Jelly used to show up at Leak's Lake after midnight:

> The man who ran Leak's Lake out in Watts used to hire me to play piano. Watts was an after-hours place, they didn't open until 11 o'clock. There was gambling and they sold whiskey [during Prohibition]. They had tables and a place to dance. All the sporting class of people from Los Angeles and Hollywood came out there after one o'clock at night. It would be loaded with white people and black people and stayed open until five or six in the morning. Round about two thirty or three Jelly Roll and "Singin' Mitch," I called him, came in. Mitch was a great entertainer. Everybody on the coast knew him. . . . He and Jelly used to go every place and break up any place they went. When they came in people would scream for them to play and sing.[127]

Spikes sold out within about a year after it opened because he used to spend his weekend nights walking around outside to discourage the bootleggers that roamed the Watts area plying their trade, and "that fog would have me all wet down to here, see, and I got down in the bed, and I was down 'bout a year and a half with . . . just stiff as a board with rheumatism, so I sold it out to . . . the boys, and they ran it—the band ran it."[128] In addition to Morton, the musicians who bought in to the place were Jesse Smith, Everett Walsh, and Pops Woodman: "I think Woodman had most of the money. Woodman was pretty close, you know. He saved his money, and I think he had more money in there than any of 'em."[129] In the interview with Russell, Woodman clearly states that it was he who bought the club: "Spikes bought Leak's Lake. When things got rough, he sold it to me. It was a 'white elephant.' I got stuck with it; I mortgaged my home and gave him a down payment on it, but I paid him off. It was just a big plain hall, about seventy-five by a hundred feet long, with no trimming, no porch, or nothing."[130] Woodman says that he too had trouble with the police about bootleggers and for that reason eventually sold out.

Given that Leak's Lake opened in the summer of 1921 and that Morton was back in Los Angeles by January of 1922 or sooner, it is possible that he worked there steadily, weekends at least, between January and whenever he left Los Angeles later that year; certainly, he was quite active there in the spring and summer of 1922, when he managed to lure King Oliver to Los Angeles from the Bay Area, where Oliver's band had been playing at the Pergola Dancing Pavilion in San Francisco since 12 June 1921.[131] Morton regarded the engagement as rather a coup: he boasted that "Wayside Park is the place King Oliver made much fame when I introduced him there in April, 1922."[132] Evidently, Jelly assembled a band especially for the occasion, for none of the personnel he lists in a January 1938 interview in *Down Beat* were in the band Oliver brought west from Chicago. According to Jelly, the band included Mutt Carey and King Porter, who joined Oliver in the trumpet section; Gerald Wells, Paul Howard, and Leon Hereford, saxophones; "Al Woodward" on trombone; and "Ward [*sic*] Wilson," bass; with "Ding [*sic*] Johnson" on drums and Jelly himself on piano, of course.[133] The "Al Woodward" on trombone was no doubt Pops Woodman, who was also a trombonist. Morton seems to have had a penchant for getting Woodman's name wrong: in Lomax's book, he calls him "Pops Woodward," and when Patricia Willard reads that passage to Spikes in the Rutgers interview, Reb says emphatically, "Well, that's Woodman he's talking about."[134] Woodman himself corroborates Spikes's story: "I'll tell you when we had a good week. Jelly Roll knew King Oliver, and when Oliver came down through here from Frisco he played a week with us at Leak's Lake. We packed them in that week. . . . Oliver was our guest and just sat in with Jelly Roll's band." [135] It appears that Jelly had a falling-out with Dink Johnson, because he says that he fired him and replaced him with Ben Borders at some point. Also, Buster Wilson, who had become Morton's protégé, alternated with Jelly on piano from time to time, according to Wilson himself. [136] In addition, it is possible that Oliver brought his own band to Los Angeles for at least part of the Wayside Park engagement. According to Martin Williams, "With various changes of personnel . . . the Oliver band played in Los Angeles[,] where Oliver also played with a large one led by Jelly Roll Morton." [137] In a conversation with Floyd Levin, Buster Wilson recalled that "when King Oliver's Creole Jazz Band came to California in 1921, they were invited to Wayside Park," and Levin himself recalls that "in an early interview with Reb Spikes, he told me that the Oliver band, with Wilson on piano, made a few recordings in Santa Monica for the Spikes brothers' Sunshine label. He assumed that the wax masters were among those that melted during shipment across the hot desert to an eastern pressing plant." [138]

Whatever the length of the engagement, whatever the personnel, Morton's reunion with one of the most dominant New Orleans musicians of all time must have had a powerful impact on Jelly, not to mention the fact that King Oliver's Creole Jazz Band included old friends and acquaintances from New Orleans: Johnny Dodds, clarinet; Jimmy Palao, violin; Honore Dutrey, trombone; Lil Hardin, piano; Minor "Ram" Hall, drums; and Ed Garland, bass. (Garland decided to stay on the West Coast and was replaced in Chicago by none other than Jelly's brother-in-law, Bill Johnson; Hardin was born in Memphis and came west with the band from Chicago.) Morton must have been reminded of what it had been like to be surrounded by musicians of that caliber. In fact, one wonders if Oliver's influence may have had some bearing on Jelly's decision to return to Chicago. Oliver evidently had offers of work in the Bay Area, but he was "soon back in Chicago, despite an assurance of continued success in the Bay Area."[139] Oliver knew where the action was, and his powerful presence and determined departure may just have reminded Jelly of that fact.

Morton must have begun to consider leaving California at about this time, if not sooner. In *Mister Jelly Roll*, he says, "The tracks were treating me very dirty these days, and, somehow, my luck in California was running out."[140] Considering his own words on "The Pearls" and "Kansas City Stomps," and the rather robust state of his musical activity generally, he must have been talking about things other than music—certainly gambling and the track, and possibly his nemesis in the form of George Brown. Whether he continued to make trips south to Tijuana on a regular basis is not certain, though as we have already seen, he did return to work at the Kansas City Bar at least once during the summer of 1922. He was also busy at Leak's Lake during that summer, so it does not seem possible that he could have spent much time at the Kansas City. According to Woodman, "Jelly played at the hall about a year."[141] Even if that was his only trip south of the border that year, no doubt Jelly had enough time to lose a bundle: he had a knack for losing a lot of money in a short time.

But, true to form, he attributes his bad luck "mostly to the moves of my old enemy, George Brown." Sometime in 1922, Morton was arrested and detained briefly on two occasions. First, a woman working as a servant in Pasadena was arrested for stealing from her own employer, and she named Jelly as her accomplice. When he confronted her at the jail, however, she backed down and confessed that she had never seen him before. Then Morton found out from "one of the police . . . that it was George Brown that helped to frame me."[142] On the second occasion, the charge was much more serious: murder. A grocery man had been murdered the day before on the corner of Fourteenth and Central, and a maid's description of the killer matched Jelly exactly. Again, his accuser let him off the hook: "This time I had no alibi, but, fortunately, when the maid saw me, she said I was not the man." Even though he had narrowly escaped a charge of murder, finding out who was behind the whole mess put him in a murderous mood:

> Again, I discovered that it was George Brown, the half-hand big-shot, who was responsible for naming me. I walked into his place that evening [Brown was involved in the nightclub business on a regular basis] with my hand on my gun. I told George off and I was about to draw, when Bill (Bojangles) Robinson walked in, laid his hand on my arm and said very quietly, "Jelly boy, what's the matter with you? You must be going crazy."
>
> Bill led me out the door and took me home to Anita. A couple of days later, when we were on our way to a show, a cop stopped us and Anita was so rattled by this time, she yelled, "We're goin to the theatre, can't you leave us alone."
>
> That cop turned out to be an old friend who just wanted to say hello, and we apologized. But, somehow or another, that was the end of California for me.[143]

He must have meant "the beginning of the end," though: his next statement is, "It actually came about this way," and he then begins to tell the story of his relationship with the Spikes brothers.[144] Aside from saying that those events happened in 1922 or 1923, it is impossible to date them more precisely.

Morton's statement that the decision to leave California "actually came about this way" implies those two near-arrests were not the immediate cause. The cause, he claims, was instead his involvement "in the music-publishing business with Reb and Johnny Spikes."[145] I use the word "claims" for two reasons: First, there is no evidence that Morton was ever actually a partner in the Spikes brothers publishing business at this time, although they apparently did come to an informal agreement to publish some of his music. His name appears on the sheet music for "Froggie Moore" and "Wolverine Blues" only as coauthor with the brothers. Second, Anita's statement to Lomax suggests that Morton left because of problems in their relationship: "Well, we had a misunder-

standing and he left for Chicago in 1922."[146] The cause-and-effect relationship implied by the two parts of that statement, however, may just
be Anita's perception of things. To complicate matters even further,
Morton's own last words on the subject imply that maybe the trouble
stirred up by George Brown really did precipitate the move: "On account of all the things that had happened around L.A., Anita urged me
to leave."[147] No doubt all those factors played a role in the final decision, but the single most likely cause was the music business—not the
Spikes brothers publishing business alone. Although that was certainly
very important, events having to do with music in California and elsewhere may have convinced Jelly it was time to move on. The years Morton spent on the West Coast coincided with the years when the recording business, first in Chicago, then in New York, discovered that there
was a market for jazz and blues recordings. I will discuss the overall impact of those developments later in this chapter, but obviously the man
who claimed to be the "originator" of jazz and its very best exponent
must have grown restless as he watched from afar while others cashed in
on his "stuff." When, finally, the Spikes brothers took "The Wolverines"
to sell to Melrose Music Company in Chicago as "Wolverine Blues" by
Spikes-Morton-Spikes, Jelly had to make his move.

Morton's comments on the Spikes brothers are typical of what he
would say about any musician he didn't consider to be in his league:
"Johnny played piano, and Reb, sax. They could read, but had no ideas.
Occasionally, I condescended to play with these cornfed musicians."[148]
On that score, even Reb Spikes himself would not have given Jelly much
of an argument. In *Jazz on the Barbary Coast*, Reb admits, "I was never
much of a jazzman. I played baritone sax, and I never could play a lot of
hot jazz. I played a lot of counterpoint like cello parts."[149] Spikes may
have been no more than a journeyman as a performing musician, but he
was smart enough to face that fact and make use of his real strength as an
entrepreneur. During its nearly ten-year run on the corner of Twelfth
and Central (1919–1927 or 1928), the Spikes brothers music store was
the center of black music in Los Angeles. As we have seen, even Holly-

wood movie stars would send their chauffeurs to the store to pick up the latest record releases, and he would often provide extras and musicians to the studios. As broker, agent, music publisher, composer, club owner, and record producer, he became the major force in the business of African American music in Los Angeles—perhaps even in the state of California. Not that he stopped performing: he kept a band going that included some of the best local talent—Sonny Clay; Adam "Slocum" Mitchell; Pops Woodman, patriarch of the Woodman brothers clan; and Lionel Hampton, among others. In fact, Lionel Hampton moved from Chicago to Los Angeles at Spikes's invitation. Spikes needed a drummer, and all it took was Les Hite's recommendation.[150] Los Angeles eventually became the launching pad of Hampton's career.

Spikes eventually became a wealthy man, though not through the music business: the source of his wealth was some astute real estate investments. Although he never again became quite the kingpin that he was during the heyday of the Spikes brothers store, he continued to have some influence on the music scene in Los Angeles through the years. As we have seen, Morton's return to Los Angeles in 1940 was in part motivated by the prospect of a business collaboration with Spikes. In 1942, just a year after Morton's death, Spikes opened an arts center, Music City, on the corner of Jefferson Boulevard and Normandie Avenue. Though the center stayed open only for three or four years, it was the place where the young Norman Granz started the jam sessions that would lead to the Jazz at the Philharmonic series. In his Rutgers interview, Spikes remembers that Granz's first concert, at Music City, featured Nat Cole and Illinois Jacquet, among others.[151]

The year 1919 marks the point when Spikes turned decisively to music as business—on the 15th of December, to be exact. The ad in the *California Eagle* of 13 December announces the "Big Opening" of "Spikes Bros. & Carter," the "'So Different' Music House"—the latter courtesy of Sid LeProtti's So Different Orchestra. The next line says it all: "MUSIC PUBLISHERS—DEALERS IN EVERYTHING MUSICAL."[152] On the 20th, seven days after the first ad and five days after the opening, a second ad appeared in the *Eagle*, announcing in triple boldface "BIG SUCCESS" and explaining, "Their store at 1203 Central Avenue was crowded from morning to night with Colored music lovers and well-wishers of Los Angeles"; and then, adding a personal touch: "We take this opportunity to thank the Colored people of Los Angeles for making the opening a grand success; those present had a grand treat, through the kindness of the famous Black and Jazz [*sic*] Orchestra, Dominant Orchestra, Mr. G. Wells, Wood Wilson, E. B. Douglas, Mrs. Fay Allen, Bert Johnson, and others."[153] Such statements may be no more than advertising hype, but if that is the case here, certainly the store rapidly lived up to the hype. Spikes was onto something, and he knew it: "After that [the opening], I got into the business end of music more."[154] By the time Morton returned from the Pacific Northwest via Denver, Reb Spikes either controlled or had a hand in every aspect of black music in Los Angeles.

Of some importance to the dispute that arose between Morton and the Spikes brothers over authorship of "Someday, Sweetheart" is the fact that the 20 December ad calls the tune "THE SEASON'S LATEST SONG HIT"—sheer self-promotion, at this point—then, "OUR FIRST PUBLICATION," to which it adds, "BY JOHN C. SPIKES." On 10 January 1920, yet another ad for Spikes Brothers and Carter credits John C. Spikes as the composer.[155] When Melrose eventually published "Someday, Sweetheart" in 1923, the credit went to both brothers, but as noted earlier, in *Mister Jelly Roll* Jelly maintains that the tune was his idea. He explains that Kid North, "an old racetrack friend of mine" who was working with Bob Rowe, used to play a tune called "Tricks Ain't Walkin' No More." According to Jelly, "Since the Kid knew that I was a writer and we had been friends for quite a while, he told me I could have that tune," which was the basis of the verse in "Someday, Sweetheart."[156] Jelly must have been involved with the racetracks on the West Coast long before 1921, and if he and Kid North were friends "for quite a while" they must have known each other before the California days. Jelly probably would have passed the strain that he got from Kid North to Reb or John Spikes in Oakland, where they played together just before Morton went to Seattle in 1919, which in turn means that he would have picked up the strain from North during his first stay in Los Angeles, about 1917 or 1918.

In the Library of Congress recording, he shouts out "the verse" when he gets to the strain in "Tricks" that became part of "Someday, Sweetheart," as if to identify it for Lomax. In "Tricks," it appears as the second strain and acts as a bridge for the return of the first strain. In "Someday, Sweetheart," it serves as the verse leading into the chorus—and it serves very well indeed, rising slowly through a complex set of chords and modulations, seamlessly setting up the transition to the first strain of the chorus, whose simple romanticism contrasts nicely with the rather intricate verse. To put it another way, the tension that builds slowly and surely in the verse is released with a kind of sigh in the first notes of the chorus. Morton plays it exactly that way in the 30 October 1923 version on the Gennett label, with a quintet that includes himself, Natty Dominique on cornet, Zue Robinson on trombone, Horace Eubanks (with whom he had played in Seattle) on clarinet, and an unknown drummer. Oddly enough, in the 16 December 1926 version with the Red Hot Peppers—by far the more widely known—he omits the verse altogether and puts in its place a four-bar intro that creates none of the drama of the original. On its own, the chorus has a pleasant enough melody but is a bit bland compared to Morton's most characteristic work; with the verse, his entirely characteristic skill in juxtaposing contrasting themes comes to the fore.

Whatever Morton's reasons for deleting his own contribution to "Someday, Sweetheart" in 1926, the fact that the ad promotes the tune in December of 1919 means that it had been written sometime between that year and the summer of 1917. In his comments to Lomax, he is uncharacteristically generous and forgiving about the "theft": "Of course, my name doesn't appear on that song, but I'm not jealous. I hope the boys write ten million other ones like it, but, since this story is for the Archives where you're supposed to give the facts, the truth might as well come out. The song was practically wrote at the time Reb and I were working together in a cabaret in Oakland [1918], but they left my name off it."[157] The chronology is exactly right: the gig in Oakland came just before Spikes moved to Los Angeles to open the music store where the tune was first mentioned in the ad for the grand opening.

The marketing strategy that eventually led to "Someday, Sweetheart" becoming the 1920s version of a "hit" tune was quite simple. As Reb describes it, "Well, we published them so we could sell 'em. You know, publish them first to get 'em popular[,] . . . [to get them] started . . . [;] then you turn them over to a publisher. You get a better deal. See, we published 'Someday, Sweetheart' I think twice before we got it in to a big publisher's. And if it starts to pick up a little bit, they give you a better deal than they do if you just send them something that they don't know nothing about."[158] Alberta Hunter was the first to record the tune, around May of 1921. "Someday, Sweetheart" and three other tunes were among the first recordings put out by Harry Pace's black-run, but unfortunately short-lived, Black Swan Records.

In the Rutgers interview, Spikes tells Pat Willard that he stopped making records under his own Sunshine label for two reasons: first, because of a dispute between himself and Arne Andrae Nordskog, owner of the recording studio where Spikes recorded "Ory's Creole Trombone," over the labeling of the product; second, because of the appearance of Black Swan Records in New York. He explains, "[Sunshine Records] was a lot of trouble, a lot of work and expense afterwards, you know. Then the reason I didn't make any more is because then the Black Swan Record [*sic*] opened up back East, and I made records with Fletcher Henderson. You know, they made records for me back there. . . . Fletcher Henderson recorded [Spikes's tunes] with his band but for Black Swan Records."[159] Henderson's band backed up the singers that Harry Pace had signed up for his label, including Ethel Waters, whose version of Alberta Hunter's "Downhearted Blues" became Black Swan's big hit; Henderson also functioned as musical director (A&R, or "artists and repertoire," as we say nowadays). Spikes must have sent "Someday, Sweetheart" along with some other tunes, and Henderson evidently liked what he heard. Even though the tune did not enjoy the instant success of the Waters recording, the very fact that it had been recorded must have been a selling point to the Melrose brothers, who had the copyright transferred to their firm in 1924, by which time Alberta Hunter had become about as popular as Ethel Waters. The strategy did not always meet with such resounding success, of course, and when the brothers tried it on Morton's "The Wolverines," Jelly cried foul. But more on that later.

The Spikes brothers may have been "cornfed musicians" to Jelly, but when he returned in the summer of 1921, and for most of his last year in Los Angeles, all roads in black music in Los Angeles passed through the Spikes brothers music store, in particular, through Benjamin Franklin "Reb" Spikes. When Morton left Los Angeles in 1919 for San Francisco and eventually the Pacific Northwest, Kid Ory and Mutt Carey arrived from New Orleans and moved in on the gigs at the Cadillac and elsewhere. When Morton returned from the Pacific Northwest to Los Angeles in 1921, Ory and Carey were well established. But there was still plenty of room for Jelly, and the city was treated to a taste of real New Orleans hot music climaxed by King Oliver's appearance in Wayside Park. And that was only the beginning of a trend that saw more and more New Orleans musicians settling in Los Angeles in the 1920s, as Lawrence Gushee has noted. Reb Spikes wisely conceded the preeminence of those musicians as musicians, and took over everything else for just short of a decade.

As for "The Wolverines," Morton tells the story this way: "I did get hot about how they handled *Wolverine Blues*, which they misnamed because it is not a blues. I first wrote *Wolverines* in Detroit in the early days." Then he adds, "The tune got to be famous around Chicago[,] and Melrose wrote and offered a $3,000 advance for it. Somehow the Spikes brothers got the letter and jumped up and wrote some words and published my song as written by Spikes-Morton-Spikes. Right there we had an argument, because they just wanted to drag me over the fence, to tell the plain truth. I decided to go on to Chicago and demand that the tune be changed over to my name, when Melrose published it." [160] Lawrence Gushee has discovered a contemporary account of the same story told from a Chicago perspective in a periodical called *Talking Machine World*, dated 15 May 1923. The story corroborates Morton's account just about to the letter: "According to Walter Melrose, manager of the Melrose Bros. Music Co., the history of 'Wolverine Blues' was very interesting. Some few weeks ago the number was introduced locally by Joe Oliver, known as 'Wizard on the Cornet,' and the requests Mr. Oliver received for copies of the publication were very numerous. Mr. Melrose, in making the inquiry, discovered that the number was unpublished and, upon investigation, learned from Mr. Oliver that the writers of the number lived on the Coast. He lost no time in getting in touch with them and negotiations for publishing by the Melrose Co. were completed within a few days by wire." [161] The plural "writers" means that the "publication" Oliver got so many requests for must have been one of the Spikes brothers' in-house printings intended to lure bigger publishers, like Melrose (though at the time the Melrose brothers ran a fairly small operation). Obviously, Oliver had brought the sheet music along with him when he returned to Chicago—probably along with the music to "Froggie Moore," which Oliver recorded in Richmond, Indiana, in April of 1923.

"Froggie Moore" was another of Morton's compositions attributed to Spikes-Morton-Spikes simply because one or both of the brothers wrote lyrics to it. With "Wolverine Blues," Reb Spikes's marketing strategy worked quite well—too well, as far as Jelly was concerned, and too fast. If the phrase "Some few weeks ago" is accurate, Oliver introduced the number in late April of 1923, and Melrose moved so quickly that by the time Morton arrived in Chicago (May of 1923, by his reckoning) it was already a hit. He arrived, a red bandanna tied around his neck and a ten-gallon cowboy hat on his head, at the entrance of the Melrose Brothers Music Store and saw "a great big banner hung out front—WOLVERINE BLUES SOLD HERE—and I could hear one of the Melrose boys trying to play my tune."[162] As Lester Melrose described it twenty-five years later, Jelly walked into their store and "hollered[,] 'Listen, everybody, I'm Jelly Roll Morton from New Orleans, the originator of jazz.' He talked for an hour without stopping about how good he was and then he sat at the piano and proved he was every bit as good as he claimed and better.'"[163]

The speed with which the negotiations over "Wolverine Blues" had taken place—"within a few days by wire"—suggests that Oliver must have had the Spikes brothers' published version, words and all, to show Melrose, who then would only have had to get the brothers' permission to publish it under the Melrose banner. The negotiations would have taken much longer had they gone through the mail, as Morton suggests. If Jelly left the Coast as quickly and suddenly as the account in Lomax suggests, he was still in Los Angeles when the chain of events began and he felt impelled to go at once. The chronological evidence fully supports such a rapidly unfolding sequence: Morton was still in Southern California on 17 March, Oliver introduced "Wolverine Blues" and recorded "Froggie Moore" in April, and Morton arrived in Chicago in May. Perry Bradford's recollection that sometime in 1923 Jelly wrote him from Fort Wayne, Indiana, about the possibility of making records fits that chronology very neatly.[164] If that means Jelly had not recorded yet, the note would have been written before June of 1923, when he made his first recordings, for Paramount, "Big Fat Ham" and "Muddy Water Blues," most likely in late April or early May, when Jelly knew he had to make his move.

Anita's statement to Lomax that Morton left Los Angeles in 1922, before the controversy over "Wolverine Blues" broke out, and that his motive had to do with a rupture in their relationship cannot be accurate: "Well, we had a misunderstanding and he left for Chicago in 1922. He told me, 'Baby, I don't think I can live away from you. I'd want to die first.' He said he would send for me and I waited. Then he wrote me that he had a thousand dollars and when he got two, he'd send for me. Then he got sick. He never did send. He went and took up with another

woman. But I was the only woman he ever really loved."[165] It seems odd
that a woman of her financial resourcefulness had to wait for Morton to
come up with the cash for her to make the move, especially considering
the apparent ease with which she moved up and down the Coast with him
as she bought into and out of one business after another. But then, to
move as far as Chicago would have been another matter altogether, and
perhaps she would have had to let go of whatever sources of income she
had established in Las Vegas and Los Angeles. Besides, she still had her
mother to look after and no doubt would have had to bring her to Chicago too. Whatever the reason for the delay, Anita did wait for approximately two years. As she puts it, "Then he got sick. He never did send."
The illness seems to have been the point at which she gave up all hope
that he would ever "send." According to Lomax, Morton fell ill about
two years after he left Los Angeles.[166] Lomax quotes one of Jelly's sisters
(which one, he never mentions), who says that she went to Chicago in
1925 to help nurse him through his illness. In a 1969 interview with
William Russell, Morton's younger sister, Frances Morton Oliver, confirms that she was the one who spent six months supposedly nursing her
brother, from April to October 1925.[167] As for the nature of his ailment,
he never told her, and he never even let her do much nursing: "He went
out to work at some nightspot . . . and come [*sic*] right back home and
get in bed and sleep all day. He said his nerves were shot to pieces." She
makes it clear that her brother was scuffling financially at the time, living in a rented room and "riding in his old piece of a Marmon car that
wasn't running half the time."[168] The year Jelly's sister gives for his illness would seem to be exactly right: in 1925, Morton recorded only two
numbers, both in the month of May, drastically reduced from the twenty-
nine recordings in 1923–24 and from the great burst of creative activity
represented by his Red Hot Peppers recordings of 1926–27. Anita's reference to "another woman" must mean Mabel, whom he courted around
1926–27, when he was flush with the money and success that his Red
Hot Peppers recordings brought about, so maybe Anita waited that long

before finally giving up altogether. Certainly, the success of those recordings would have voided any excuses for a further delay in bringing Anita to Chicago, had he needed them.

Morton spoke only once about the breakup of his relationship with Anita, in December of 1938, at the last of the recording sessions with Lomax in the Library of Congress. He strums a guitar as he speaks, and, aside from a few light moments, his voice fairly drips with regret as he remembers the events of some sixteen years earlier. Lomax asks, "How were you and Anita getting along?" and Jelly answers, "Oh, we [was] gettin along swell. It's a day that I don't like to bring back, because I never realize how happy I was until after I left her. There was nothin under the sun that I ever wanted that I didn get during that time but two things. And those two things, one of em was a yacht n the other was a cow." [169]

Though Lomax's response is inaudible, he is obviously perplexed by the cow. Jelly responds, "A cow. I never did have a cow. I wanted that, see, and I wanted a yacht." He never says anything more about the cow, but instead moves rapidly on to a discussion of how devoted Anita was to her mother, who lived with them:

> Of course, Anita was devoted to me[,] more so than to her mother.
> If I told her to do something, she listened to everything I said and
> she respected me as her husband, as few women today respect their
> husbands. Aside from that, Anita was a very beautiful woman and
> she dressed very handsomely with plenty diamonds to elaborate the
> condition. I couldn't wish for a finer woman than Anita. In fact, I
> don't believe there was ever one born finer than Anita[,] and I know
> I've missed an awful lot by leaving her. It was all a mistake, but nevertheless it happened.[170]

Whether or not the breakup was actually brought about by the "misunderstanding" that Anita refers to, Jelly's sober assessment of the matter sixteen years later is certainly unusual for a man who could hardly ever bring himself to admit that he was wrong about anything. His words, uttered in December of 1938, are especially poignant because as he spoke them he was still with Mabel, who had convinced him to move back to New York from Washington, D.C. They left in the thick of a blizzard two days before Christmas. He was a sick man—sicker than he knew at the time: he had only two and a half years to live. Already he was planning a possible return to Los Angeles. As he speaks his last public words about Anita to Lomax, he says little about the exact shape the mistake took, except for the obvious: leaving her in the first place. But the words on the page convey little of the depth of feeling in Jelly's voice as he speaks them in the middle range of his rich baritone voice, his rhythms and inflections not mournful or solemn, but elegiac. Perhaps it might not be too fanciful to call his words an informally spoken elegy for a lost Eden. From the perspective of December 1938, his California years must have seemed a golden age, full of sunshine and diamonds, music and youth, twelve-cylinder motor cars and trips to Alaska—and Anita.

7

In Mabel's observations of Jelly at work writing music, she includes some obvious matters of routine—how an idea would strike him in the middle of the night and he would get up and "begin whistling and then go to dotting it down"— but then she adds that "lots of times he liked to get in the car and go out in the country, maybe look at an old house or some scenery and he'd write a song from that."[171] The titles of Morton's compositions would seem to support Mabel's comments, which in effect imply that much of his opus consists of program music, in the sense of music intended to evoke a concrete image, event, mood, or personality: "Jungle Blues," "Mamanita," "The Pearls," "Kansas City Stomps," "Bert Williams," and "Deep Creek," to name just a few. Jelly's own comments on "The Pearls" lend further support to the idea. In that event, it should be fairly easy to identify the compositions written on the West Coast simply by the content of the titles: tunes like "Mamanita," "Sweet Anita Mine," "Seattle Hunch," and "The Pacific Rag," with their obvious references to West Coast places and people, could be roughly dated as having been written sometime between 1917 and 1923. There are at least two problems with that formula, however. First, the ideas that struck him "in the middle of the night," as Mabel describes them, were probably musical, not programmatic. When a composer gets up in the middle of the night humming or whistling a melody that he is in a hurry to write out, chances are that the musical idea has come first. Morton may eventually have settled on a programmatic title, but that is another matter. If the inspiration was primarily musical, then the connection between the composition and a specific time, place, or person becomes rather tenuous. Second, Morton would occasionally change titles in a way that apparently nullified their original programmatic intent: "London Blues" became "Shoe Shiner's Drag," "Stratford Hunch" became "Chicago Breakdown," "Black Bottom Stomp" began as "Queen of Spades," "Wild Man Blues" as "Ted Lewis Blues," "Fickle Fay Creep" as "Soap Suds," and "Tom Cat Blues" became "Midnight Mama" to fit the lyrics added to it later.[172] And apparently Morton changed the title of "The Pacific Rag" to "Bert Williams" simply because the great comedian expressed his admiration for the tune.[173] The music of "Bert Williams" betrays the rather arbitrary switch of titles: although it has to rank as one of Jelly's best pieces, the thematic material of the tune does not come anywhere near as close as Duke Ellington's "Portrait of Bert Williams" to expressing the nature of its subject. Ellington's "Portrait" is just that—it sounds as if it were written with the comedian in mind; it has the same mix of humor and pathos expressed so vividly in Ann Charters's biography of Williams, *Nobody*. Morton's title, while sincerely intended as a tribute to the comedian, is more dedication than portraiture.

With that cautionary note in mind, the possibility that the titles may contain clues that help to place the compositions chronologically should not be dismissed entirely. "The Pearls" and "Kansas City Stomps," the only two surviving compositions that can be definitively placed as products of the West Coast years (aside from "Someday, Sweetheart," a collaborative effort), Morton himself connects directly to the Kansas City Bar in Tijuana and, in the case of "The Pearls," specifically to a pretty

barmaid. And his comments to Lomax on the Library of Congress re-
cordings contain a tantalizing reference to a forgotten tune that was inspired directly by a California locale, this time the Cadillac Cafe in Los
Angeles. As he recalls it, as soon as he opened at the club, "I wrote . . .
'The Cadillac Rag.' I've forgotten that tune now, it's quite a hard tune,
I use ta play it on the piana . . . and it's one of those things where the
singers would sing it, you know . . . and I'd have an answer in it. And the
'Cadillac Rag' got to be kind a pretty fair." [174] Then there is the interesting "Tia Juana (Tee Wana)," recorded as a piano solo in July of 1924.
Even though the piece is not Morton's own composition, the fact that
he recorded it during his first year in the recording studios, along with
four pieces from the West Coast years, can be seen as a sign of nostalgia
for that place and time. (The other pieces are "Kansas City Stomps,"
"The Pearls," "Someday, Sweetheart," and "Mamanita"—the last one
recorded twice.) In addition to the geographic reference in the title, the
themes of "Tia Juana" evoke a south-of-the-border feeling. The rather
elaborate introduction has a highly syncopated "Spanish tinge" feel to it.
The rhythm of the first strain is straight ragtime, but the second modu-
lates to a tango-habañera beat. Then, after the first strain is repeated,
with its straight-ahead time, the third strain makes its first appearance
with a habañera rhythm and a melody that is pure mariachi. In the rest of
the performance, Morton "rags" the third strain, plays some variations
on it, and brings it to a conclusion. It's as if he is making a musical statement about the bicultural experience of playing jazz in Tijuana, Mexico,
in a place called the Kansas City Bar. Of the three pieces directly connected to his work in Mexico, "Tia Juana" is the only one to evoke the
musical particulars of his experience there, even though the composition is not Morton's own. Great as they are, "The Pearls" and "Kansas
City Stomps" could have been written anytime, anyplace. Jelly seldom
recorded anything but his own material; that alone makes "Tia Juana"
unusual in the Morton canon.

The tunes connected directly to Anita should be ranked next to those
above as most likely to have been written on the West Coast: "Mama-

nita," "Sweet Anita Mine," and "Dead Man Blues." "Mamanita" is a lovely "Spanish tinge" piece that Morton recorded three times: twice in 1924, little more than a year after their separation; and once on the Library of Congress recordings. Quite possibly, Jelly could have written the piece during the interval between his departure from Los Angeles and his first recording of it in April of 1924, but there can be no doubt that he wrote it with Anita and his West Coast years in mind. To my ears, his best performance of the composition by far is the Library of Congress version. He takes it at a slower tempo in that rendition, and the performance is infused with an elegiac nostalgia entirely missing from the two earlier versions, whose brisk tempos suggest an optimism appropriate to the status of their relationship at the time, when Jelly was supposed to be saving his pennies to bring Anita to Chicago. As for "Sweet Anita Mine," it was not recorded until 1929, and it's anyone's guess whether it was written while Morton was on the West Coast or after. It has none of the nostalgia that one would expect to hear in the piece if it were written in Chicago or New York. It's a sprightly if undistinguished piece of music, at least as performed by the rather large band assembled for the occasion—eleven pieces, to be exact. Morton never quite got the knack of writing jazz for large ensembles, at least not at that time; the recorded evidence usually sounds more like a society band at work (except for the solos, of course) than a jazz orchestra, and "Sweet Anita Mine" is no exception. This is his only recording of the tune, so maybe it would have fared better in a small-group or solo-piano treatment. I have already commented on the lyrics of "Dead Man Blues" in an earlier chapter; most likely Anita wrote them while Jelly was still on the West Coast. Had she written the words after he left, she would have had to rely on her memory to fit the words to the music. It could have happened that way, but it is more probable that she wrote the lyrics when Jelly was still around and the music was fresh in her mind. Of course, the music could have been written before 1917–23 and the lyrics sometime during that period. At any rate, the lyrics are not particularly memorable, and the classic recording of the tune is not the vocal version by Edmonia Henderson recorded in July of 1926 but the instrumental Red Hot Peppers version from September of the same year.

Sometime in July or August, Morton also recorded "Dead Man Blues" on a Q.R.S. piano roll.[175] This time around, Jelly follows the form of the vocal—that is to say, of the lyrics: intro (an eight-bar quotation of the funeral march "Flee as a Bird to the Mountain"), ABAAA, and coda ("Flee as a Bird" again), with a couple of interesting changes. First, he plays two choruses instead of just one, so that "Flee as a Bird" makes three appearances, as intro, interlude, and coda. Second, an even more striking change, the "A" theme is played to the habañera-tango rhythm that Morton referred to as the "Spanish tinge" element in jazz, something entirely absent from the other two versions. For the final recording in September, he completely recast the tune, using "Flee as a Bird" only as an intro, dropping the original B strain altogether and adding a new strain, played by a clarinet trio, that was evidently composed especially for this session. The new arrangement is: intro, A strain, clarinet solo (one chorus), cornet solo (two choruses), B strain (two choruses, with trombone obbligato on the second chorus), A strain, and coda (the first two measures of the B strain). In effect, Morton has abandoned the lyric version of the tune altogether and turned the composition "from a mere novelty to a fine blues piece," in James Dapogny's words.[176] The odd thing about the flurry of activity over "Dead Man Blues" in 1926 is that Morton never recorded it again. Perhaps the obvious explanation is that Jelly himself never regarded the piece as anything more than a novelty number, in spite of the aesthetic and critical success of the final version. Surely, the three recordings—especially the vocal version—reminded Morton of Anita. On the lead sheet he sent for the copyright, he was careful to note, "Words by Anita Gonzales, music by Ferd Jelly Roll Morton."[177] Without more evidence, however, it is impossible to tell whether his sudden but short-lived interest in the piece had anything to do with the state of their relationship as of 1926. Most likely, Anita had given up on Jelly by the summer of that year, and it is tempting to surmise that the final, recast version of the tune was symbolically a musical farewell.

But the thematic material of "Dead Man Blues" provides some clues to another of Morton's compositions that may have originated on the West Coast: "London Blues," recorded twice during Jelly's first year in the recording studios and later retitled "Shoe Shiner's Drag." When James Dapogny says that the last chorus of "London Blues" ends each time, in the 1923–24 versions, with "the same four-measure phrase," he is describing the same four-bar phrase that ends each chorus of "Dead Man Blues." Not only that, but the third strain of the melody is accompanied by the same ostinato bass figure that announces the third strain of "The Pearls." By the time Morton recorded the composition as "Shoe Shiner's Drag" with the Red Hot Peppers in 1928, the motifs that link it to "Dead Man Blues" and "The Pearls" had been completely submerged in what amounts to a composition that stands on its own, without the motifs that originally supported it. But the presence of those motifs in the early versions of "London Blues" suggests that they came from the same melodic matrix that produced both "The Pearls" and "Dead Man Blues," perhaps even from the same chronological period. Since we cannot date the composition of any of the three pieces, it is impossible to say where the motifs first appeared. However, the recording dates of "London Blues," both versions, and of "Shoe Shiner's Drag" may contain a clue to Morton's attitude toward the composition. The piece had certainly been altered enough to justify a change of title, and the new title expresses more clearly the potential programmatic implications of the composition than "London Blues" does. The thematic material has nothing of "London" in it. In all of his travels, Morton never left continental North America, though he would not have been the first composer to have written music about a place he had never seen. One of the earlier titles, "London Cafe Blues," may be an indication that, similar to the case of "Kansas City Stomps," the piece was originally written when Morton was working at a place called the London Cafe—though it never appears in any of the newspaper ads, and Jelly himself never mentions to Lomax a cafe by that name.

The title of "Seattle Hunch" puts that composition in the running to make the list of West Coast compositions, but the connection goes a bit deeper than that. James Dapogny has identified the piece as one of a cluster of three compositions with thematic or structural similarities. The other two are "Mamanita" and "Frances" (also known as "Fat Frances"). As Dapogny points out, the similarity is most striking between "Mamanita" and "Frances": "*Mamanita* has similarities to the later *Frances:* it is a three-strain work with the second strain returning to close the piece. The third strain itself is very similar to that of *Frances*, being in the same key and using the same chromatically rising left-hand gesture." Dapogny also notes that Morton used the three-strain format of "Mamanita" in only two other compositions, "Frances" and "Seattle Hunch," and adds that "neither of them was as successful as 'Mamanita' because neither had the interrelationships among strains that 'Mamanita' had, nor so suitable a second strain for closing the piece."[178] Structural and thematic echoes of that kind do not necessarily mean that the pieces are related in any other way—that is, either chronologically or biographically—but the fact that Morton never used that formal three-strain format elsewhere does leave the door open to the possibility that he was experimenting with that format at one time and then went on to other things. But even if he wrote "Mamanita" and "Seattle Hunch" after he left the Coast, the titles suggest that he was thinking of those years as he wrote them. The copyright dates on "Seattle Hunch" (28 September 1929) and "Frances" (10 January 1931) place both pieces at some chronological distance from 1917–23, but considering Morton's tendency at times to copyright his compositions some years after he wrote them, the dates may have little to do with when they were actually written.[179]

As for "Bert Williams," Roy Carew's list in appendix one of *Mister Jelly Roll*, arranged chronologically according to copyright date, cites the title with the parenthetical notation "originally *The Pacific Rag* from the California years."[180] However, Rudy Blesh and Harriet Janis's *They*

All Played Ragtime assigns the date 1911 to the piece, supposedly "named for vaudeville comedian Bert Williams after Williams had heard and admired it."[181] The early date makes sense, because it seems unlikely that Morton crossed paths with the great comedian during the 1917–23 period, when Williams was securely anchored in the Ziegfeld Follies in New York and Jelly was busy with one hustle or another up and down the West Coast. However, Blesh and Janis supply no source for their dating, and, considering how closely Morton worked with Carew toward the end, the latter's statement about the piece being written during "the California years," should carry some weight. Perhaps the original title, "The Pacific Rag," is a reference to Jelly's earlier trip to California, sometime between 1908 and 1911. The encounter between Morton and Williams may have occurred in 1911—Williams's second year with Ziegfeld, when the Follies left New York for a West Coast tour—or perhaps in Chicago sometime between 1911 and 1917.[182] "Bert Williams" may eventually provide a clue to the exact date of Morton's first foray into the Wild West, but the piece does not seem to have been the product of his second, five-year stay.

In short, the evidence about Morton's compositional activity during the years 1917–23 allows only a handful of tunes to be credited with any certainty to that time. At the top of that list is "The Pearls," "Kansas City Stomps," "Someday, Sweetheart," and the lost tune "The Cadillac Rag." The next group, only a bit less certain chronologically, includes "Mamanita," "Dead Man Blues," "Seattle Hunch," and perhaps "Sweet Anita Mine." The third group includes tunes that Jelly recorded in 1923–24, immediately after his return from the West Coast—excluding, of course, those known to have been written earlier: "King Porter Stomp," "New Orleans Joys" (also known as "New Orleans Blues"), "Wolverine Blues," and "Jelly Roll Blues," as well as a half dozen or so written by others. That leaves "Big Fat Ham," "Muddy Water Blues," "Grandpa's Spells," "Froggie Moore Rag," "Tom Cat Blues," "Stratford Hunch," "Perfect Rag," and "Fish Tail Blues." Those tunes may well have been written on the West Coast, but there is no evidence—not even in the titles—to contradict the possibility that they were written either before or after that period. To that group can be added an even more hypothetical category: tunes written on the Coast but not recorded or copyrighted until much later. (The title of "Shreveport Stomp," recorded in July of 1924, seems to suggest a much earlier date—if the title means anything.) A case can be made for placing "Creepy Feeling" and "The Crave" in this category. Sid LeProtti's recollections indicate that "The Crave" had been written by 1918, the year he and Jelly had the dispute over the tune after it became popular with the Hollywood crowd at Baron Long's. As much as Morton resented LeProtti's use of the tune, the popularity of "The Crave" and of the tango in general as a dance at that time may have inspired Jelly to try his hand at a couple other tangos—"Creepy Feeling" and "Mamanita." And the three compositions are remarkably similar in mood and musical structure: when Morton plays them back-to-back on the Library of Congress recordings, they sound like they could be grouped in a three-part suite, with *The Spanish Tinge* as the general title. At any rate, Jelly didn't record "The Crave" until he was near the end of his life—once for Alan Lomax sometime between May and July of 1938, and then for the General label in New York on 14 December 1939; the lead sheet for the copyright is dated 20 December 1939, over twenty years after it had become the rage in Los Angeles. "Creepy Feeling" was not copyrighted during his lifetime and was recorded only twice—once for Lomax and once for an obscure Washington, D.C., label, Jazzman, in December of 1938, which means that it was not effectively available to the public during his lifetime. Why Jelly neglected for so long two pieces that have to be considered among his best work is mysterious.

Finally, of the twenty-seven recordings made by Morton in 1923–24, twenty were his own compositions; subtracting the four known to have been written earlier, sixteen possible candidates for West Coast compositions remain—80 percent of the recordings of his own tunes, or slightly more than half his total recorded output for his first two years in the studios. And if we count only the eight compositions that can be ascribed to the 1917–23 period with any certainty, they would still represent 40 percent of his recordings of his own work during those first two years. Either way, Lawrence Gushee's guess that much of Morton's early recorded work was composed on the West Coast seems to be correct. Those eight—possibly as many as sixteen—represent some of his best work, some of his finest contributions to the jazz repertoire. On the other hand, if we consider Carew's copyright list, the only compositions that Jelly himself dated earlier than 1917 are "Jelly Roll Blues" (1905), "Frog-i More Rag [*sic*]" (1908), "King Porter Stomp" (1902), and "New Orleans Blues" (1902–3)—only four pieces.[183] They may not be, and probably were not, his only works before 1917, but there may not have been many more, considering that during those early years he did not make an unequivocal commitment to music, and that he often regarded music as a "front" for his activities as a pool shark and pimp. And even if his total output before 1917 equaled that of his West Coast years, this would mean that it took him twelve to fifteen years to accomplish what took only five years after 1917—relatively speaking, a creative outburst of sorts. Certainly, by the start of 1923 he had created a body of work impressive enough to have ranked him eventually among the great jazz composers, even if he had written nothing else beyond that point.

Morton must have had at least an inkling of that eventuality when he left Los Angeles for Chicago, and his experience with the Spikes brothers—with Reb, in particular—showed him how easy it was for those on the business end of music to put their names on the work of others and to cut them out of not only the profits but the recognition as well. Surely, Anita, with her head for business, would have understood that reality and would have encouraged Jelly to return to Chicago and lay claim to his rightful place in the music world.

8

Jelly Roll Morton's West Coast years mark a crucial period of transition in his life and work, a transition that was to a large extent precipitated and paralleled by a radical transformation of the music business, especially African American music, at that time. The years 1917–23 are momentous in the history of black music and neatly marked by three events: first, in 1917 the Original Dixieland Jazz Band, a white group from New Orleans, recorded "Livery Stable Blues," as far as anyone knows the first jazz recording ever, and it was an instant hit; second, in 1920 Mamie Smith became the first black blues artist to record, and her "Crazy Blues" sold thousands of copies within the first few months of its issue; finally, though little noted at the time, in 1921 Reb Spikes produced on his own Los Angeles–based Sunshine label the first jazz record to feature black musicians, "Ory's Creole Trombone," featuring Kid Ory himself, Papa Mutt Carey, and others. Because of limited production and distribution, the Kid Ory record had little impact outside of Los Angeles, though it must have attracted Morton's attention. The other two recordings, however, because of their popularity, had a tremendous impact. After the Original Dixieland Jazz Band's success, the word "jazz" began to appear everywhere to denote a new fad in popular music. Though it was exploited at first primarily by white musicians like Paul Whiteman, who dubbed himself "King of Jazz," even the locally popular Black and Tan Orchestra began to insert the word "Jazz" between "Tan" and "Orchestra." And Mamie Smith's success with "Crazy Blues" forced the major recording companies of the day to realize that there was a fortune to be made recording black jazz and blues artists for primarily black audiences. In no time at all, most recording companies established a "race record" division, a designation that was to persist for some two decades.

The importance of these events in the history of jazz and blues has often been discussed. They affected every musician in the field, not excluding Jelly Roll Morton, even though he never commented publicly on any of the three recordings. In 1917, when "Livery Stable Blues" came out, Jelly was already twenty-seven years old and well established as both composer and pianist. But whatever fame he had achieved was the result of doing things "the old-fashioned way"—by constantly traveling from one major urban center to another, challenging and vanquishing the local talent and then moving on. It is hard for most people nowadays, in 2001, to think of life without television, but Morton came to maturity as an artist even before radio and before the phonograph became a common household item. He adapted quickly to the challenge of the phonograph record as a new medium through which to disseminate his art and, by 1926, with his Red Hot Peppers sessions, had mastered the demands of having to make his musical statements within the confines of a three-minute recording. But he was still a child of his age, and it took a long time for him to realize that it was not enough simply to have his name next to the titles of his compositions on sheet music and on recordings. Like many musicians of his generation, he was careless about the practical aspects of the music business, especially about copyrights. The commercial success of his Red Hot Peppers recordings created a demand for in-person appearances, and the money kept rolling in—for a while. Only when the flow became a trickle did he realize that he had been exploited. Then he complained loudly and at length about how he was being robbed; but he had unwittingly aided and abetted the theft. From 1923 to 1934, most of the copyrights for his music were held by either Melrose Music Company or Southern Music Company.[184] He would spend the rest of his life trying to get both companies to give him a fair share of the royalties, but the damage was done. Around 1938, with the help of the collector and music enthusiast Roy Carew, he set up Tempo Music Publishing Company, which enabled him to copyright older material that the other companies had missed and the newer material he wrote during his last years. But he had already lost control of many of his most popular pieces, in particular "King Porter Stomp," which was in the book of just about every swing band during the 1930s.

In many ways, his West Coast years mark the end of one era and the beginning of another. Far removed from the centers of the growing music industry in Chicago and New York, he could continue living his life as he always had, moving effortlessly among the various roles he had assumed in life—piano player, composer, showman, pimp, gambler. The combination had always worked before, and it was still working for him.

He had Anita at his side, a twelve-cylinder automobile to drive, and a large following that would gather enthusiastically whenever he played, especially in Los Angeles. He could still afford to be naive about matters like copyrights and recording contracts. It was, as we have seen, a kind of golden age. But signs of the age to come were already appearing, and it was to be an age in which naïveté could prove fatal to a career in music.

Was his return to Los Angeles in 1940 an attempt, psychologically, to recapture that lost innocence, to reenter his lost Eden? Maybe so. But to paraphrase the poet C. P. Cavafy, we all know what these lost Edens really mean.

CHAPTER 4

The Scrapbook

1

In June of 1952, a scant two months after the death of Anita Ford, two good friends, Dick Russell and Joe Marvin, were watching a prizefight on television in a Santa Monica bar. They were celebrating their recent graduation from the University of California at Los Angeles. Dick Russell was the real prizefight fan—to this day, he keeps an archive of fight lore and memorabilia in his home. Joe Marvin liked prizefighting well enough, but his real passion was jazz, especially classic New Orleans jazz.

Alone in the next booth sat a rather loudmouthed older man who was also watching the fight, which involved a black and a white boxer. "Hit that nigger!" he shouted; "Kill the black sonofabitch." Finally, Joe, the jazz fan, got tired of listening to the man's mouth and complained to him about his use of the word "nigger." As some white folks do in such situations, the older man immediately became defensive: he really had nothing against Negroes—why, he had known and worked and even lived among Negroes all of his life. It seemed like nothing more than the tired old "some of my best friends are Negroes" gambit.

But then he made his next move: grinning broadly at them and pointing to one of his front teeth, he declared "See this? This is the diamond of Jelly Roll Morton I've got in my mouth." Even more skeptical now, the two young men didn't know exactly what to do or say next, except to think that the man must be a blowhard who had had a few drinks too many. In the course of the conversation, Joe Marvin had mentioned that he was a jazz fan, so it was easy to take the older man's declaration as nothing more than an attempt to impress the two younger men, or to throw them off balance. When they expressed their skepticism, however, the man countered by introducing himself as Jack Ford, and invited them to follow him to the parking lot. He had something more to show them. In the lot, he climbed into a well-kept, still sleek-looking 1930s vintage Cadillac, slipped the key into the ignition, and started the car. As Joe Marvin remembers it now, the car was so well-tuned that he could not hear the engine running. Looking up at them from inside the car, Jack Ford said, "This was Jelly Roll Morton's car." Of course, the young men had no more reason then to believe Ford than they had had earlier, in the bar. Not to be deterred by their skepticism, Ford countered with: "Look, get in your car and follow me up the Pacific Coast Highway to my motor inn in Malibu, and I'll show you something that will make believers of you both." Joe and Dick took a quick look at one another, and immediately decided to take up the old man's challenge, even though they still couldn't bring themselves to believe him.

In about half an hour, they arrived at the Topanga Beach Auto Court, and soon found, to their astonishment and delight, that Jack Ford was as good as his word. When they entered the cabin that he used as his residence, he sat the young men down, disappeared for a moment, and came back carrying a suitcase. When they saw what it contained, they did become believers, as Ford had predicted. "We thought he was a real phony," Joe Marvin wrote some forty-five years later, "but he showed us a real collection of Jelly Roll Morton material that Ford's wife, *Anita Gonzales* ("Mamanita") had kept—no doubt this was the *real* thing."[1] (See fig. 13.)

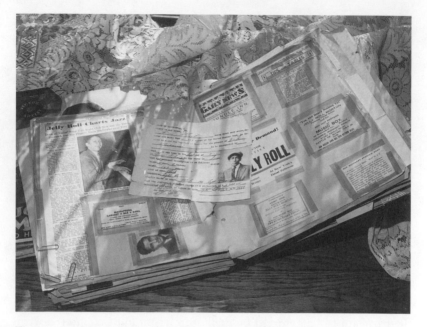

Figure 13. Morton's scrapbook, probably compiled in late 1938. Courtesy Historic New Orleans Collection.

2

In February of 1997, after following a series of leads that took about a year to develop, I found out that Jeanne Ford—widow of Henry Ford, adopted son of Anita and Jack Ford—had inherited the collection of Jelly Roll Morton memorabilia that Joe Marvin and Dick Russell had seen that night in June 1952. I heard their story only after my own discovery made the newspapers in the spring of 1997. When Joe Marvin read about it in the *San Jose Mercury News*, he wrote me a letter with a short version of the above story; in the rather long telephone conversation that ensued, he spelled out the details as I have set them forth. A phone conversation with Dick Russell verified the story that Marvin told.

The story corroborates what I heard from the Ford family in Portland, Oregon, in February of 1997: Anita got the collection from Morton when he died in July 1941, she kept it until her own death in April 1952, and Jack then inherited it from Anita. The rest I also learned from the Ford family: Henry Ford inherited it from Jack when he died, just a few years after Anita. Henry kept the stuff in a suitcase —perhaps the same one Jack Ford had shown Marvin and Russell—in his office at Ford's Restaurant in Portland. When Henry died in 1996, no one bothered to open the suitcase to check its contents until about a year later, when Jeanne took a peek, realized what it contained, and took it home to keep it out of harm's way. The collection includes a fifty-eight-page scrapbook that contains, among other things, newspaper clippings, letters, contracts, and publicity material. The scrapbook has a dark green, imitation leather cover and measures 14¾ × 13 × 3½ inches. Jelly used clear cellophane tape to mount the items; naturally, the tape is no longer clear, having yellowed enough to obscure parts of some of the items. (See fig. 14.) Most of the material dates from 1935 to the fall of 1938, the bulk of it from 1938. The stabbing incident that nearly killed Jelly took place in the late summer or early autumn of 1938, so it is possible that he put the scrapbook together during his recuperation. He did not take the trouble to arrange the items in chronological order, so there are items from 1938 at the beginning of the book and others from 1935, or even earlier, at the end. In some cases a single page holds items from three or four different years. The scrapbook contains no internal evidence to prove definitively that Morton himself compiled it, but he is the most likely candidate for a number of reasons, which I will discuss shortly.

The pile of unorganized clippings and documents is at least equal in volume to the stuff in the book. Indeed, some of the most valuable material—from a biographer's standpoint, at least—never made it into the scrapbook: for example, the work visa, mentioned earlier, from October 1921, which allows us to date his gig at the Kansas City Bar in Tijuana, where he says he wrote both "Kansas City Stomps" and "The

Figure 14.   Flyer for Morton and his Red Hot Peppers, from his scrapbook (note the yellowed cellophane tape), date unknown. Courtesy Historic New Orleans Collection.

Pearls," two of his most masterful compositions;[2] and the appointment card for the hospital in New York where he was treated after his heart attack in 1939 and where he made his follow-up visits in 1939–40. In contrast to the scrapbook, the loose material is far more diverse and far less focused. It includes material from as early as 1919 and as late as November of 1941, four months after Jelly's death—at least three items are posthumous: the guest register from the funeral, and two receipts for postal money orders, both dated 18 November 1941, sent from Riddle, Oregon, a town close to Canyonville, where the original Ford's Restaurant was located. One can only assume that Anita was still taking care of unfinished business related to Morton's estate and therefore added the receipts to the collection. The contrast between the loose material and the scrapbook puts the latter in a rather surprising perspective: as unorganized as the scrapbook seems, there is definitely a principle of selection at work, a focus on a fairly well-defined slice of time. The year 1938 was a time of backward glances, as far as Morton was concerned: it was the year of the Lomax interviews at the Library of Congress and the year of the public debate between Morton and W. C. Handy over who was the true "originator" of jazz; and it was at about this time that Morton wrote the few autobiographical sketches that he started and never finished. At any rate, Anita Ford was raising her family—or families—on the West Coast in late 1938 and could not possibly have had access to the scrapbook until Jelly brought it with him to Los Angeles in November of 1940. The loose material is another matter: the three items that must have been added by Anita after Jelly's death open the possibility that some of the material could have been left with her when he departed California for Chicago in 1923.

The link between the scrapbook and the recuperation is not the only factor that points to Morton as the compiler. Above all, it is more than just a scrapbook. It does contain the kind of material that usually finds its way into scrapbooks: notices of appearances, articles about him in newspapers and magazines, fan mail, and the like. However, Morton also used it as a kind of crude business file and included things like letters from the musicians' union and booking agents, contracts from booking agencies—even, on one page, about a dozen standard American Federation of Musicians contracts, signed by Morton as employer, with everything filled out in his own hand except for the names of the musicians, which he left blank. In fact, David Stuart, who got to know Morton at the end, in Los Angeles, indicates that Morton had more than one scrapbook in his possession when he died: "After he died, I got his scrapbooks and a few photos. . . . I wound up with only the photos, because I made the great mistake of loaning the scrapbooks to Mabel Morton. She said she'd return them, but naturally she didn't do so. It's a shame, because the scrapbooks were wonderful, filled with newspaper clippings and things like that."[3] That Morton used the scrapbooks as a kind of business file is corroborated by one of his letters to Roy Carew, on 7 February 1939. In reply to a question Carew asked about "the names of those tunes Southern messed up for you," Morton says, "At the time it will be impossible to give you the titles of many of the numbers that S- [Southern] have, they are listed in my scrap book & the Agent have that, at present."[4] The date of the letter and his use of the singular "scrap book" suggests the possibility that the scrapbook Jelly had loaned the agent was the very one that wound up in the Ford Collection—it would have been the most recent and up-to-date. The statement also suggests that the scrapbook was similar in function to the portfolios kept by actors, musicians, and entertainers to this day: a kind of self-advertisement.

In *Mister Jelly Roll*, Mabel tells Alan Lomax that "Ferd did all his own bookings by letter or in person."[5] The scrapbook corroborates that statement only in part. Actually, during his glory years as a popular Victor recording artist, the Music Corporation of America (MCA) handled his bookings, but Mabel was around for only the last year or so of that period.[6] In stark contrast to his relationship with Anita, for most of the twelve years he was with Mabel he never discussed business matters with her: "Jelly was always very close about his business affairs," she tells Lomax, and explains, "He never told me what he made a year, and he never let me know exactly what was going on."[7] She was evidently unaware that, after he was dropped by Victor and MCA, he did his own bookings most often out of necessity rather than design. Material in the Ford Collection clearly indicates that, through the 1930s, Jelly continuously shopped around for an agency to handle his affairs; however, by then even small agencies considered him a has-been. Had Mabel compiled the scrapbook, she would have known those facts. Stuart gives no indication of exactly when he "loaned" the scrapbooks to Mabel; Russell's footnote to the interview merely states, "The scrapbooks were almost certainly lost at the time of Mabel's death in New York, in or before 1969."[8]

That leaves Jelly as the only person likely to have put the scrapbook together. And that, in turn, leaves us with an invaluable set of clues about what was on his mind toward the end of his life, just before he left on his last trip to California. This book is not the place for a close look at the full collection. Certainly, the collection merits examination, but carefully and with close attention to detail—a project in itself. My purpose here is to see what the collection might tell us about Morton's return to California, specifically what light, if any, it sheds on his motives. With the help of Lomax's book and the letters Morton wrote to Roy Carew, the collection enables us to construct a fairly accurate, detailed account of his activities and concerns up to November 1940. From that perspective, the word "collection," for me at least, includes the recollections of the Ford family, who have preserved the material and generously permitted me not only access to it but also a hand in determining its fate. What I have learned from both sides of the family is as much a part of "the collection" as the thing itself.

3

This much is certain: the scrapbook is littered with evidence of Morton's craving for the attention he had once gotten. Understandably, one of the most frequent entries has to do with the famous controversy ignited by Robert Ripley, who in a March 1938 broadcast of his "Believe It or Not" radio program introduced W. C. Handy as "the originator of jazz, stomps and blues." Morton, an avid fan of the show, immediately fired off a letter to Ripley, denouncing Handy as a liar and announcing that he, Morton himself, had "originated" jazz in 1902.[9] The scrapbook contains what appears to be an original typescript of the letter—five pages, single spaced and full of typographical errors. He addressed it to Ripley but also sent a copy to *Down Beat* magazine, which had already run a two-part feature on him in the December 1937 and January 1938 issues. *Down Beat* published the entire letter, in two parts, in the August and September 1938 issues, quoting Jelly on the August cover as saying, "W. C. HANDY IS A LIAR!" [10] Morton kept everything he could find in print: both *Down Beat* articles, of course, a long article in the *Baltimore African-American*, and many others. He was making headlines again.

Before the Ripley affair, Morton had become the forgotten man of jazz. He kept trying to find ways back to the limelight, but nothing worked—for very long, at least. Twice, he landed what were intended to be regular radio shows featuring himself on piano and vocals: one, on WINS radio in New York, lasted barely a month, from August to September 1934; the other, according to the *Washington Daily News* of 23 June 1936, was to have been a series called *The History of Jazz*, on radio station WOL in the capital. Letters from WINS in the Ford Collection document the fate of the New York show. The only evidence for the Washington, D.C., program in the collection is the news item cited above, which Morton saved in the scrapbook. Both programs were on long enough to attract some fan mail, at least some of which Morton kept and eventually taped into the scrapbook: a dozen letters in all, most of them handwritten, some in pencil. Morton held fast and long to recognition from even such humble sources.

But easily the most important of the fan letters that he kept has nothing to do with the radio shows—a five-page, handwritten letter dated 30 March 1938 from a self-professed amateur jazz writer named Earle Cornwall, a postal worker who lived in Los Angeles. About half the letter attempts to solicit biographical data for an article Cornwall intended to publish in an unnamed British periodical. The rest is a reply to a letter from Morton in which he had evidently asked Cornwall about what was going on in the Los Angeles jazz scene. Certainly, Morton must have heard that Central Avenue had become a haven for jazz clubs and after-hours joints, and Cornwall's responses to the inquiry clearly indicate that Jelly's letter had voiced his desire to return to Los Angeles. However, Cornwall offers little or no encouragement. He tells Morton to "think it all over very carefully" because "the country here is full to the overflowing of orchestras, musicians, writers, etc." He even tells him that he would "be surprised at the young folks who very likely would not know who the celebrated Jelly Roll *was!*" He then adds, "Another point: considering the *art of piano* playing. Here again, *times* have changed. Listen to Art Tatum's solos—& Teddy Wilson's. The boys are getting more and more complex & involved. Radio is educating the public every day more & more. Scott Joplin's 'Maple Leaf Rag' would sound out of place today."[11]

We need not strain to imagine Jelly's response to the idea that his kind of jazz was out of date. The literature abounds with his replies to younger musicians like Chick Webb who implied or stated outright that his music was old-fashioned—his basic message was always, "If you're playing jazz, you're playing Jelly Roll." Cornwall was right as far as Central Avenue was concerned, though: even when Los Angeles became one of the centers of the New Orleans revival in the 1940s, it never found a home on the Avenue. The revival tended to attract a mostly white audience and thrived in clubs in and around Hollywood. The significance of Cornwall's letter, however, is that it offers clear evidence of Morton's desire to return to California, and that it fully corroborates other evidence, if only in bits and pieces. For example, in *Mister Jelly Roll*, Morton tells Lomax that, when he still had an office in New York, he had hired a West Indian man to run it: "As I had decided to form a monopoly and put my money behind a lot of my type bands with the main offices located in Los Angeles, I needed a confidential partner to handle the New York end."[12] The fact that he could still afford to rent an office outside his home and had enough money to consider such a scheme places this almost-event at about 1930, perhaps earlier. Morton went broke soon after and blamed his bad fortune on a voodoo curse supposedly placed on him by the West Indian.[13]

In Floyd Levin's article, "Jelly's Last Days," Anita Gonzales tells Levin that Morton actually did pass through Los Angeles, around 1936, as the anonymous accompanist for a burlesque act known as "Brownskin

Models." Anita's description of the act is detailed enough to suggest that she saw the show and that she and Jelly were reunited, if only for a brief visit: "They played at the Burbank Theatre on Main Street down on skid row. The girls didn't strip—they did a lot of posing behind sheer curtains. It seemed quite risqué at the time. Peg Leg Bates was the headliner. Jelly's name was not used in the advertising. He only played in the pit and was not featured at all—what a waste. But those were depression years and Jelly was glad to have the work."[14] Levin himself supports this story: a great-uncle of his, Jack Rothschild, and Irvin C. Miller were booking agents for the show. Rothschild offered to take his nephew to the show, free pass included, of course, and, knowing Floyd's growing passion for jazz, mentioned that Jelly Roll Morton was the accompanist. Although he later regretted it, Floyd turned down the offer—he was more interested in Benny Goodman and swing music and did not know much about Morton at the time. In the light of this anecdote, it is especially puzzling that Morton, in *Mister Jelly Roll*, tells Lomax he "never seen [*sic*] either Los Angeles or Anita again."[15] Surely Jelly could not have forgotten such a trip in a few short years. There seem to be only two possible explanations: either Morton is lying, or Lomax's transcription is faulty. Perhaps Jelly's pride stopped him from admitting that he had been reduced to taking work as an anonymous accompanist to a burlesque act.

Barney Bigard's autobiography contains an important recollection of Morton talking about a return to California a few years before his final return. Bigard mentions the 1930 recording session—a trio with himself, Morton, and Zutty Singleton—and says,

> After those records I saw Jelly off and on[,] and then it seemed like he was out of the picture for a few years[,] or maybe I was travelling so much [with Duke Ellington's orchestra]. I saw him years later coming up 125th Street. He was all bundled up with his coat up high against the icy wind. "How's things going, Jelly[?]," I asked him.
>
> "Boy, those booking agents are smart people. They know if they

hold Mr. Jelly down, they can hold the rest of those cats down," he
replied.

"Come on, Jelly. That's not like you," I said.

"I'm getting ready to go to California," said Jelly Roll.

A few years after that I saw him again one more time. This time
it was actually in Los Angeles. He said, "I'm doing good out here.
Got a place out in the country. Everything's all right. I'll make it."
Next thing I heard, he had died.[16]

Bigard doesn't even try to guess the dates of his last meetings with Jelly
Roll, but what he does recall fits the chronology of Morton's activities
during the 1930s. The period when Morton seemed "out of the picture
for a few years" could be the 1935–38 period, when he was living in
Washington, D.C. The winter meeting in New York most likely took
place during the winter of 1938–39, just after his return from Washington—that is, if Bigard remembers correctly that he last saw Jelly "a
couple of years later" in Los Angeles. That last meeting would have happened somewhere between November 1940 and April 1941; after that,
Morton was permanently bedridden.

It may be no coincidence that the Earle Cornwall letter and Bigard's
winter sighting of Morton happened within about a year of one another,
between March 1938, when Jelly was still in Washington, and the winter of 1938–39, just after his return to New York. Evidently, while he
was moving north he was considering, if not planning, a move west, even
though Anita and Mabel later gave Lomax the impression that the move
was sudden and unplanned. The stabbing in Washington left Morton in
a weakened and deteriorating state of health, and he may have had no
choice under the circumstances than to return to New York with Mabel, at least temporarily. Her own words to Lomax indicate that she did
in fact force the issue of the move.[17] The blow to Jelly's ego must have
at least equaled the physical trauma he had sustained: during his last
years Morton was so weak that he had to rely on the women in his life to
help him get to the finish line—that is to say, on Mabel first and then

on Anita. It is fairly certain that the trauma precipitated the heart attack Mabel describes in *Mister Jelly Roll*, though the heart condition must have been latent. The scrapbook preserves a letter to Morton from his brother-in-law, J.P. Oliver, M.D., who ran his own Oliver Sanitarium in Lubbock, Texas. In the letter, Oliver acknowledges a letter, dated 7 May, from Jelly to his sister Frances, in which he complained of both poor health and union problems. Dr. Oliver mentions both problems and urges Morton to come to Lubbock "for a month or until you feel able to resume your work." Unfortunately, the year is not mentioned anywhere in the letter, but it is possible to date it approximately: the scrapbook contains nothing after 1938, and in May of that year Jelly had not undergone either the stabbing incident or the heart attack. The scrapbook does contain a considerable amount of correspondence about union problems, most of it from 1935. On 31 May of that year, Morton had contracted with an agency, Cosmopolitan Entertainments, to take a band for a quick one-week tour of upper New York State during the week of July 4. Evidently, Jelly bungled the job and tried to blame the musicians in order to take the heat off himself. The case he brought against the musicians dragged on until the autumn of 1935, when Jelly lost by default (he failed to show for the last hearings). He kept all the correspondence and eventually placed it in the scrapbook, along with a few letters having to do with other union or labor disputes. By May of 1936, Morton had moved to Washington, D.C., and no doubt would have written his sisters, Frances and Amide, about what had happened—in Lomax's interview of Amide and other members of Morton's family, it becomes clear that Jelly kept in close touch with his family over the years. An educated guess would date Dr. Oliver's letter to May 1936; at any rate, it gives a strong indication that Morton had complained of health problems long before the 1939 heart attack—even before the 1938 stabbing incident. Indeed, in the notes in the Library of Congress from interviews that were not recorded, Morton reveals that he had had a serious bout of some kind of venereal disease in his early youth, when he was about sixteen or seventeen years old: "At that time, there was something called the 'whore's itch,' which broke out all over Jelly Roll. He would scratch and scratch until he almost poisoned himself. A big cake of a sore formed between his thighs. . . . He cured himself with sulphur, lard, and bluestone."[18] If the undiagnosed malady was syphilis, Jelly's cardiovascular problems may possibly have been the symptoms of the tertiary stage of that disease. We know now that the only certain cure for syphilis is penicillin or one of many forms of antibiotics now available, but those drugs were not available to cure the illness until after Morton's death.

Morton's stay in Washington, D.C., which lasted roughly two years, was itself a strange affair, and as might be expected, the scrapbook includes a fair share of mementos from those years. He told Mabel that he was going to the capital to try his luck with prizefight promotion, and the scrapbook does show evidence of his activities in the fight business—particularly a flyer announcing that Ferd Morton is representing K. O. Clark ("A REAL BOX OFFICE ATTRACTION"), who at the time supposedly held the featherweight and bantamweight championships of Florida. The flyer lists the names and weight classes of five other equally obscure boxers, the most well-known of whom was Lou "Tiger" Flowers, whose main claim to fame was being Joe Louis's "most successful sparring partner." But, according to Mabel, Jelly wrote her that the boxers "wouldn't keep training, drank all the time, and so that went flop and he didn't know what he would do next."[19]

Then she did not hear from him for almost two years. If she ever suspected that Jelly was doing his best to leave her, she apparently never showed it. With her characteristic persistence and loyalty, she finally located him, and he wrote her a number of apologetic notes that are full of his own characteristic evasiveness about his activities. When she forced the issue by showing up in Washington, D.C., she understood both the silence and the evasions: he had taken up with a woman by the name of Cordelia Rice Lyle, proprietor of a D.C. nightspot variously called the Jungle Inn or the Music Box. (See fig. 15.) "I saw what the situation was," Mabel says to Lomax; "You can sense those things." Mabel's response

Figure 15. Newspaper ad for the Music Box–
Jungle Inn, circa 1936–38. Courtesy Historic
New Orleans Collection.

was typically self-effacing: "Immediately the help at the place accepted
me as his wife. They expected some sort of big blow-up, I suppose, and
then nothing happened. Cordelia was very polite and nice to me and I
was the same to her, but I soon saw that it was the wrong spot for Jelly."[20]
Morton's attempts to improve the club and its clientele are reflected in
the many ads he saved in the scrapbook (some fourteen), but Cordelia
seemed more intent on catering to her friends than running a successful
business. Even after the stabbing incident, Mabel had a hard time con-
vincing Jelly to leave. Perhaps he was finally convinced when the young
man who had stabbed him got only thirty days in jail because Cordelia

"couldn't do nothing against the child of a schoolmate of hers" and, a few weeks after his release from jail, he was back at the Jungle Inn again.[21] Finally, his health irreparably damaged, Jelly allowed himself to be convinced to return to New York, where his heart attack in the spring of 1939 spelled the beginning of the end.

Among the loose material in the Ford Collection is, as mentioned earlier, Morton's appointment card from the Vanderbilt Clinic on 168th Street and Broadway in New York. That document and the letters Morton wrote to Roy Carew during this period allow us to set down an accurate chronology for the ups and downs of Jelly's condition—far more accurate than what we find in Lomax's book, at least. According to Lomax, Mabel says that Morton was in the hospital for three months, and her letter to Roy Carew informing him of the heart attack is dated 17 April 1939.[22] However, Morton's stay was nowhere near the three months that Mabel supposedly remembers. In a letter to Carew dated 8 May, Jelly writes, "I was released from the hospital Sunday May 7th at 1 pm."[23] His hospital stay, in other words, was about three weeks, not three months. In another letter to Carew, this one dated 30 May, Jelly mentions the follow-up appointment during which the doctors advised him to stop playing for reasons of health. That would have been the appointment on 29 May, noted on the Vanderbilt Clinic card (stamped on the right-hand side). The next follow-ups noted on the card are 14 August and 21 August. (See figs. 16a and 16b.) One can only assume that having two appointments so close together indicates some kind of crisis—otherwise, they tend to be spaced at intervals two to three months apart; the next are on 16 October and 11 December, which would indicate that Morton's condition had stabilized or improved. But then his next appointment is 8 January 1940, less than a month after his December visit, and is followed by another exactly a week later, on 15 January.

Suffering a New York winter must have put a tremendous strain on Morton's heart and must have made him remember rather wistfully the mild winters of Southern California. But a letter to Carew on 6 February 1940 attests to the fact that Los Angeles was on his mind at this very

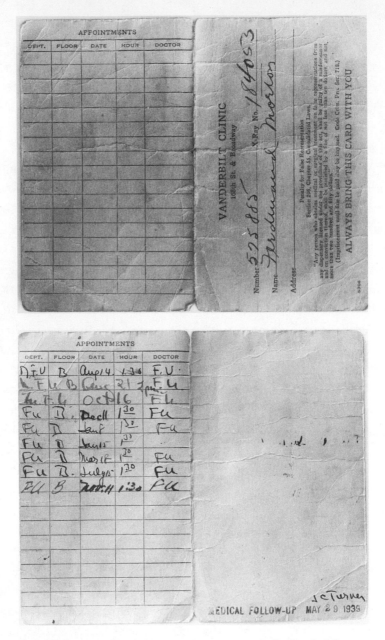

Figures 16a and 16b.   Morton's appointments at the Vanderbilt Clinic, 1939–40, following a heart attack. Courtesy Historic New Orleans Collection.

time for reasons apart from the weather: "It is true that warm weather is due in short, I am sure I won't be in New York to greet it. . . . My last near relative is . . . on a death bed in Los Angeles . . . and the other is stone blind. . . . These two was responsible for my little musical education, and just the same as my mother and father. . . . It seems I just can't get things to roll my way as I have in past years, this is God's work and no one can do anything about it."[24] Three days later, on 9 February, he writes, "My relative passed away yesterday, I feel very badly over it."[25] That relative was, of course, Laura Hunter, whose final illness and death coincided exactly with Morton's closely spaced visits to the Vanderbilt Clinic in December and January. Perhaps the spacing was no mere coincidence: the death of someone so close to Morton could easily have caused a setback in his own condition. The next three appointments on the card—18 March, 15 July, and 11 November—certainly suggest that the three visits so close together, from 11 December to 15 January, were an anomaly. The spacing of the next appointments after 18 March— four months in each case—indicate that his condition had improved somewhat; at any rate, he was gone from New York by 11 November, the last date on the card. Morton's weakened condition certainly would explain why he did not leave for Los Angeles in the spring of 1940, as he had intended, according to the letter to Carew. But if Jelly's condition had improved enough by 18 March that another visit to the clinic was not deemed necessary until 15 July, why did he wait until November for his coast-to-coast trip? Stranger still, a letter to Carew on 19 September places Jelly in Cincinnati, Ohio, following a lead on a gig in that city.[26] Why go back to New York only a month and a half later, before heading west again? The most obvious answer would be that he was doing all he could, given his condition, to raise as much cash as possible, as his letters to Carew indicate. We should remember too that the letters express his determination to continue playing music, in spite of his doctors' advice.[27]

The trip to Cincinnati was only one of a number of failed prospects. Another such reversal was a gig at the Hunt's Point Palace in New York. On 6 April 1940 he writes to Carew, "I planned the starting of a band circuit with what money I could get ahold of . . . but before we could get under way the Union stepped in and raised the scale so high . . . we could only stay one night."[28] The Ford Collection has preserved the contract for that engagement, and the document clarifies what Morton says about starting the circuit "with what money I could get ahold of": signed on 6 May, the contract states that Morton agrees to pay "50.00 nitely" for the privilege of using the Grand Ball Room ("Can use Casino if Main Hall is taken"). (See fig. 17.) In addition, the letter to Carew includes a flyer that makes it clear that the engagement was not just for a solo piano but involved two big bands, Morton's and another led by Baron Lee. Evidently, Morton, still the gambler, was betting that he could pay the rent on the hall and the musicians' salaries out of his own pocket and recoup his losses from whatever money the job raised and, eventually, from the royalties of increased record sales that a successful engagement might inspire. The only other possibility is that Morton had found a backer. He certainly did not have much money at that time: a receipt from 21 October 1939 in the loose material of the Ford Collection shows that Morton could afford only a two-dollar deposit on three used tires costing a total of twelve dollars. Where was he to come up with fifty dollars a night? Could Anita have already been lending him a hand? No hard evidence exists to support that possibility. We may never know how Morton intended to finance the engagement, but it was to have lasted, according to the terms of the contract, from 12 May 1940 "until May 1941," and it would have forced him to postpone his trip to Los Angeles indefinitely. Perhaps the trip to Cincinnati was cut from the same cloth: Jelly was a desperate man, living under a sentence of death, willing to do anything to turn his fortunes around. And perhaps the move to Los Angeles was his ace in the hole, to be played only when all else had failed. He knew he would have to play it sooner or later and was hoping for some measure of control over exactly when he would show his hand. By late October, he knew the time had come, before his health failed completely and he would be unable to make the trip.

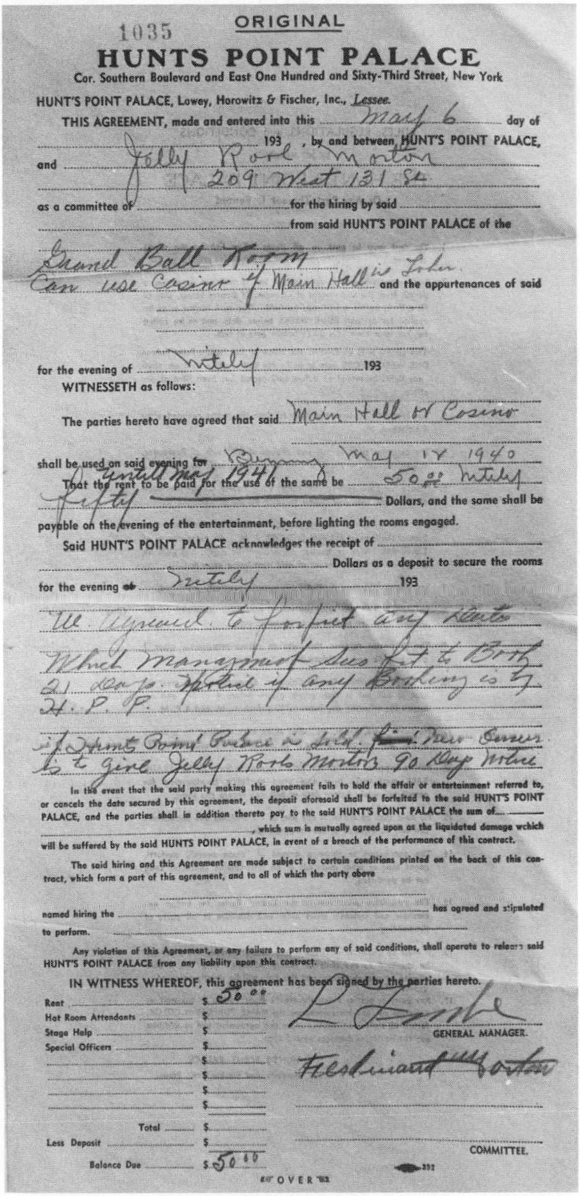

1035

ORIGINAL

HUNTS POINT PALACE

Cor. Southern Boulevard and East One Hundred and Sixty-Third Street, New York

HUNT'S POINT PALACE, Lowey, Horowitz & Fischer, Inc., Lessee.

THIS AGREEMENT, made and entered into this May 6 day of 193 , by and between HUNT'S POINT PALACE, and Jelly Roll Morton 209 West 131 St as a committee of for the hiring by said from said HUNT'S POINT PALACE of the Grand Ball Room Can use Casino of Main Hall and the appurtenances of said

for the evening of Nitely 193

WITNESSETH as follows:

The parties hereto have agreed that said Main Hall or Casino shall be used on said evening for Begining May 18 1940 until May 1941

That the rent to be paid for the use of the same be 50.00 Nitely Fifty Dollars, and the same shall be payable on the evening of the entertainment, before lighting the rooms engaged.

Said HUNT'S POINT PALACE acknowledges the receipt of Dollars as a deposit to secure the rooms for the evening of Nitely 193

In the event that the said party making this agreement fails to hold the affair or entertainment referred to, or cancels the date secured by this agreement, the deposit aforesaid shall be forfeited to the said HUNT'S POINT PALACE, and the parties shall in addition thereto pay to the said HUNT'S POINT PALACE the sum of , which sum is mutually agreed upon as the liquidated damage wchich will be suffered by the said HUNTS POINT PALACE, in event of a breach of the performance of this contract.

The said hiring and this Agreement are made subject to certain conditions printed on the back of this contract, which form a part of this agreement, and to all of which the party above named hiring the has agreed and stipulated to perform.

Any violation of this Agreement, or any failure to perform any of said conditions, shall operate to release said HUNT'S POINT PALACE from any liability upon this contract.

IN WITNESS WHEREOF, this agreement has been signed by the parties hereto.

Rent $ 50.00
Hat Room Attendants $
Stage Help $
Special Officers $
Total $
Less Deposit $
Balance Due $ 50.00

GENERAL MANAGER.

COMMITTEE.

OVER

Figure 17. Morton's contract for a proposed engagement at Hunt's Point Palace, 1940. Courtesy Historic New Orleans Collection.

Which brings us back to Mabel. Her words to Lomax in *Mister Jelly Roll*, cited earlier, are clear and unambiguous: "In November of 1940 the news came to Ferd from Los Angeles that his godmother had passed away. He got terribly restless. He was worried because his godfather was blind, and he said anybody could step in and take advantage of the old man. He felt like he ought to get out and take care of the money and the jewels his godmother had left."[29] Perhaps Mabel was the one from whom he was hiding his ace in the hole. Lomax is guilty of occasional lapses, like writing "three months" where Mabel must have said "three weeks," but those are usually obvious slips of the pen on a single word. But Mabel's statement could not involve such a slipup. Mabel simply could not have said "February" instead of "November"—the entire statement would make no sense whatsoever. If the statement is accurate, it must mean that Morton kept the news about his godmother from Mabel until he needed it as an alibi for his sudden departure for Los Angeles. And it also means that Anita must have been in on the plan. Why else would she continue the deception, even after Jelly's death, in her statement to Lomax: "Laura taken sick in 1940 and here came Jelly Roll driving his Lincoln"?[30]

Incredible though the deception might seem, it is entirely consistent with the way he treated Mabel throughout their relationship. As noted earlier, he told Mabel nothing about his income or about his handling of the business end of his music. And he insisted on complete control even over their personal affairs, right down to his practice of carrying their marriage license in his inside coat pocket:

> Now I think back, it's a peculiar thing that he always insisted on carrying our marriage license and wouldn't never give it to me to keep. I used to ask him why couldn't I have it framed and put up on the wall and he'd tell me, "Look, now, May, the way we travel up in Massachusetts and all that where they have those strict laws about entertainers being married, I need to carry this license at all times. I'm the man of the house and you just let me bother about these things."

So I didn't worry my head about it and let it go. I was just dumb to the fact, that's all I can say now.[31]

In one of his letters from California to Mabel, Morton writes:

> Don't pay any attention to any of those [rumors]. I never told her [an anonymous gossip] no such thing. She ask if you were home and I said no and did not give them any satisfaction. . . . Pay no attention to them. . . .
> I never told anyone you wasn't my wife.[32]

The wedding ceremony that took place in Gary, Indiana, in November 1928 "at the sign of Justice McGuire on the highway" could very well have been a fake.[33] If so, her words about her first encounter with Jelly in Chicago are loaded with unintentional irony: "As soon as he saw me he said he was going to kidnap me, but that took some time, it really did."[34] Jelly adamantly refused to have their marriage blessed by the Roman Catholic Church in New York circa 1939–40, however, which makes sense only if the civil marriage was a lie or if he was planning to leave Mabel, or both. His embrace of the Church at the end of his life seems to have been sincere, and he must have known that a civil marriage was not accepted as valid by the Church. In the eyes of their religion, Jelly and Mabel were living in sin, as Father McCann, Mabel's priest, must have mentioned when he urged that they be married in church.[35] Jelly may have made good his threat to kidnap Mabel in 1928.

Danny Barker's recollections of his last visit with Jelly and Mabel in New York confirm that Morton was indeed restless and unhappy there, and that his relation to Mabel was strained, to say the very least. Barker happened to run into them as they were talking to some priests in front of St. Aloysius Church, and they invited him up to their apartment. "I sat for a couple of hours," Barker says, "listening to Jelly speak sadly of all the misfortunes that he had been through, and how completely disgusted he was with New York City as well as the music business. He told me that he was spending most of his time at the church and the rectory with the priests. Mabel said nothing as she started dinner, she just looked sadly at Jelly and then looked at me. I don't think she realized she was shaking her head as she moved about the kitchen and dining room. When I left the apartment, I was real shook up."[36] The concern he expresses in that last sentence must have been as much over Mabel as Jelly. The extent to which both of the Mortons trusted Barker can be measured by Mabel's statement that Jelly was so jealous that he usually refused to have even friends over for dinner.[37] At any rate, Barker's words offer a cameo of a restless man about to make a desperate move.

One further piece of evidence points clearly to a plan to move west. In an interview with Laurie Wright, Morton's discographer, Reb Spikes reveals that he and Morton were planning to go into business together upon Jelly's return to Los Angeles.[38] In another interview, Spikes talks about the plan in greater detail: "When he came back [to Los Angeles] the BMI Music Association was opening up to try to be like ASCAP, and they sent for us [Spikes and Morton], and, and we went out there and they wanted us to come in with them 'cause we had a cataloge [*sic*] you know. They didn't have nobody with any catalogue of music so we told them . . . Jelly and I was getting ready to open up a music publishing [*sic*], and he died. That was about '38 I think it was and that ended that."[39] The date is a long way off if Spikes means that Morton died in 1938. Could he instead be remembering when he and Morton began to talk about joining forces again? Perhaps, but Spikes's citations of dates are often imprecise in the Rutgers interview. At any rate, the 1 January 1941 issue of *Down Beat* announces, in a short note, that Spikes and Morton had come to an agreement with BMI.[40] Since Morton had arrived in Los Angeles just a month and a half earlier, he and Spikes may have discussed the plan before Jelly left New York—perhaps as early as 1938. It seems highly unlikely that the idea not only occurred to them but also came to fruition so soon after Morton's arrival in Los Angeles. If Morton wrote to a complete stranger like Earle Cornwall about his prospects in Los Angeles, he may also have contacted the two people he had lived and worked with on the West Coast from 1917 to 1923: Reb Spikes and

Anita Gonzales. Clearly, Morton either had maintained contact with the two over the years or had revived the contacts near the end of the 1930s. Anita, a successful businesswoman by that time, had the means to help finance Jelly's comeback and was evidently secure enough in her relationship with her husband to be able to follow Morton from Canyonville, Oregon, to Los Angeles, where her own family, the Johnson brothers and their offspring, could help out. And Spikes, though no longer at the hub of the music scene in the city, still could provide important connections there, as well as the partnership in the BMI venture. And then there were Jelly's New Orleans home boys—Mutt Carey, Kid Ory, Bud Scott, Minor Hall, and Ed Garland—waiting and ready to rehearse and to bear witness to the revival of Jelly Roll Morton and his music.[41]

4

The story of Jack Ford and Jelly's legendary diamond does have an ending, and it deserves to be told, even though it leaves the question about the gem's ultimate fate unanswered. Just about everyone who has talked or written about Morton mentions the diamond, so much so that at times its gleam seems the light that illuminates the legend itself. It was the last of the many diamonds that Morton had sported at the peak of his career in the 1920s, and he managed somehow to hold onto it through the poverty and neglect he suffered during the 1930s. Lomax's book records the rumor that Anita Gonzales paid for the diamond, so it may be linked in more ways than one to the person Jelly called "the only woman I ever loved."[42] And, as noted earlier, according to Jelly himself his love of diamonds was first inspired by his beloved godmother: "She kept boxes of jewels in the house and I always had some kind of diamond on. Through her I came to be considered the best dresser [among his peers]."[43]

The fact that it was missing when he was buried was established early on, though it turns out that no one had a clear idea of how or why it turned up missing. Again, Lomax is the source of this information: "Two persons at the funeral knew that something was missing out of the coffin.

'I've always lived with my diamonds and I want to be buried with them,' he had said time and again, but now beneath the cold lips forever sealed, the gold inlay in the front tooth showed a ragged hole. The diamond was gone. It was curious that no one accused the undertaker."[44] Unfortunately, Lomax's account raises more questions than it answers. Who told Lomax that the diamond was missing, and just who were the "two persons at the funeral" who knew about it? If Anita herself was the source, Lomax doesn't say so explicitly, though the likelihood is clearly implied by the context of the story as Lomax tells it. But then who is the second of the two persons? Lomax offers not a single clue, unless he means Morton himself and intends the reader to understand the statement as a figure of speech. And—even more curious—why should anyone have suspected the undertaker? Surely, the absence of the diamond would have to have been noticed before Morton's body was delivered to the undertaker: after the undertaker had done his work, Jelly's lips would truly have been sealed—literally—and no one could have noticed its absence. Until now, the only other suspect was fingered by Danny Barker, who says in his autobiography that the dirt was done by "an old underworld acquaintance of Jelly's, a dope fiend and a notorious thief" who "sneaked into the undertaking parlor during the night and, with a chisel and a hammer, removed the four-carat diamond from Jelly's front tooth."[45]

Like Lomax, Barker says nothing about his source, but at this point neither story matters much except as testimony to the extent to which the diamond had become a part of the Morton legend. Curiously, David Stuart, one eyewitness who spent a lot of time with Morton near the end, says the diamond was gone when Jelly arrived in Los Angeles.[46] Had he pawned it temporarily, as he often had done with his diamonds over the years when he was broke? Certainly Anita would have noticed. Whatever the case, both Jeanne Ford and Mike Ford, Jack and Anita's grandson, have verified Joe Marvin's story that Jack did have the diamond. As for the question of who removed it and why, the most likely answer, aside from the possibility that Anita simply redeemed it from a pawnshop, is a very practical one, and not at all as sinister as Lomax would have it: the risks involved in burying someone with jewelry are simply too great under most circumstances. In fact, it would have been foolish to leave it on him in the nursing home or hospital. Even jewelry that can be seen on the deceased during the funeral, like rings and bracelets, can too easily be removed by an unscrupulous undertaker or assistant after the coffin has supposedly been sealed. It would have been easier still for whoever prepared Morton's body to remove the diamond before his lips were permanently sealed. Anita was nobody's fool; it would have been completely out of character for her not to understand that Morton's wish to be buried with his diamond was impractical and that to honor his wish would have been foolish. If Lomax's innuendoes were intended to suggest that Anita did something sinister or unscrupulous, they are entirely out of place here. Anita may not have removed the diamond herself—she may have asked someone in the family to do it for her; but no matter who actually did the deed, Anita would only have been following the dictates of common sense.

As for the diamond itself, it seems to have been fated to disappear. When I asked Jeanne Ford about it, she couldn't remember what had happened to it. Mike Ford, however, told me that Jack died suddenly of a heart attack and that when Mike's father, Henry, went to identify and claim the body, the diamond was missing, along with a diamond ring Jack was in the habit of wearing. Like most grave robbers, the person who stole it probably had no idea of its history and acted out of sheer greed. Should anyone ever come forth with a diamond and claim that it is Jelly's, there would be no way to either verify or dispute the claim: diamonds don't talk and, as everyone knows, dead men tell no tales.

CHAPTER 5

Last Days

1

Morton's trip west was truly Odyssean—storms all the way—and the job of driving through one storm after another was made even more difficult by the fact that he was trying to tow one of his two cars through it all. He could not blame the wrath of the god Poseidon, as Odysseus could, though no doubt it crossed his mind at least once that the weather was the work of an old voodoo curse once again; this time, though, he counted on the support of the God he had turned to just recently, or on the "blessed mother," the instrument of God's grace. In a note from Eureka, California, he writes to Mabel on 9 November 1940:

> I thought I would drop a line, to let you know I am safe. I started
> and decided to go west, and, believe me, when I hit Pennsylvania
> and every state thereafter I met a terrific storm—as follows, Penn
> sylvania, Ohio, Indiana, Illinois, Missouri, Kansas, Wyoming, Idaho,
> Oregon, California.
>   I slid off the road in Wyoming in a sleet storm and damaged the
> car a little. The blessed mother was with me and I did not get hurt. I
> had to leave one of the cars in Montpelier, Idaho, on account of the
> weather was too dangerous. And the next couple of nights I was

caught up on a mountain in Oregon near the town of John Day. The snow was very slippery and deep. The police car had to pull me out and I was not hurt. Yes, the blessed mother really taken care of me in a-many ways in all the storms and danger I had to confront me. I did not get a chance to make many novenas on the road on account of driving all the time, but I said lots of prayers just the same.

I am trying to find some kind of good climate and will soon or I will keep roaming till I do.[1]

"I had a mighty dangerous trip," he writes to Roy Carew on 13 November from Los Angeles. "I was in a storm clear to Calif. [*sic*] the types were rain, snow, hail, sleet and wind. I came near serious accidents three different times but with the help of God I made it."[2]

The itinerary he spells out to Mabel is the northern transcontinental route. When he writes that he "decided to go west," he means due west as opposed to southwest and the southern route. Morton makes it seem that he made the decision after he hit the road, but that little ruse was for Mabel's benefit; the route was determined by Anita's presence in Oregon and nothing else. The southern route would have made much more sense, above all because it was more of a straight line between New York and Los Angeles than the northern route; getting to Southern California through Oregon is quite a detour. But Mabel seems not to have noticed that Morton had taken a rather roundabout way to his destination. Perhaps she overlooked that detail in her relief that he had survived the trip at all. In her comments to Lomax, she says that she was more concerned at the time about the possibility of bad weather and about "how Jelly was going to travel without any money" than anything else.[3] Even that, along with many of the questionable circumstances attending his apparently sudden move, would have aroused suspicions in anyone even slightly less trusting and naive—not to say gullible—than Mabel. When Mabel suggested that she accompany him on the trip, he answered with an evasion: "No, I know my condition. I know if something was to go wrong, you'd have hysterics and it would make my heart attack worse."[4]

Small thanks to someone who had seen him through at least two major medical crises.

There is little doubt that Morton left New York with a plan that he had already discussed with Anita, who by then had apparently agreed to act as patron of his West Coast comeback. We will probably never know the exact details of the deal they struck at the time, though the papers in the file concerning Jelly's last will and testament contain some clues. Obviously, part of the deal was to keep Mabel in the dark about Anita's role in Jelly's affairs, and not only her role in the present but in the past as well. He never mentions Anita in any of the eleven letters to Mabel that Alan Lomax has preserved in *Mister Jelly Roll*. When Mabel says to Lomax, "Anita? I never heard of her till later," she apparently means she heard nothing of Anita until after Morton's death, which in turn would mean she had heard nothing of the relationship between Jelly and Anita during the period 1917–23.[5] Evidently, Morton assiduously avoided any mention of Anita to Mabel, even during the time when Anita could safely have been considered someone from the fairly distant past. After all, Jelly and Mabel married in 1928, six years after he had left Anita in Los Angeles, and they were to be together as husband and wife for a total of twelve years after that, minus the year or two he was on his own in Washington, D.C. Twelve years—eighteen, counting the time from 1923, when he left Anita in Los Angeles—is a long time to keep such a secret. Perhaps Morton was merely sticking to a policy of not telling his current mate about any of his previous loves unless he absolutely had to. Possibly, too, he could have been worried that any talk of Anita would inevitably betray the depth of his feelings about her as *the* love of his life. It is hard to imagine that Morton's silence about Anita was part of a twelve-year plan to deceive Mabel in the fall of 1940, but one thing is certain: had Mabel known about the nature of the relationship between Anita and Jelly, she would have had firm grounds for suspicion about any move to the West Coast that did not include her.

Exactly when he left New York is unclear. According to Mabel, it was in November, but he sent a letter to Carew from Rock Springs, Wyoming, on the fourth of November—a lot of ground to cover in four days, especially considering the weather conditions he describes. At any rate, the gap in his correspondence between 4 November and 9 November, when he wrote Mabel from Eureka, California, defines his itinerary for that part of the trip: he left Rock Springs with one of his two cars still in tow sometime around the fourth; he abandoned one of the cars, the Lincoln, in Idaho; he was pulled out of the snow in John Day, Oregon, before making it in his Cadillac to Ford's in Canyonville, and he wrote the letter from Eureka—all in about five days. Four days later, on 13 November 1940, he writes both Mabel and Carew to announce that he has arrived in Los Angeles. He promises Mabel that he will send her money so that she can return home to New Orleans—a refrain in almost all his letters to her from Los Angeles—and adds, " The weather is warm here and I feel some better. Even my eyesight have [*sic*] improved a bit."[6]

The total mileage of his itinerary from Rock Springs, Wyoming, to Eureka, California, was something like 1,232 miles, which means that he would have had to average 246 miles a day for five days to make that trip between the fourth and the ninth of November, leaving little or no time for any kind of visit in Canyonville; subtract the two nights he was stuck in the snow in John Day, Oregon, and he would have had to travel an average of 400 or 500 miles per day. One wonders how a man in such fragile health survived the ordeal, or whether the dates and place-names were another part of the plan of deception designed to keep Mabel in the dark. He was thoroughly practiced in the ways in which letters could be sent to, and mailed from, places to create the impression that he was in a given place at a given time. In fact, he suggests just such a thing to Mabel in a letter dated 16 January: "I am writing a letter to Mrs. V——. I want you to mail it from New York and we will see if you get an answer from this."[7] In this and other letters, he encourages Mabel to put up a front implying that he is still living with her in New York and is on the road in places like Los Angeles purely for business reasons. In a larger sense, though, his health didn't survive the ordeal: every mile he drove through rain, snow, and sleet must have shortened his life. We will never

Figure 18.   Ford's Restaurant, Canyonville, Oregon, owned by Anita and Jack Ford, date unknown. Courtesy Henry Villalapando Ford Collection.

know how long he might have lived had he not made that trek, or if he had done it at a more sensible time, at a more leisurely pace.

At any rate, although the detour through Oregon obviously had to do with Anita, it is not clear exactly why he had to see her before he got to Los Angeles. One would think that perhaps he went that route to pick up Anita to accompany him on the last leg of his trip—he surely would have welcomed some help with the driving at that point. But two witnesses attest to the fact that Anita did not join him in Los Angeles until some weeks after Morton arrived there: in an interview with William Russell, Gene Colas, Morton's nephew, says that Anita arrived in Los Angeles "within a few weeks" after Morton; and in another interview with Russell, the jazz enthusiast Bill Colburn, who rode the Southern Pacific from San Francisco to Los Angeles just to meet Morton, says that "Jelly at first stayed with his 'brother-in-law,' Dink Johnson[,] and his wife[,] Stella, at 2340 Damon Street," and that "Anita had not yet come down from Canyon, Oregon, to stay with Jelly."[8] (See fig. 18.) Whatever the exact reason for the detour, his visit to Ford's must have been a quick one; besides, his presence in Canyonville would certainly have raised questions about race that Anita would rather have avoided.

The mild, sunny weather that greeted Morton on his arrival in Los Angeles had a bracing, tonic effect on his health at first. That is to say, although he was by no means a healthy man, on 2 January 1941 he could write to Carew, "My health has been kind of up and down, but altogether I believe I will be better off here." From about February on, however, the news is mostly down, even about the weather, until he writes Carew a final letter from the Los Angeles Sanitarium on 21 June to complain that "I tried to make it in the worst way. I don't know if I will be able, I get up one day and go back to bed three and four weeks. . . . I am just about at the end of the rope."[9]

Most reports of his activities in Los Angeles refer to the period between November 1940 through January 1941, when he evidently still had enough energy to get out and about. Rose Mary Johns remembers Anita and Jelly paying her family a visit in San Bernardino, for example—that would have been a good two- or three-hour trip one way in those days, and Jelly would hardly have been in shape for it after February. As mentioned earlier, Reb Spikes remembers going with Morton to the offices of the newly formed BMI to negotiate a deal for the catalogue they could offer: "They didn't have nobody with any catalogue of music so we told them we, we was belonged [*sic*] to ASCAP . . . and Jelly and I was getting ready to open up a music publishing."[10] That must have been before the New Year; the 1 January 1941 issue of *Down Beat* declares, "Jelly Roll to Help BMI Get Negro Writers":

> Hollywood—Broadcast Music, Inc. has signed to take the entire output of a new publishing company formed here by Jelly Roll Morton, famous old-time blues pianist and singer, and Benjamin "Reb" Spikes, songwriter . . . and one time bandleader. . . .
> Harry Engel, Coast chief of operations for BMI, said Spikes would be the composer in the new firm and that Morton would watch for and select songs by other Negro composers. Morton can

function only as a publisher in the Spikes-Morton firm due to the fact that he is bound to ASCAP as a composer-member, but not as a publisher.[11]

The papers in the Ford collection include the manuscripts of two songs, "Floatin' on Air" and "Thoughts," by Henri Woode and Les Cauldwell, mailed by Cauldwell from Chicago to Morton at the Spikes-Morton Music Company, Hollywood, California, in care of Harry Engel, Broadcast Music, Inc. The address is corrected by hand to 4052 South Central, Hollywood. The street address is one of three connected to Morton in Los Angeles, but Central Avenue is nowhere near Hollywood. On the postmark, the day and month are not legible, but the year is, 1941, so perhaps the manuscripts were sent in response to the news item in *Down Beat*. In a 1969 interview with William Russell, Spikes remembers seeing Morton "several times" in 1940–41 during the brief negotiations with Harry Engel: "We were getting ready to go into the publishing business. They tried to get us to come to BMI, which was just starting out at that time. They tried to get us to come to BMI, but we were ASCAP members and had to refuse."[12]

Some of the most detailed information about Morton's activities in Los Angeles comes from the record-store owner and collector David Stuart: "I had my Jazz Man Record Shop, and Jelly used to come in, and we became friendly. He loved to talk about the past, and he had a terrific memory. . . . Sometimes we'd take him out to hear music in the evening—Kid Ory and Mutt Carey, old New Orleans people like that. The musicians called him 'The Roll,' and when he appeared they'd all stand up and say[,] 'Here comes The Roll.'"[13] In another 1969 interview with Russell, Stuart remembers a fairly active Jelly Roll Morton in the early months of his return to Los Angeles. Although Stuart never got to know Anita very well, he recalls that when Morton was staying with Anita's brother Dink Johnson and his wife, Stella, "I heard him play quite often on Dink's piano. In fact, he played any place there was a piano; he simply loved to play."[14] And Jelly still had enough energy to engage fellow entertainer Peg Leg Bates in a battle of words that recalls the legendary Morton–Chick Webb jousts outside the Rhythm Club in New York:

> I remember one time when Jelly Roll was standing on a corner on Central Avenue talking to the one-legged tap dancer Peg Leg Bates. Jelly was telling him the most outrageous stories you've ever heard, but they probably were all true, except that you could hardly believe them. And with Bates standing there, Jelly said things like, "You know, I can tap dance better than anyone in the world." Peg Leg said, "You can't tap dance as well as I can. I'm much better even with just one leg." Jelly said something like, "I could cut my feet off at the ankles, man, and whip you." They would argue at the corner, with a big group of people always standing around whenever Morton was talking, just listening to those horrendous stories.[15]

And Stuart recalls that when Morton would visit him at his record store, "we'd drive around in Jelly's old Cadillac. Jelly and I would sit in front and I'd ask questions, and Charlie Campbell, who'd been a secretary and could write shorthand, sat in the back seat and took it all down."[16] One of the first times Stuart and Campbell went out with Morton, they took him to the Silver Dollar, a saloon on Main Street in Los Angeles, where Jelly's old friend Mutt Carey was playing: "I remember Jelly got up and played *The Finger Breaker* [*sic*]. It broke them all up. They couldn't believe he still played that way."[17] According to the bassist Ed "Montudie" Garland, there were other visits to the Silver Dollar: "Mutt had the band there. The bandstand was upstairs on the balcony. We used to go up there and sit in. The people there liked to hear Jelly play. He was a drawing card."[18]

Garland is the best source on the subject of the big-band rehearsals Morton held before he became too ill to continue. Garland had received a phone call from Morton in the fall of 1940. He told Garland that he was planning a trip to Los Angeles to look after his godmother's estate and asked him to get an orchestra together to rehearse for a recording session: "Since Morton indicated he was very ill and would probably not play the piano, Garland selected Buster Wilson, an apprentice of Morton's two decades before, to stand by." [19] Garland recalls that "we rehearsed at the Elk's Hall, 4016 South Central Avenue[,] . . . right off Jefferson. We rehearsed two or three times a week, sometimes almost every day, because he had this big job in mind. I think he was going to make records or a movie." [20] In spite of his frail health, Morton was quite an active presence at the rehearsals, according to Garland: "Jelly played piano now and then with the big band to show just how he wanted his arrangements to go. If someone didn't play their part right, Jelly'd run over it on the piano to show them." [21]

Morton's love of playing often overcame his weakened state. As Garland recalls, "Sometimes Jelly would be at the Elk's club before we started rehearsing and he'd play the piano. He loved to play and had a gift for sitting at the piano and making up things." [22] The orchestra included Mutt Carey and Pee Wee Brice, trumpets; Kid Ory and Jug Everly, trombones; Theodore Bonner, Robert Garner, and Alfonso George, saxophones; Atwell Rose, violin; Bud Scott, guitar; Ed Garland, bass; Minor Hall, drums; Buster Wilson, piano; and Morton himself as conductor. "He had written parts for four trumpets and five saxophones," Garland explains, "but he revised the arrangements to fit the smaller band I put together for him." [23] Morton's body may have been frail, but his spirit was still strong, and he was determined to make a go of his comeback. The orchestra never recorded, however, and they never performed publicly. According to Anita, Morton was unable to play any gigs when he returned to Los Angeles: "When he arrived the last time, he was too sick to play—he kept thinking he would get well enough to take some of the jobs he had been offered. He never could take any of those jobs." [24] She must have meant that he was too sick to play all night at a dance hall or a nightclub; obviously, he was still able to summon enough energy to play, even to sit in occasionally at a place like the Silver Dollar, but an extended engagement of any kind would have been unthinkable.

The dozen or so new arrangements that Morton rehearsed with the band represent one of the most tantalizing gaps in his biographical record, though part of the gap may have been filled recently. Buster Wilson, Morton's substitute on piano for the rehearsals, still had the arrangements in his possession in 1952, as Floyd Levin recalls:

> Jelly's hand-written scores remained in Buster Wilson's home as late
> as 1952. They were in a large trunk in Buster's small house on Central Avenue. The trunk was draped with a silk Spanish shawl on
> which stood a tarnished brass lamp with a beaded shade. Buster was
> in poor health in 1952, but he promised to sort through the old
> trunk "some day" and wanted me to have those old manuscripts. I
> repeatedly reminded him of his offer, but he never managed to open
> the trunk. After Buster died, his widow moved from the city[,] and
> several attempts to obtain the promised legacy proved fruitless. It
> is regrettable that Jelly Roll's last writings will probably never be
> located.[25]

As we shall see, Levin's pessimism about the scores has recently proved to be unjustified, a result of their discovery among William Russell's papers. From what Ed Garland says about the music, even though so many of the musicians involved were New Orleans originals (many of whom, like Kid Ory, had retired from the music business during the Great Depression), the arrangements were in the then-contemporary swing-band style and not the revivalist stuff that was to be very popular in Los Angeles and San Francisco just after Morton's death. As Garland tells the story, "Those arrangements were very interesting. Jelly was aware that some of his tunes were being successfully played by the swing bands—Goodman had a hit record of his 'King Porter Stomp' and Lionel Hampton's 'Shoe Shiner's Drag' was heard every day on the radio. He thought he would show those swing bands how his music should be played."[26]

The most obvious musical problem Morton faced was the fact that his chief soloists—Ory and Carey in particular—were New Orleans traditionalists whose style may have sounded anachronistic in the setting of contemporary swing arrangements. But Morton's last band recordings in New York indicate that the problem was potentially solvable.

Even though the repertoire of those 1939 Victor recordings included many New Orleans chestnuts like "High Society" and "Oh, Didn't He Ramble?" and the personnel included New Orleans musicians like Sidney Bechet, Wellman Braud, and Zutty Singleton, the overall stylistic thrust is more contemporary swing than New Orleans revival, especially on tunes like "Winin' Boy" and "Don't You Leave Me Here." On those recordings, the days of banjos, tubas, and two-beats are gone. The rhythm section—piano, guitar, bass, and drums—propels the band with a swinging 4/4 pulse that does not sound dated even today (bassist Wellman Braud had in fact played with Duke Ellington in the 1930s).

The nucleus of the Los Angeles orchestra eventually went on to become Kid Ory's band during the New Orleans revival that began around 1944–46 (Ory, Carey, Buster Wilson, Garland, and either Minor Hall or Zutty Singleton), but all the recordings of that band have a distinctly "retro" feel to them, especially in comparison to Morton's last sessions. Ory may simply have been providing his audience with what it wanted to hear. The predominantly white audience of revivalist enthusiasts had very particular ideas about what the "authentic" New Orleans style was supposed to sound like—ideas that often spelled a return to banjos, tubas, and two-beats (to his credit, Ory never went that far). We will never know whether Morton would have been offended by a revivalist audience that regarded him as a relic or whether he would simply have climbed on the bandwagon, but the new arrangements were not anticipations of the revivalist trend. Instead, Morton seems to have been intent upon proving the contemporary relevance of his music.

Those intentions have been at least partly verified recently by the discovery—in the William Russell Collection, which is part of the Historic New Orleans Collection—of eight manuscript arrangements that may have been among the twelve Morton brought west with him at the end of his life. Since neither Morton himself nor others, such as Garland and Buster Wilson, have ever named the specific tunes that were rehearsed in Los Angeles, it is not possible to state definitively that those are in fact the "missing" arrangements; however, some of them do reflect in a general sort of way what both Morton and Garland have said was the stylistic mode of the pieces played at the rehearsals. The guide for the Jelly Roll Morton Manuscript Music Collection in the Russell archive, prepared in 1996 by Richard Jackson and Nancy Ruck, lists five big-band arrangements of familiar, previously recorded Morton material: "Finger Breaker"; "Mamie's Blues"; "We Are Elks," recorded in 1940 as "Swinging the Elks"; "Good Old New York"; and "Mr. Joe" (a variant spelling of "Mister Joe"), a tribute to King Oliver that Morton had recorded in 1928 as "Buffalo Blues." But three brand new additions to the Jelly Roll canon are also listed: "Oh Baby," "Stop and Go," and "Gan-Jam."[27] Four of the eight were performed in the Economy Hall Tent at the 1998 New Orleans Jazz and Heritage Festival by Don Vappie leading a thirteen-piece orchestra: "Mister Joe," "Oh Baby," "Gan-Jam," and "We Are Elks." The reviewer Barry McRae notes that the first and last pieces were "perhaps a little more identifiable" than the other two as Morton works, especially "Mister Joe." The other two, however, were another matter altogether: "*Oh! Baby* . . . was Luncefordian and one could imagine the score having been written by Sy Oliver. It made use of established big band dramas[,] and the solos (written or extempore) were distinctly in the then flourishing swing style. A further contrast was offered by *Gan-Jam*. This suggested a touch of Eastern promise rather than a Spanish tinge[,] and it used a brass and reed mix that owed nothing to the accepted patterns of 1940 big band fare. If anything, it looked forward to *Pithecanthropus* Mingus but with breaks rather than all-ins and with a decidedly off-centre relationship between melody and rhythm."[28] In the *Chicago Tribune*, Howard Reich's review expresses his similar reactions to the performance, and notes the ambivalence in the style of the retro "Mister Joe," the contemporary-swing feel to "Oh Baby," and especially the forward-looking "Gan-Jam," which he describes as "an orchestral tour de force that defies the big-band conventions of the late '30s and early '40s. Beyond its exotic chord progressions and unusually sinuous and chromatic melody lines, the piece changes texture, tone and color many times over."[29]

Recordings of the newly found material have yet to be issued commercially, but Don Vappie was generous enough to send me an audiocassette of the performance. As McRae and Reich say about the four arrangements, they express Morton's ambivalence toward his ties to New Orleans traditions and his need to be perceived as up-to-date, or even as ahead of his time, a pacesetter to the end. The style of "Mister Joe" is entirely consistent with orchestrations for the ten- and eleven-piece bands Jelly recorded in the late 1920s. "We Are Elks" is played as a four-square march, plain and simple, as one might expect from its origins: it is the product of a scheme hatched by Morton and Roy Carew to take advantage of an Elks convention that took place in New York during the summer of 1939. The subject of an exchange of letters from June to September of that year, it was written specifically with the purpose of peddling it to the Elks.[30] Jelly and Mabel tried selling the piece at convention halls, hotels, and bars frequented by the members, but the Elks were not buying. Morton made good use of it during his last commercial recording session for General in 1940, though. Retitled "Swinging the Elks," the recording expresses perhaps more fully than any other the direction Morton wanted to go with his music. After a swinging 4/4 intro by the ensemble, the opening chorus betrays the tune's origins as a march, with Wellman Braud's two-beat on the bass making it literally a march song; however, once Henry "Red" Allen starts his sizzling hot, muted trumpet solo, Braud kicks in with a propulsive 4/4 beat that delivers the "swing" promised by the title. The two-beat feel returns for the second strain, played and embellished nicely by Eddie Williams on alto sax; and for Claude Jones's trombone solo, the rhythm section lays down a distinctly marchlike shuffle beat, led by Zutty Singleton's snare drum. Finally, on the "out" chorus, the rhythm section shifts up to a swinging 4/4 again, with Red Allen's open horn soaring majestically above the ensemble—surely, along with his earlier muted solo, some of his best work on records. Certainly, "Swinging the Elks" is the most artistically satisfying of the band numbers recorded at that last session. The fusion of swing, march, and New Orleans–style ensembles is absolutely seamless. Morton reminds us here that, like that of most great jazz composers (Ellington, Monk, and Mingus come to mind), a summation of his best work cannot be reduced to a single style or era—it is "beyond category," to cite Ellington's favorite phrase.

On the Vappie ensemble's recording of "Oh Baby," Jelly sounds quite comfortable with the big-band idiom of the swing era circa 1940, a verification of Morton's claim that Mister Jelly Roll could not be relegated to the status of a relic. But "Gan-Jam" is another matter altogether, an absolutely unique addition to the Morton canon—in fact, it's hard to place in the spectrum of Morton's stylistic range. The only anticipations of the piece among Morton's compositions are the superficially "modernistic" composition "Freakish"—a 1929 effort intended to rival similar pieces by James P. Johnson ("You've Got to Be Modernistic") and Eubie Blake ("Dictys on 7th Avenue")—and "exotic" pieces like "Jungle Blues," "New Orleans Bump," and the third strain of "Mamanita," with their use of ostinato bass parts. McRae is absolutely right to compare parts of "Gan-Jam" to "*Pithecanthropus* Mingus," for at times its use of dissonance does sound like the Charles Mingus of the late 1940s. However, though there may be faint echoes in "Gan-Jam" of Morton's earlier work, they are mostly superficial. Seldom had he ever used pedal point and ostinato bass figures so extensively. Never before had he so completely abandoned conventional song form and allowed his melodies to develop their own organic form, like free verse in poetry. Never had he used such a variety of exotic scales, like the eight measures based on the double harmonic minor scale.[31] "Gan-Jam" is so unlike anything Morton had ever done that the obvious question becomes whether it is indeed his work. But the manuscript is in his own hand. It is odd, however, that he never once mentions the piece in any of his letters to Carew, especially since they set up Tempo Music particularly to secure the rights to new work and to previously uncopyrighted material. It must be said, though, that the same is true of two other pieces in the Russell collection, "Prologue Opening" and "Stop and Go," neither of which is mentioned in the Morton-Carew correspondence—or elsewhere, for that matter.[32] "Stop and Go" provides another example of Morton experimenting with modern dissonances in his orchestral scores. As William Russell says of the piece, "In some sections, Jelly Roll may have experimented with a more dissonant—or what he believed to be more modern—harmonic style than usual. At times, his ninth and eleventh chords produced tone clusters in sections G and H. . . . He frequently uses major seventh dissonances, such as in the piece's final chord."[33] Interestingly enough, similar tone clusters appear throughout "Gan-Jam," not in just a few sections. Without offering any support for his statement, Russell says that "Stop and Go" "probably dates back to the thirties," but the fact that Morton never mentions the piece in any of the Carew correspondence renders that bit of speculation unlikely.[34] For now, both compositions raise many unanswered questions. One thing is certain, though: both show that he "had ears" for fairly advanced harmonic and melodic conceptions.

Had he lived, Morton would have been faced with a dilemma. On the one hand, given the state of his finances, it would have been difficult to resist the temptation to cash in on the New Orleans revival trend that was soon to give his friend Kid Ory a second career, and he no doubt would have been gratified to get recognition at last as one of the originators of the music. On the other hand, that was not really the direction he wanted to go, and one can imagine that he would have fiercely resisted any attempt to treat him or his music as a museum piece. In fact, he had already been forced to wrestle with that dilemma in Washington, D.C., and New York: the Library of Congress recordings, although they would not be available commercially until after his death, had set the tone for his comeback if only by word of mouth, and commercial recording companies like Victor and General wanted more of the same— they were not much interested in the "new" Jelly Roll.

Left to his own devices, as he was on a private recording session in Baltimore in 1938, he recorded three versions of Fats Waller's contemporary hit "Honeysuckle Rose," and on the Library of Congress recordings he managed to sneak in his version of Waller's "Ain't Misbehavin'.'" On the last commercial recordings in New York, he included a few of his more recent compositions, like "Swinging the Elks" and "Sweet Substitute." For the most part, though, what the recording companies wanted from Jelly was more of the New Orleans stuff that he had revived for Alan Lomax, and his awareness that he was being forced to conform to that stereotype was at least one of the reasons that he headed west. In his first letter from Los Angeles to Carew, on 13 November 1940, he writes, "I thought my chances were very slim in N.Y."[35] On 30 November, he writes again, explaining himself a bit more fully: "I think I did the best thing leaving N.Y. . . . I think little by little I will make the grade. . . . I don't ever try to do things with inferior material, but what can you do when things are forced on you, and that's the east method."[36] Evidently, Morton had come to regard the West Coast as a place where his new material was more likely to find a receptive audience, especially among record producers. We may never know if that assumption was more than wishful thinking; there is no tangible evidence that a recording session was actually in the works. And then the great irony: Jelly could not have predicted that the New Orleans revival, primarily a West Coast phenomenon, would have forced him, had he lived long enough, to face the same dilemma he thought he had avoided by heading west.

His last address, 1008 East Thirty-second Street, within a block of Central Avenue in Los Angeles, would have provided him with access to a suitable arena in which to test the new material. At the time, the Avenue was not only the heart of the African American community in Los Angeles but also the center of a thriving jazz and blues scene that has been compared favorably by musicians and writers alike to New York's Fifty-second Street and Kansas City's Eighteenth and Vine in their heydays. But it was definitely not an environment hospitable to the revivalist style, which flourished primarily in Hollywood and in white areas of Los Angeles. The music that dominated the Central Avenue scene in the 1940s was swing, early bebop, and early rhythm and blues. The Elks Auditorium, where Morton rehearsed his last band, often hosted the popular swing bands of the day and was conveniently located just a few blocks from his last residence. About ten short blocks north, the Lincoln Theatre regularly featured the likes of Duke Ellington, Count Basie, and Cab Calloway. Just six blocks north of that, at 1710 Central, Local 767 of the American Federation of Musicians provided a nerve center for black musicians in Southern California. Ten blocks south of Thirty-second Street was the Dunbar Hotel, at 4225 Central, which housed most of the big-name black entertainers who passed through Los Angeles at that time and was the center of a cluster of nightclubs and after-hours joints that included the Downbeat (4201 Central), the Last Word (4206), and the Club Alabam (4215). *Central Avenue Sounds*, a recently published oral history of that era, chronicles the reminiscences of musicians who remember the time as a kind of golden age of creative cultural and social activity. Jack Kelson's comments are typical of those memories:

> That's my favorite spot on Central Avenue, the spot in front of the Dunbar Hotel, because that to me was the hippest, most intimate, key spot of all the activity. That's where all the night people hung out: the sportsmen, the businessmen, the dancers, everybody in show business, people who were somebody who stayed at the hotel. . . .
>
> From corner to corner there were stores. The Dunbar was on the northwest corner, and the next corner would be the Downbeat nightclub, and across the street would be the Last Word. . . . That was the heart of Central Avenue for me.[37]

Just as it had during Jelly's first stay in Los Angeles, the black nightlife of Central Avenue attracted people from the Hollywood film industry, both black and white:

> There was Stepin Fetchit with his long white Auburn-Cord or Packard or whatever it was, with a lion sitting in the back. That wasn't far-fetched. . . .
>
> And Central Avenue was quite the focal point of many people in the film industry. The movie stars would come over there, because

there was more glamour, in a sense, on Central Avenue. There was a magnetism about it that was at a much more personal level than the magnetism that drew people's interest to Hollywood Boulevard.[38]

The Jelly Roll Morton of old would have found the Central Avenue scene a perfect setting for his own brand of flamboyance, glamour, and musical artistry, and he would have staged his entrance with the practiced eye of an experienced vaudevillian. Instead, he entered unnoticed, as an extra, and in his letters to Mabel and Carew his silence about the Central Avenue scene is deafening. When I asked them about it, none of the musicians from the *Central Avenue Sounds* project remembered seeing Morton on the scene during that time. Among his old New Orleans buddies—Mutt Carey, Kid Ory, Ed Garland, and others—he was still "The Roll," of course, and had a standing invitation to sit in with them at their regular gig at the Silver Dollar. The Silver Dollar was on Eighth and Main, not far geographically from Forty-second and Central, but in terms of visibility it might as well have been in Siberia. Just short of his fifty-first birthday, pale and thin, weak of heart and short of breath, he had every right to stand in front of the Dunbar Hotel on the corner of Forty-second and Central and loudly proclaim that he, Jelly Roll Morton, had first put the Avenue on the map, as far as jazz was concerned, some twenty years earlier, and that the infatuation of Hollywood stars with the Avenue had begun with him at the Cadillac Cafe in 1917. And perhaps he did, when he first arrived, if the encounter between Morton and Peg Leg Bates is any indication.

But who among the younger generation would have believed him?

2

On the twentieth of November in Los Angeles, Jelly writes to Mabel:

Hello Angel
    Tell Miss H—— when she asks for me, that I went out of town with some musicians to see if I could plan some way to put a band to

work. I will never be satisfied holding my hands doing nothing, because I like to make my own living. . . .

My godfather told me of many diamonds that my godmother
left—all was stolen and not one left. Some of their friends told me
the same thing too.[39]

It is the last time that Morton uses the story about his godmother's diamonds to explain his trip to Los Angeles. Once in California, he disposes
of the story with a single sentence in the letter to Mabel and never mentions the diamonds or the godfather again. There very well may have
been diamonds, or some sort of estate to settle—Laura's fondness for diamonds is well chronicled in *Mister Jelly Roll*—but the sense of urgency
over their fate is a dramatic invention entirely of Jelly's own making. As
noted earlier, well before he left New York for California he knew that
Anita was in charge of his godmother's affairs. Nothing short of a conscious plan by both Anita and Jelly can explain how Mabel was kept in
the dark for so long about Laura's death. And if that much of the trip was
so carefully planned, there is no reason to doubt that all of it was worked
out in some detail before Morton left New York.

There is also little reason to doubt that Jelly was largely dependent on
Anita, at least financially, during his last days in Los Angeles. The recording that was supposedly the goal of the rehearsals never material-
ized, and he was too sick to work. His only income seems to have been
the royalty checks from ASCAP, but he complains to Mabel on 16 January that, though he had recently received a check, "this town takes
money to live, so that is about all gone."[40] On the "Petition for Probate
of Will," the list of property value for the Morton estate includes a check
from ASCAP for royalties in the amount of $185.00, which gives some
idea of how much the quarterly checks may have been. On the 28th he
tells Mabel, "I received the check from Melrose. $52.00. I seen a lawyer.
He advised me not to cash it, so I will institute suit against them."[41]
The "Creditor's Claim Form" filed in the Superior Court of the State of
California on 15 August 1941 itemizes Anita's claim on the estate for a

total of $538.00, which includes $45.00 for his stay at the Los Angeles Sanitarium and $63.50 for the grave, and lists three items for which Anita claims "Cash advanced decedent": $35.25 from 4 February 1941 to 12 June 1941 for a piano; $65.00 from 24 February 1941 to 8 October 1941 for furniture; $295.00 from 25 November 1940 to 8 October 1941 for "Cash advanced to pay on Cadillac Car." [42] Obviously, her generosity came with strings attached; ever the shrewd businesswoman, she was not about to start giving her money away without collecting receipts. Ever the gambler, Morton seems to have bet on his ability to stay alive long enough to repay Anita for her investment in his comeback.

It would have been entirely in character for Morton to bet his future royalties in exchange for immediate financial relief. After all, aside from the issue of his health, a comeback was not really a long shot; in fact, he had made a good beginning, though his frail health would not let him take advantage of it as well as he might have otherwise: *Down Beat* had featured him in a series of four articles in 1937–38; the 1938 Library of Congress interviews, though not yet available commercially, had already achieved an underground, cult status; the W. C. Handy controversy about who was the "originator" of blues and jazz had gone a long way toward removing the tarnish from his claim to celebrity; and the 1939–40 recordings in New York had proved that, in spite of his failing health, he was still a formidable presence as a musician after a hiatus of some eight years from the recording studios. Sadly, perhaps the clearest proof that his comeback had not been just a matter of wishful thinking, the 1 August 1941 edition of *Down Beat* announces in a headline at the top of the front page, "'Jelly Roll' Morton Passes On," and then adds: "For Story See Pages 1, 4, and 13"—in other words, it devoted no fewer than three articles to his death. Two of the articles attempt an assessment of Jelly's contributions to jazz—and succeed fairly well so far as his work through the 1920s and his Library of Congress recordings are concerned—but they make no mention of his recent attempt to rehearse a big band. He may have been sick and broke, but he was no longer the Forgotten Man, as he had been just a few years earlier; in fact, George

Hoefer Jr.'s lead article dubs Morton the "Dizzy Dean of music," a title that smacks of more than a little condescension.[43]

Although he was no longer a forgotten man when he arrived in Los Angeles, he was a dying man. In his last full letter to Mabel on 22 February, he begins with an apology and then lists some ominous symptoms: "Your letter was received but due to illness I was unable to answer until now. Up to now I have had two different doctors. My breath has been very short like when I had to go to the hospital [in New York] and have been spitting blood and other symptoms too numerous to mention, but I am some better this morning."[44] His last note to Mabel is dated 26 April 1941: a blank money order form on which Morton has scribbled the words "will write soon[.] Still sick."[45] Rose Mary Johns remembers visiting the home of one of her uncles in Los Angeles at about this time: Anita was present, the adults all had sad and somber faces, and the children were told to be quiet and stay out of the way; Morton himself was confined to one of the bedrooms, out of sight. On 21 June he wrote his last message, cited above, to Carew from the Los Angeles Sanitarium; by then, he had given up hope of surviving. He signed his last will and testament a week later, on 28 June. According to his death certificate, he was admitted to Los Angeles County General Hospital eleven days before his death, which would have been 30 June, two days after he signed his will; he died on 10 July. David Stuart remembers visiting him in County General: "He got sick before he died, and they put him in a kind of broom closet in the hospital, and they treated him shabbily. I'd go over in the afternoon and sit with him. He'd hold my hand hour after hour, even though I'm sure he had no idea who I was anymore."[46] In his 1969 interview with William Russell, Stuart paints an even more vivid portrait:

> He was pretty thin, and with the beard that he grew he looked like a black Jesus. Yes, he let his beard and mustache grow. He had this big black full beard on and he looked absolutely fantastic. He actually looked like a black Christ, a magnificent-looking man.

But I didn't expect him to last long, because he was pretty miserable and unhappy, and I don't think he gave a damn whether he lived or died. He was really far-out at the end. . . . He never talked, and I really don't think he was capable of talking. He wouldn't answer if you asked him a question. I'd sit by the bed and he would just hold my hand. I always thought he recognized me, but I couldn't be sure. He would smile at me. I was there a day or two before he died.[47]

As noted earlier, Anita recalls his final moments this way: "He died in my arms, begging me to keep anointing his lips with oil that had been blessed by a bishop in New York. He had oil running all over him when he gave up the ghost."[48] The rather sharp contrast between the two versions of Morton on his deathbed is hard to explain: Stuart has him virtually comatose and unaware of his surroundings, while Anita's version has him alert enough to call for his holy oil. Not only that, but it is curious that Stuart, whose wording implies his visits were regular ("I'd go over in the afternoon . . ."), says nothing about crossing paths with Anita at the hospital. Perhaps Anita was dramatizing what actually happened on Jelly's last day. In Floyd Levin's article about Levin's negotiations with Anita over who would be allowed to put a gravestone on Morton's grave, her voice would fill with emotion and her eyes with tears whenever she talked about Jelly, even though she had done nothing about a gravestone in the nearly ten years since his death, a performance that left Levin wondering why she felt so strongly about something she had put off for so long. And what she says about Morton is remarkably close in both wording and detail to what she tells Lomax in *Mister Jelly Roll*, suggesting a carefully rehearsed performance rather than a spontaneous display of emotion.

The funeral on 16 July 1941 at Saint Patrick's Church in Los Angeles is described by an anonymous obituary in the 1 August edition of *Down Beat*. Among the guests were what the article calls "Kid Ory's band of the Sunshine record period of 1921": Ory himself, Mutt Carey, Dink Johnson (called "Jelly's brother-in-law"), Ed Garland, Fred Washington, and Ben Borders. Ory, Carey, Washington, and Garland are named among the pallbearers, along with Paul Howard, by then secretary of Local 767, and Spencer Johnson and Frank Withers, described as "old friends of Jelly who had worked with him in bygone years." Also in attendance was David Stuart, the "one white man . . . among the approximately 150 people who attended the church service and accompanied the funeral service to the cemetery." Stuart also gave Reb Spikes a ride from the church to the burial site. The article explains that Spikes "didn't have a car and almost didn't make it to the cemetery. Stuart saw that Reb was about to get left behind and took him out in his car. 'Sure appreciate that,' said Reb. 'Wanted to go as far as I could with Jelly.'"[49]

The obituary adds, "Observers noted that Mrs. Morton, who was accompanied by Jelly's sisters, seemed to take it pretty hard, especially at the cemetery."[50] The Mike Ford Collection, a small but valuable set of memorabilia separate from the Henry Villalapando Ford Collection, contains a funeral guest register that clears up some of the confusion in the above statement about Anita and "Jelly's sisters." The sisters' names appear in a short list of those who wired messages of condolence to the funeral: "Mrs. Amide Colas, La." and "Mrs. Mime [*sic*], Oliver, Tex." The next name listed is "Mrs. Mable [*sic*][,] N.Y.," obviously Mabel herself, her first name misspelled and her last name omitted entirely. The "Mrs. Morton" named in the obituary was Anita, not Mabel. The sisters would have been Anita's sisters-in-law, who are listed under "Relatives Attending" along with their husbands, Anita's brothers: James Johnson and his wife, Mary; Dink Johnson and his wife, Stella. Both James and Dink are identified by the abbreviation "Bro." for brother, rather than the more accurate "brother-in-law," as Jelly often called Anita's brothers. And Ed Hunter, Jelly's godfather, is listed as simply "Father"; his name appears on the list of those who sent flowers. Also, among the names that appear under the heading "Friends Who Called" is "Mr. Hugh MacBeth" [*sic*], the lawyer who signed as witness to Morton's last will and testament and who served for many years as executor of his estate; he also represented Anita and, later, her daughter Hattie, in legal disputes over the estate. The fact that Macbeth called to express condolences suggests that he was quite likely the lawyer Morton mentions in his letters to Mabel and Roy Carew about his dealings with ASCAP and his two publishers, Southern and Melrose.

The facts about who was informed of Morton's death, and when, and about who was or was not at the funeral, are material to questions raised by the controversy and the legal disputes that arose over the estate. The will was bound to stir up trouble, leaving, as it does, the bulk of Morton's estate to "my beloved Anita Gonzales," whom he describes as "my beloved comforter, companion and help-meet for many years, and whose tender care I sincerely appreciate." To Anita went all of his royalties from ASCAP, Southern Music Company, and Melrose Music Company, as well as "all property of every kind personal and otherwise wherever located." The only other heirs named are his sisters: Amide Colas, to whom he left his share of royalties and interest in Tempo Music of Washington, D.C., the corporation set up in collaboration with Roy Carew in order to take out copyrights on previously uncopyrighted material; and his other sister, named as "Frances Morton, now married," who appears in other court papers under her nickname and married name, Minnie Oliver, to whom he left the paltry sum of one dollar. The royalties from Tempo did not amount to much, at least at this stage: in the "Petition for Probate of Will," four royalty checks from Carew totaled $51.01, while the check from ASCAP alone is listed as $185.00. There can be no doubt that Anita got the lion's share of the estate. Mabel, his wife of twelve years, is not even mentioned.

The content of the will is handwritten on a standard printed form, quite possibly by Anita herself. (See fig. 19.) A comparison of her name as it is written in the will and her signature on her claim against the estate for a total of $538 reveals a very close similarity. It is definitely not Morton's own handwriting, which appears only in his signature. His weakened state is apparent in the way he signed the document: his first name, Ferdinand, is signed well below the dotted line, and, though his middle and last names are on the line, he has omitted the "h" in Joseph. Oddly

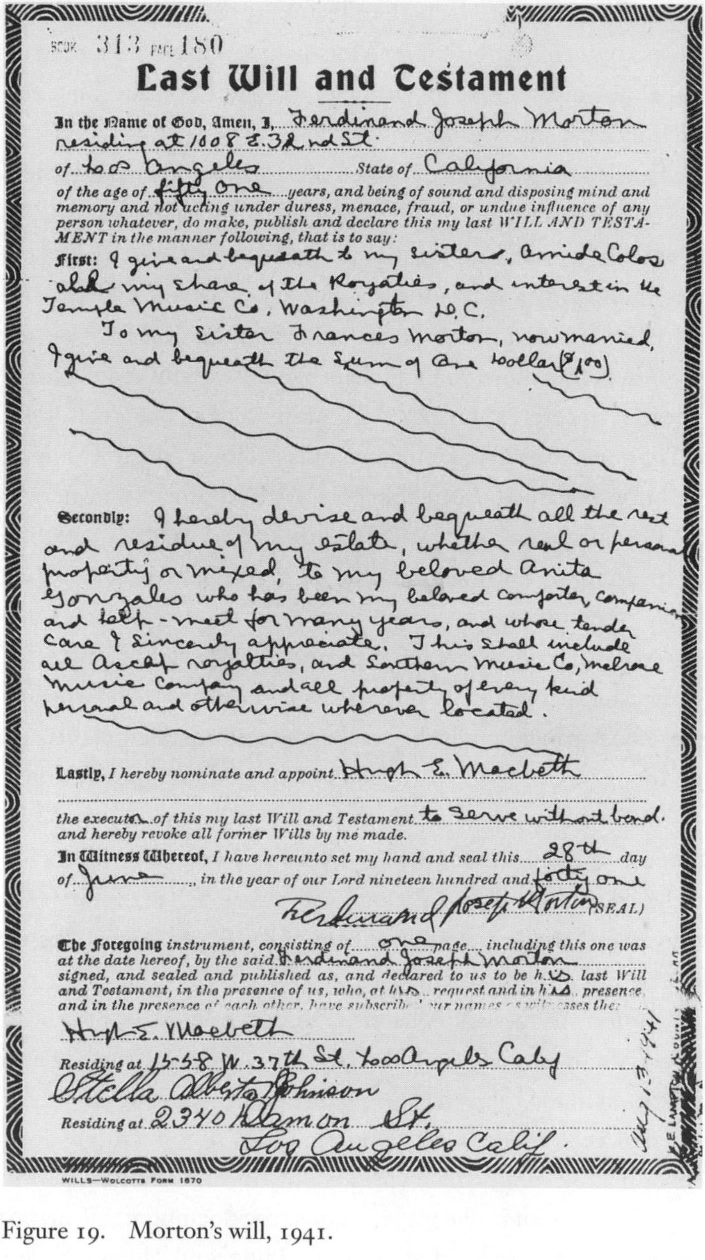

Book 313 Page 180

Last Will and Testament

In the Name of God, Amen, I, Ferdinand Joseph Morton residing at 1008 E. 32nd St. of Los Angeles State of California of the age of fifty one years, and being of sound and disposing mind and memory and not acting under duress, menace, fraud, or undue influence of any person whatever, do make, publish and declare this my last WILL AND TESTAMENT in the manner following, that is to say:

First: I give and bequeath to my sisters, Amide Colas also my share of the Royalties, and interest in the Temple Music Co, Washington D.C.

To my sister Frances Morton, now married, I give and bequeath the sum of One Dollar ($1.00)

Secondly: I hereby devise and bequeath all the rest and residue of my estate, whether real or personal property or mixed, to my beloved Anita Gonzales who has been my beloved comforter, companion and help-meet for many years, and whose tender care I sincerely appreciate. This shall include all Ascap royalties, and Southern Music Co, Melrose Music Company and all property of every kind personal and otherwise wherever located.

Lastly, I hereby nominate and appoint Hugh E. Macbeth the executor of this my last Will and Testament to serve without bond. and hereby revoke all former Wills by me made.

In Witness Whereof, I have hereunto set my hand and seal this 28th day of June, in the year of our Lord nineteen hundred and forty one

Ferdinand Joseph Morton (SEAL)

The Foregoing instrument, consisting of one page including this one was at the date hereof, by the said Ferdinand Joseph Morton signed, and sealed and published as, and declared to us to be his last Will and Testament, in the presence of us, who, at his request and in his presence, and in the presence of each other, have subscribed our names as witnesses thereto.

Hugh E. Macbeth

Residing at 1558 W. 37th St. Los Angeles Calif

Stella Alberta Johnson

Residing at 2340 Harmon St. Los Angeles Calif.

July 1? 1941

WILLS—WOLCOTTS FORM 1870

Figure 19. Morton's will, 1941.

enough, his age is given as fifty-one, though he had nearly three months to go before he crossed that threshold. That would make the year of his birth 1889, the same year Anita gave as his birth date on the death certificate. In his last years, Morton often lied about his age in order to lend credibility to his claim that he was the "originator" of jazz, but the year he would give was 1885; stating the year as 1889 would add only one year to his real age and would have no effect on his claim. At this point he must have been very weak, and either he himself misstated the year, or he was so out of it that Anita had taken complete charge and simply guessed wrong. Within two days of 28 June, when the will was drawn up, Morton was transferred from the convalescent home to what David Stuart described as a "broom closet" of a room in County General, a move that suggests how hopeless Jelly's condition had become. Perhaps he was already lapsing into the semicomatose state that Stuart describes. The presence of lawyer Hugh E. Macbeth, who signed as both executor and witness, may explain the legalese ("I hereby devise and bequeath all the rest and residue of my estate, whether real or personal property or mixed . . ."). The second witness is Stella Alberta Johnson, Dink's wife, who gives her address as 2340 Damon Street, Los Angeles—the same address that Anita gives as her home on the death certificate and on the court documents relating to the probate of the estate.

It would be fairly easy to read a sinister intent into all the misinformation that Anita disseminated on official documents relating to Morton's death and his will, especially since all of the misinformation consistently helps to expedite the processing of the case. But we may never know definitively whether Anita had Morton's blessing in those matters—whether, in effect, he had struck a deal with her and promised the royalties in exchange for her help.

Harrison Smith, a small-time booking agent and promoter who at one time had worked not only with Morton but also with Duke Ellington and Fats Waller, wrote a series of articles in jazz journals like *Record Research* and *Storyville* in which Anita emerges as a self-serving manipulator who all but defrauded Jelly's sisters and wife, Mabel, of their rightful share of the Morton estate. Since Smith's allegations, both explicit and implicit, have so far gone unanswered, I cite the entire statement he gave to *Storyville:*

> By virtue of having resided in New York City for more than 12 years, Jelly Roll Morton had established legal status as a resident of that City and State [*sic*]. This is contrary to the certification, made under oath and prepared for him to sign as his "death-bed will" that he was a resident of the City of Los Angeles in the State of California. He had died there during a seven-month visit made to ascertain the possibility of acquiring any estate left by his deceased grandmother [*sic*].
>
> The New York licence [*sic*] plates on his automobile bore mute testimony to the proper status of his legal residence.
>
> The lawyer who devised the will was appointed executor of the estate of Ferdinand J. Morton and was thereby enabled to collect remuneration of 15% commission and "expenses" for his duties. Jelly's estate comprised royalties from his publications and records, and ASCAP fees from public performances of his compositions.
>
> The "death-bed will" designated Mrs. Anita Johnson-Gonzales-Ford, described as his "beloved comforter, companion and helpmate [*sic*] for many years" as the principle legatee and made meagre bequests to his two sisters, to whom he was very devoted.
>
> In discussing the matter with his sister, Mrs. Frances Morton Oliver, she advised me that they didn't know he had died until after his burial, and in view of her financial contributions on his behalf, she could not reconcile herself to the authenticity of the will[,] which bequeathed her "the sum of one dollar"!
>
> Mrs. Ford, sister of famed Bill Johnson, and Jelly were sweethearts in the days of their youth, when she authored DEAD MAN BLUES and he dedicated SWEET ANITA MINE and MAMANITA to her. Until his return to Los Angeles a short time before he died they had not seen each other for over twenty years. During the intervening years she had twice married and had had children. At the time the will was

written it appears that she was still married to Mr. Ford, with whom she operated a motel.

Presentation of the will for probate purpose to [the] Surrogate's section of the Los Angeles Superior Court resulted in no-one protesting the alleged claim of Jelly being a resident of the City and State [*sic*]. Such being the case, acceptance was made of the claim as authentic information and the will was probated as valid.

Time marched on. Mrs. Ford and the lawyer passed away[,] and the irony of the matter is that now Mrs. Ford's daughter, who Jelly Roll Morton never saw, claims executrix-ship of his estate, by being executrix of her mother's estate, which in turn was originally Jelly's, much to the chagrin of his two sisters and his wife, who after twelve years of marriage, was left behind in New York when he went "for a short visit" to California. . . . the visit from which he never re- turned. . . .

Deep were the roots of love planted by Jelly and Anita during their youthful days so long ago.[51]

The problem with Smith's claims is that they contain as much mis- information as Anita's various misstatements of facts on official docu- ments. First of all, the will itself says nothing about Morton's legal sta- tus as a resident of Los Angeles; it simply attests that 1008 E. Third Street, Los Angeles, was his current address. It is the death certificate that claims he was a resident for four years, not the will, and the death certificate says nothing about swearing under oath. As for the license plates, according to the "Petition for Probate of Will," filed on 22 July 1941, Morton's convertible Cadillac sedan had California plates: "Cal. 1941 Lic. No. 77-V-656." Of course, that does not change the fact that Anita lied about Morton's length of residency on the death certificate, but Smith's lie is careless. One wonders how he could have known what plates were on the car; he certainly underestimates Anita's careful atten- tion to detail—she made sure that the New York plates would not give the lie to her statements that Jelly had lived in Los Angeles for four years.

One also wonders how he could have been sure that Morton never knew Hattie, Anita's daughter and executrix; there is simply no evidence, one way or the other, but it seems highly unlikely that Morton never knew her or even knew of her, either in Biloxi or Los Angeles. At any rate, if Jelly wanted to leave the bulk of his estate to Anita, it must have occurred to him that Anita, in turn, would leave her estate to whomever she wished. Nor is there any evidence to support Smith's statement that "during the intervening years" after Morton left California and then returned, Anita had "twice married and had had children." Aside from Jack Ford and possibly Jelly, her only husband of record was Fred Seymour, Hattie's father, whom Anita had left in Biloxi sometime between 1905 and 1910; her only child aside from Hattie was Henry, whom she and Jack adopted at some point.

Smith also gets some of the smaller details wrong: Morton was in Los Angeles for nine, not seven, months and was supposedly there to look into his godmother's estate, not his grandmother's. A more serious bit of factual error is sister Frances's claim that she and Amide "didn't know he had died until after his burial"; as we have seen, both sisters and Mabel had sent wires to the funeral. As for her claim about "her financial contributions on his behalf," there is no evidence of such contributions; in fact, Amide told Lomax that Jelly was sending her money to the very end.[52] In another article, published in *Record Research* in October 1961, Smith's penchant for misstating facts shows up again: he reproduces a bowdlerized version of the original, handwritten form of the will by whiting out the names of the executor and witnesses. And Smith's implication that the misrepresentation of Jelly's residential status in effect rendered the will invalid may well be true, but in fact no one with a claim on the estate ever successfully made an issue of it in court, and that includes the two sisters, Mabel, and Harrison Smith himself.

Smith's tendency to stretch the truth, to put it mildly, surfaces again in his 1970 interview with William Russell, where he declares that "Dink Johnson's wife rushes out and gets this bum lawyer. She dug him up—Jelly didn't."[53] In fact, Hugh Macbeth was a prominent and well-respected attorney in Los Angeles, as a front-page article in the 17 November 1938 edition of the *California Eagle* attests. The article, titled "Let Your Own Defend You," is accompanied by a large photograph of Macbeth among other prominent lawyers of the day, whose caption reads "ATTY. HUGH MACBETH, Liberian consul and outstanding civic leader . . . will speak at the Town Hall Forum of Scott M.E. Church Sunday night." —definitely not a "bum lawyer," as Smith would have it.[54] As for his concern over Mabel, he complains to Russell that she "didn't get a nickel," but then repeats an unsubstantiated rumor that she was a pickpocket and has Morton say that he wants to dump her, to boot: "In New York, [Morton] had Mabel hanging on to him. 'I wish I could get rid of her,' he'd say, but he couldn't manage it. They tell me she was a pickpocket—I don't know. They say when Jelly had a crowd on the dance floor she would work her way through—I don't know. I used to get on him for treating her so mean."[55] Smith thus portrays himself as, at once, Mabel's defender and character assassin.

What Smith never mentions in any of the articles is that he was currently, and would be until 1972, contesting Morton's will over royalties for Morton compositions that Smith claimed were either partly or wholly his own. That information would certainly have made his insinuations about Anita appear rather self-serving. Nor does he mention that his claims on the estate were based largely on a brief period when Smith and Morton shared an office in New York. According to Lawrence Gushee and William Russell, Smith was the "West Indian guy" that Morton took on as "confidential partner" to handle the New York end of a booking agency whose main office was to be in Los Angeles. The partnership was in trouble from the very beginning. Jelly told Lomax, "I assured him I didn't want to make him an office boy, but the son-of-a-gun was jealous of me. He didn't want to handle the music counter and told me I was high-hat because I kept my door closed. I had to have quiet for my arranging and composing. I guess he hated me because he was such a poor excuse for talent, himself—if you told him to rhyme 'ham,' he would say 'Pontchartrain.'"[56] After Morton found out that Smith was involved with voodoo, things got worse:

> Well, I found out that this West Indian not only couldn't do accounting, he could hardly count on his fingers, much less type. Then I discovered that he was stealing my music and selling it to a big, high-powered firm and I knew I would have to kick him out. . . .
>
> He wouldn't admit to anything. I told him that our contract didn't mean anything if one of the partners didn't play fair. I showed him I had the goods on him. He told me, "Morton, everything in this office is in my name and belongs to me." We started to fight and the super of the building came running and hollering, "Don't hit him here. He will sue the building." That gave the West Indian a chance to escape, which he did. He hollered back, as he ran away, "Jelly Roll Morton, you will lose everything you have."[57]

After that incident, Morton became convinced that Smith placed the voodoo curse on him that accounted for all his bad luck in the early 1930s. Billy Young, an actress and singer that Jelly hired to do some office work from time to time, said "she had noticed that people would come to the door, and stop, seemingly unable to cross the sill; that was strange to her, because formerly a lot of people came to the office. We pulled up the rug near the door and there, underneath, were four different colors of powder—gray, white, brown and pink. We found powder sprinkled everywhere, even in the woodwork of the desk. There wasn't a piece of stationery that was clean of it."[58] One day, Young was afflicted by a "horrible-looking rash" after handling the stationery, and when she "took a drink out of a paper cup at the water cooler[,] . . . her lips swelled up as big as the bumpers on a box car."[59] Morton then contacted his own voodoo person to counteract the curse he believed had been put on him, but the chain of events precipitated a downward spiral in his fortunes that he attributed entirely to Smith's voodoo machinations. Even Mabel, who did not give much credence to voodoo, verified the outlines of the story:

> I think . . . it was some kind of poisonous powder for insects. But I saw it all over the office, some kind of pink stuff. There was a girl drank out of a paper cup and her lips swole up till you couldn't recognize her. And then my husband started to go to fortune tellers. I tried to talk to him and tell him that was all baloney. "You have the wrong idea, honey. It's those people's racket, it's their line, just the same as you're a musician, they'll send you to the cleaners."[60]

Over the years, Smith stubbornly persisted in his claim on Jelly's royalties. According to a letter from William Russell to Floyd Levin, Smith's purpose was "to prove that he, rather than Jelly Roll, was the actual composer and copyright owner of possibly 20 to 30 tunes which Jelly claimed that he (Jelly) had composed." Finally, in 1972, thirty-one years after Morton's death, and twelve years after the County of Los Angeles Superior Court denied his claims on the Morton estate, RCA Victor agreed to pay Smith royalties on seven tunes: "Don't Tell Me Nothing 'Bout My Man," "If Someone Would Only Love Me," "Fickle Fay Creep," "I'm Looking for a Little Bluebird," "My Little Dixie," "That's Like It Ought to Be," and "Smilin' the Blues Away"; the statement sent to Smith by RCA Victor, dated 31 August 1972, itemizes the royalties "FROM DATE OF RELEASE THRU PERIOD ENDING 8/31/72" for a total of $1,310.18.[61]

As for Mabel, her attempt to make a claim on Morton's estate was late and rather feeble. For some reason, she waited three years before pressing the claim. The citation orders her to appear "before the Judge of this Court in the County of Los Angeles . . . to show cause, if any, why you should be declared the surviving spouse and as such an heir of the Estate of Ferdinand J. Morton also known as Ferd J. Morton, Deceased" on Monday, 17 July 1944; the document is dated 19 June 1944, and in the attached "AFFIDAVIT OF SERVICE OF CITATION," the server attests that he received the citation on the 10th of July and served it to Mabel on the 13th, just four days before the scheduled court appearance. She did not answer the citation or appear in court on 17 July, and, on 13 October 1944, Judge Thomas Gould of the Superior Court signed an order canceling the citation. Any hopes Mabel may have harbored that her claim would be honored became buried and frozen in a soft snowbank of legalese that begins by referring to her as "Mabel Stein, sometimes known as Mabel Stein Morton" but in the end simply calls her "Mabel Stein":

> This matter having come before the above entitled Court on the 5th day of October, 1944 . . . ; it appearing to the Court that the citee Mabel Stein, sometimes known as Mabel Stein Morton . . . was duly served with the above Citation, and that the citee having not appeared in Court or answered to said Citation on said 17th day of July, 1944, and said hearing on said Citation having been duly continued from time to time until this day, and no one having appeared for said citee, and the Court having heard the testimony of Hugh E. Macbeth, Executor, of the Last Will and Testament of Ferdinand J. Morton, a. k. a. Ferd J. Morton, deceased, to the effect that Attorney Edward J. Kelly had consulted and personally visited the said executor in behalf of said Mabel Stein, sometimes known as Mabel Stein Morton, after the service of said Citation upon said Mabel Stein, as the alleged widow of Ferdinand J. Morton, deceased, and having assured said Executor that if said Attorney Kelly were able to produce evidence before the Court in favor of the claim of said Mabel Stein, for producing any evidence before the Court as to the marital status of said Mabel Stein as the alleged widow of said Ferdinand J. Morton, and said Mabel Stein, citee herein, at all times having failed to appear before the above entitled Court in response to said Citation,
> IT IS HEREBY ORDERED that said Citation be discharged.[62]

Where the name "Stein" came from is anybody's guess; if her maiden name was Bertrand, as she told Lomax, she must have been married to someone named Stein, either before or after her liaison with Morton. Be that as it may, apparently Morton carried their marriage license west with him in his "inside coat pocket," where he always kept it, over Mabel's protests. Whatever he did with it, evidently he never gave it to Mabel; the document would have been all she needed to prove her marital status to the court. The three years that had elapsed since Morton's death certainly gave her enough time to obtain a certified copy of the document, unless it were counterfeit in the first place. As we have seen, in her words to Lomax about the license, she blames herself more than anyone for allowing Morton to hold on to it: "I didn't worry my head about it and let it go," she says; "I was just dumb to the fact, that's all I can say now." But then she adds, "At that time, though, what could I think? I had everything in the world I wanted and I never had any trouble with Jelly and other women. . . . Anita? I never heard of her till later."[63]

We may never know whether she spoke those words to Lomax before or after her failed attempt to make a claim on the estate, so for now the court papers represent Mabel's last documented appearance in the Morton saga. None of my own attempts to determine what happened to Mabel have met with success. One thing is certain, though: whenever Lomax interviewed her, her reminiscences of Jelly were not tainted by the bitterness she was entitled to feel over the shabby treatment she had received. However much he may have admired Jelly's colorful personality and musical mastery, Lomax's own words about Mabel betray another kind of admiration—this time born of a deep well of sympathy over her plight and over the courage with which she accepted her fate: "plain, brave Mabel Morton," he calls her, "a good union member, a faithful Catholic, singled out, who knows whether by fortune or misfortune, as the companion of Jelly Roll Morton. She watched his struggles, she helped as she could, and she was the only one who cared that he was hurt."[64] Her motives for standing by him seem to have been her abiding faith in his genius and her willingness to do whatever was necessary to keep him going as long as possible. By far the most moving words spoken by anyone in Lomax's *Mister Jelly Roll* belong to Mabel: "In the 1940's," Lomax writes, "her face had a little gray and puzzled look, but, when she spoke of Jelly Roll, the vagueness departed and her strong and sweet Creole voice, which did not complain, cried out in a welter of Harlem tene-ments—'I have been loved by a great man, I have watched a genius at work in the cold, lonely hours.'"[65]

But perhaps Lomax, in his attempt to show compassion for Mabel, is needlessly sentimental, maybe even condescending. Her words are spo-ken with the air of someone simply stating the facts: she knew her man was a genius, pure and simple, and saw no reason to be modest about it. With equally unblinking candor, she enumerates his lapses and faults, clearly and unemotionally. As a result, only through her words do we get a full sense of Jelly Roll Morton as a private person, away from the hype and the spotlights. The verbal portrait she paints is not always a flatter-ing one, either to him or to her, but it has the unmistakable ring of truth about it.

Jelly himself was incapable of such candor. The courage he possessed when he faced his death was not with him when it came to telling Mabel, on two distinct occasions, clearly and unambiguously that he was leav-ing her: first, in 1935, when he left New York for Washington, D.C., and then unceremoniously dropped out of sight, and last, in 1940, when he left New York for Los Angeles. In his letters to her from California, his repeated and ultimately empty promises to send her enough money for a trip home to New Orleans seem, in retrospect, a thinly disguised at-tempt to avoid what he could not bring himself to say: that he was not going to send for her to join him in Los Angeles, as she no doubt would have wanted. In one exchange of letters, Roy Carew expresses his hope that Morton is writing to Mabel—she is "probably lonesome" since Jelly left, Carew writes, "and I am sure she is very anxious about you"; he then adds he is "sure that it would be better for both of you if she could be out there with you. She knows what diet, etc., you should have, and she would be giving you better care probably than you can get from outsid-ers. Let me know if you wouldn't like to have her out there."[66] In that last sentence, he all but offers to buy Mabel a ticket to Los Angeles. The reference to "outsiders" suggests that Carew had no idea that Anita was on the case—in fact, Morton never once mentions her in the many long letters he sent to his friend, in spite of his many protestations that he is being fully candid about his affairs. And when Carew closes the letter by again urging Jelly to write Mabel as often as he can, one senses Carew's awareness that Morton was not doing that. Indeed, Morton's letters to Mabel were far fewer and much shorter than those he wrote to Carew. Morton's response is dated 29 May 1941, exactly a month and a day after the date on Carew's letter: "I did not want my wife out here until I had fully decided that the climate was the right one for my health, but I am not quite so sure unless I show better improvement & with out this, It [sic] will harder [sic] to make ends meet. my [sic] health has blocked the whole program. If I had of made any money at all I would of sent her home to N[ew] O[rleans]. She would of been better off there." [67] In view of the fact that he was keeping both Carew and Mabel in the dark about Anita's presence in Los Angeles, Morton's response clearly avoids explicitly rejecting the thinly disguised offer on Carew's part to help get Mabel to California. He may have been sincere about wanting to pay her passage to New Orleans, but in effect the issue is a red herring that lets him evade the talk about her joining Morton in Los Angeles.

To his credit, he did send money whenever he could, even though it was not very much, and he did not disappear on her as he had in Washington, D.C.—which would have been a lot easier to do in Los Angeles, three thousand miles from New York. In fact, the notes and the money make it hard to believe that Jelly would willingly cut Mabel out of the will without even a mention of her name and without leaving her even a dollar, as he left his sister Frances. The omission raises serious and troubling questions about his intentions and about the role Anita played during his last days and after. Above all, was he aware of what he was signing when he affixed his signature to the will, or had he become so weak and confused that he would have signed anything put in front of him? Put in another way, did Anita rather ruthlessly take advantage of the situation? The evidence, scanty and circumstantial as it is, does not allow for full and definitive answers to those questions, and probably never will, but it does allow for some very tentative conclusions.

It must be admitted that the evidence, including Anita's actions at that time and after, make it easy to put her in a bad light. The fact that it took her nearly ten years to put a gravestone on Jelly's grave certainly makes her teary-eyed reminiscences to Floyd Levin and her indignant insistence that only she could finally have a gravestone installed both appear rather insincere. And Morton's last note to Mabel, a couple of sentence fragments scribbled on a postal money order form, make it clear that by 26 April 1941 he was already in very bad shape, some three months before he signed the will. However, his letter of 29 May about Mabel, and his letter from the convalescent home to Carew, dated a week before he signed his will, show that his mind was still clear enough to write a coherent letter, though he had given up hope of recovery. David Stuart's testimony about Morton's comatose state near the end, in County General, where he wound up just two days after signing the will, casts some doubt on Jelly's mental competence at the time of the signing. In his interview with William Russell, Stuart is quite explicit about his doubts over the will: "I don't think it possible for him to have written a will the last few days—no way!"[68] But Morton did not sign the will during "the last few days"; and he did not write it, he simply signed it, and the signature is in his hand—it matches the many other Morton autographs in the Ford Collection. Obviously, he was alert enough to sign, albeit with some difficulty, but the question remains, did he fully understand what the will contained?

The question is impossible to answer definitively, and so perhaps the wrong one to ask. A more relevant and answerable question, within limits, would be: Did Jelly and Anita have an unwritten or tacit agreement that, in return for her financial assistance, he would hand his affairs over to her? All of the circumstantial evidence—the timing of his departure for Los Angeles; the detour through Canyonville, Oregon; Anita's itemized list in the probate file of expenditures on Jelly's behalf; even his silence, as far as Mabel and Carew were concerned, about the very existence of Anita—strongly suggests that they had come to some such arrangement. Perhaps he felt he had no other choice, but that is another matter. In his final years, he had become increasingly strident, even paranoid, about the exploitation of his life's work by the music publishers, the record companies, and ASCAP. Given his resignation, by June of 1941, that the end was near, he must have given some thought by then, if not far sooner, to the question of who would inherit the fruits of his labor. He had never confided in Mabel about financial matters at all—from the very beginning of their marriage—and at any rate Mabel hardly had the means to follow through on his legal battles with the Melrose brothers and others, while Anita most definitely did. After all, "the estate" did not amount to anything tangible—no stocks, no bank accounts, no property to convert into cash; it did amount to royalties, but at that time they were barely enough to allow Jelly to support himself. Also, it must be said that Mabel's handling of the marriage license issue and her belated and failed attempt to make her claim on the estate give the distinct impression that she was far too naive and trusting when it came to legal matters. And perhaps leaving anything at all to Mabel in the will would have been a tacit admission that she did have some legitimate claim to the estate. Furthermore, to die without leaving any will at all—which he came close to doing more than once—would have made it easier for the publishers and ASCAP to dispute anyone's claim to future royalties, an outcome that would have horrified Morton. Like it or not, apparently he had little choice but to leave the bulk of his estate to Anita.

One aspect of the will strongly supports the conclusion that it accurately reflects his intentions: it leaves all of the royalties from Tempo Music to his sister Amide. If the will is really the product of Anita's selfish machinations, it is hard to explain what could have inspired such a burst of generosity toward Amide, whom Anita barely knew, if at all, and could not have seen in years. The Tempo catalogue contains twenty-four of the ninety-odd copyrighted compositions in the Morton canon—more than a quarter of the total. As noted earlier, Morton had created Tempo, with the help of Roy Carew, late in his life (1938), and it contains some of his lesser efforts—pieces like "My Home Is in a Southern Town" and "Get the Bucket," among others. But it also contains some of his best pieces ("The Crave" and "Sporting House Rag") and one that had been recorded by many popular singers of the day ("Sweet Substitute"). Also, Tempo smartly laid claim to two pieces that were not Morton's but had never been copyrighted by anyone: "Buddy Bolden's Blues" and "Mamie's Blues" (also known as "209 Blues"), tunes that have long been considered blues and jazz standards. The extensive correspondence in the William Russell Collection between Morton and Carew, which begins shortly after Jelly's return to New York in late December 1938 and ends just before his death in 1941, clearly testifies to the time and effort he put into Tempo during his last few years. In the 145 pages reproduced by Russell in *Oh, Mister Jelly*, Morton writes frequently about the copies of his recent compositions he is mailing to Carew and also describes casting about in a search for more material like "Mamie's Blues"— pieces that had become traditional in the jazz canon but that no one had ever bothered to copyright. Tempo Music represented Morton's last efforts to secure his legacy and frustrate the exploitation of his music that had gone on for so long. Anita got the major share of the inheritance— and it contains most of Morton's well-known, classic compositions— but Amide's is not negligible. A selfish Anita writing the will to suit herself would have wanted to keep it all.

In addition, Carew's copyright list indicates that between 1948 and 1949 some twenty-four additional compositions were copyrighted, this time by the Estate of Ferd J. Morton.[69] Anita, or someone advising her, must have discovered the existence of still more uncopyrighted Morton material and proceeded to lay claim to it. With the exception of "Mamanita," none of the newly copyrighted pieces are major compositions, but the fact that Anita made sure that they went to the Morton estate and not to Tempo can only mean that she wanted to get whatever she could, both legally and morally. This again supports the idea that the bequest of the Tempo royalties, and by extension the will as a whole, must represent Morton's wishes.

The question of why Anita waited so long to put a gravestone on Morton's grave is certainly puzzling—as is, one should add, why she then protested so loudly when she found out that the Southern California Hot Jazz Society was holding a benefit concert to raise money and finally put one on the grave. Her actions are so incongruous that it is nearly impossible to explain them all with one coherent theory. The most obvious would be to assume that her omission amounted to selfishness of the take-the-money-and-run variety. There are a number of problems with that explanation, however. First of all, there was not that much money to run with, so money could not have been a major factor in her motivation. She knew that his income from royalties amounted to barely enough to sustain him, if that much, and in 1941 she could not have foreseen that the New Orleans revival, which would not begin until 1944, would cause his stock to rise. Second of all, she had expended a good deal of time and effort—and her own money, it seems   to help him out, with no guarantee that there would eventually be any kind of "payoff"; the will was not drawn up and signed until near the very end. Finally, if she really did not care about anything but the money, why make such a fuss and insist that she, and only she, install the gravestone? She could have kept her silence and her money and let the Society do its work.

Perhaps it is wrong to assume that because the same person did A, B, and C, there must be a logically consistent explanation for those actions. In his *Poetics*, Aristotle may have been right to argue that the protagonist in a drama should have unity of action, but in real life, it often seems impossible to explain how the same person who did A also was capable of doing B. This is especially true of someone like Anita, who could be "Sweet Anita" one minute and a Fury with a fearsome temper the next. Perhaps it was her baffling, paradoxical complexity that drew Morton to Anita in the first place. Like Jelly, Anita wore many masks, and the real person behind the masks can be seen only in fleeting glimpses. In hour after hour of interviews with Lomax, Morton was engaged not only in an act of self-revelation but also in one of self-creation, and we have to be alert to catch the creator himself through the creation. One thing is certain: Anita was one of the few constants in Jelly's life, along with his godmother, Laura Hunter. Their relationship often survived months, even years of separation, not just once or twice but many times. In the end, as he had done at least twice before, Jelly dropped everything and traveled whatever distance was necessary, and overcame whatever obstacles presented themselves, to get to Anita. Finally, the epigram that best epitomizes their relationship comes from his own lips: "Anita managed me, the way she always did."

NOTES

PREFACE

1. Ellison, *Going to the Territory*, 123–4.
2. Lomax, *Mister Jelly Roll*, 76–82. This work has been reprinted by various presses over the years, and the pagination often differs from one reprint to another.
3. Ibid., 158.
4. Triem, *Ventura County*, 94–100.
5. Lomax, *Mister Jelly Roll*, 19.
6. Wright, *Mr. Jelly Lord*, 93.

1. PRELUDE TO A RIFF

1. Lomax, *Mister Jelly Roll*, 283–4.
2. Dirty Dozen Brass Band, *The Dirty Dozen Brass Band Plays Jelly Roll Morton*.
3. Lomax, *Mister Jelly Roll*, 213.
4. M. Williams, "The Roll," 56–7.
5. Lomax, *Mister Jelly Roll*, fn. 195.
6. Ibid., 77, my emphasis.
7. Ibid., xix.
8. Bigard, *With Louis and the Duke*, 60–1.

9. Stewart, *Boy Meets Horn*, 166.

10. Hulsizer, "Jelly Roll Morton in Washington," 215.

11. Lomax, *Mister Jelly Roll*, fn. 175–6.

12. Ibid., 251.

13. Quoted in M. Williams, "The Roll," 52.

14. Ellison, *Shadow and Act*, 243.

15. Murray, *Stomping the Blues*, 17.

16. Lomax, *Mister Jelly Roll*, 263.

17. Ibid., 253.

18. Ibid., 263.

19. Ibid., 52, 134.

20. Ibid., 257.

21. Morton, "Final Years of Frustration," pt. 1, pp. 2–5; pt. 2, pp. 8–9.

22. Lomax, *Mister Jelly Roll*, 298–9.

23. Ellison, *Shadow and Act*, 222, 228.

24. Lomax, *Mister Jelly Roll*, 4, 44.

25. Gushee, "Would You Believe Ferman Mouton?" 56–9.

26. Lomax, *Mister Jelly Roll*, 44. I have adopted the spelling "Amide" among the many variant spellings (Amede, Ameda, etc.) because that is the way the name is spelled in Morton's will and because that is the spelling William Russell draws from his collection of Morton memorabilia in *Oh, Mister Jelly: A Jelly Roll Morton Scrapbook*.

27. Gushee, "Would You Believe Ferman Mouton?" 56–9.

28. Gushee, "A Preliminary Chronology," 393.

29. Lomax, *Mister Jelly Roll*, 45.

30. Ibid., 41.

31. Ibid., 175–6.

32. McCrum, MacNeil, and Cran, *The Story of English*, 237, quoted by Morrison, *Van Morrison Glossary*.

33. Oliver, *Blues Fell This Morning*, 109, quoted in Morrison, *Van Morrison Glossary*.

34. Lomax, *Mister Jelly Roll*, 59.

35. Morton, *Winin' Boy Blues;* also in Morton, Library of Congress Interviews, American Folklore Society (AFS) 1687, A and B sides. This recording contains mostly music, with very little of Morton's spoken monologue.

36. Lomax, *Mister Jelly Roll*, 59–60.

37. Morton, Library of Congress Interviews.

38. Lomax, *Mister Jelly Roll*, 261.

39. Bricktop, *Bricktop*, 64.

40. Quoted in M. Williams, "The Roll," 53.

41. Rose, *Eubie Blake*, 116.

42. Foster, *Pops Foster*, 33.

43. M. Williams, "The Roll," 52.

44. Gushee, "A Preliminary Chronology," 407.

45. Lomax, *Mister Jelly Roll*, 348; Morton, *Ferdinand "Jelly Roll" Morton*, 25–7.

46. Lomax, *Mister Jelly Roll*, 214.

47. Ibid., 216.

48. Ibid.

49. Compare ibid., 214 and 217. The exact date and year of Morton's departure are uncertain, but since the last recorded traces of his presence date from 1922, I cite that as his last year in Southern California, though he may have stayed until early 1923.

50. Ibid., 210.

51. Ibid., 45 ff.

52. Ibid., 10, 11.

53. Ibid., 300.

54. Ibid., 54.

55. Wright, *Mr. Jelly Lord*, 81–3, 86.

56. Lomax, *Mister Jelly Roll*, 293–4.

57. Ibid., 296.

58. Ibid., 298–9. Until the publication of excerpts from Morton's letters to Roy Carew in the journal *Storyville* (1968), and the recent publication of William Russell's collection *Oh, Mister Jelly*, the exact chronology of Morton's hospital stay in New York had never been established. Lomax mentions neither the year nor the month; according to him, Mabel puts the stay at three months and says that Morton was in the studio within a month to record "Alabama Bound," "Good Old New York," "Fingerbuster," and "My Home Is in a Southern Town" (ibid.). In fact, according to his letters to Carew, Morton was in the hospital just short of three weeks, not months—from 17 April to 7 May 1939 (Morton, "Final Years of Frustration" pt. 1, pp. 2–3). In the Ford Collection, Morton's appointment card from the Vanderbilt Clinic records a follow-up visit on 29 May,

which would have been when he got the bad news about his condition that he relayed to Carew in the letter of 30 May cited above (3). The card also lists nine more follow-up appointments at irregular intervals from 14 August 1939 to 11 November 1940. Morton could not have made the last appointment because he was already in California by 11 November (Lomax, 301). At any rate, he made no recordings at all in 1939 until 14 September, a bit more than four months after his release from the hospital, not one month, as Mabel mistakenly remembers (Wright, 96). Even the list of tunes is wrong: each tune Mabel mentions was recorded at a different session: "Alabama Bound" was recorded as "Don't You Leave Me Here" in New York on 28 September 1939, "Good Old New York" on 4 January 1940, and "My Home Is in a Southern Town" on 30 January 1940 (Wright, 94–102). It is impossible to tell if the inaccuracies come from Mabel's faulty memory, Lomax's errors in transcription, or a combination of the two. The Washington recording of "Fingerbuster" and three other titles (none mentioned by Mabel) in December 1938 suggests that the scenario of a three-month hospital stay, followed by a recording session one month after his release, could have occurred in Washington rather than New York, especially in view of Mabel's comment that "he played so fast on that one ["Fingerbuster"], I'm surprised he didn't get a heart attack right there" (Lomax, 299).

59. Lomax, *Mister Jelly Roll*, 300–301.
60. Ibid., 311–12.
61. Ibid., 300.
62. Wright, *Mr. Jelly Lord*, 103.
63. William Russell, ed., *Oh, Mister Jelly*, 307.
64. Smith, "The Strange Case of Jelly's Will," 9.
65. Lomax, *Mister Jelly Roll*, 312.
66. Ibid., 303.
67. Ibid., 299, 303.

2. MAMANITA AND THE "VOODOO WITCH"

1. Lomax, *Mister Jelly Roll*, 208–9.
2. Ibid., 205.
3. Peter Pullman, *The Complete Jelly Roll Morton Library of Congress Inter-*

views, AFS 2489B. As yet unpublished, this manuscript was sent to me by the author. I refer to the manuscript by the AFS catalogue number of the recordings.

4. Lomax, *Mister Jelly Roll,* 187.

5. Paher, *Las Vegas,* 77–8.

6. Ibid., passim.

7. Ibid., 97.

8. Ibid.

9. Castleman, *Las Vegas,* 41.

10. Ibid., 41.

11. Pullman, *The Complete Jelly Roll Morton Library of Congress Interviews,* AFS 2489B; Lomax, *Mister Jelly Roll,* 197.

12. Lomax, *Mister Jelly Roll,* 216.

13. Ibid.

14. Ibid., 312.

15. Hines, *Adventures in Good Eating,* 235. Italics in the original.

16. Levin, "Untold Story of Jelly Roll Morton's Last Years," 40.

17. Ibid., 41.

18. Ibid.

19. Lomax, *Mister Jelly Roll,* 4.

20. Ibid., 45.

21. Ibid., 10.

22. Ibid., 51.

23. Ibid., 216.

24. Ibid., 209.

25. Ibid., 200.

26. Ibid., 4.

27. Ibid., 5, 45.

28. Ibid., 45.

29. Ibid., 130.

30. Ibid., 51.

31. Ibid., 311–12.

32. Haskins, *Voodoo and Hoodoo,* 98.

33. Lomax, *Mister Jelly Roll,* 11, my italics.

34. Rose, *Storyville, New Orleans,* 53.

35. Lomax, *Mister Jelly Roll,* 4.

36. Ibid., 311.

37. Ibid., 57.

38. Ibid., 58.

39. Ibid., 11, 58.

40. Ibid., 59.

41. Ibid., 272–3.

42. Ibid., 311.

43. Metraux, *Voodoo in Haiti*, 15.

44. Tallant, *Voodoo in New Orleans*, 80–2; Haskins, *Voodoo and Hoodoo*, 61.

45. Morton, "Final Years of Frustration," pt. 1, p. 3.

46. Lomax, *Mister Jelly Roll*, 45.

47. Ibid., vii.

48. Ibid., vii–viii.

49. Hurston, *Mules and Men*, 275–6.

50. Haskins, *Voodoo and Hoodoo*, 62.

51. Hurbon, "American Fantasy and Haitian Voodoo," 194.

52. Sonnier, *A Guide to the Blues*, 79–80.

53. Lomax, *Mister Jelly Roll*, 68–9.

54. Metraux, *Voodoo in Haiti*, 19.

55. Mintz and Trouillot, "The Social History of Haitian Voodoo," 123–4, my italics.

56. Tallant, *Voodoo in New Orleans*, 52–5.

57. Ibid., 72–3.

58. Ibid., 75.

59. Ibid., 73.

60. Ibid., 72.

61. Ibid., 80–1.

62. Ibid., 80–2.

63. Ibid., 80.

64. Ibid., 55.

65. Lawrence Gushee, e-mail to author on the subject of Marie Laveau, 20 November 1997.

66. Gushee, "A Preliminary Chronology," 393.

3. L.A. JELLY, 1917–1923

1. Gushee, "A Preliminary Chronology," passim.

2. Ibid., 404.

3. Lomax, *Mister Jelly Roll*, 189, 194.

4. De Graf, "The City of Black Angels," passim.

5. Lomax, *Mister Jelly Roll*, 158, 194.

6. See Bryant et al., eds., *Central Avenue Sounds*, 409, n. 39: "The spelling of 'Leek's Lake' by Levin, Lomax, and other scholars seems wrong. Advertisements in the *California Eagle* . . . , one of them a Spikes brothers ad, spell the location 'Leak's Lake.'"

7. Ibid., 194.

8. Ibid., 194–5.

9. Ibid., 194.

10. Ibid., 195; Pullman, *The Complete Jelly Roll Morton Library of Congress Interviews*, AFS 2488A.

11. Pullman, *The Complete Jelly Roll Morton Library of Congress Interviews*, AFS 2488A.

12. Howard, Interview, 42–3.

13. Gushee, "New Orleans–Area Musicians," 3.

14. Pullman, *The Complete Jelly Roll Morton Library of Congress Interviews*, AFS 2488B.

15. Bontemps and Conroy, *Anyplace but Here*, 252.

16. Levin, "I Remember Buster Wilson," 6–7.

17. Russell, *Oh, Mister Jelly*, 526.

18. De Graf, "The City of Black Angels," 330–2.

19. Lomax, *Mister Jelly Roll*, 195.

20. Spikes, Interview, 83–4, 104–6.

21. Ibid., 20–1.

22. Stoddard, *Jazz on the Barbary Coast*, 47.

23. Ibid., 47.

24. Ibid., 48–9.

25. The listing for his name in the 1918 *Los Angeles City Directory* gives 1218 East Eighth as his home, and adds "restaurant at 553 Central," the address of the Cadillac Cafe.

26. Lomax, *Mister Jelly Roll*, 189.

27. Pullman, *The Complete Jelly Roll Morton Library of Congress Interviews*, AFS 1658B.

28. Lomax, *Mister Jelly Roll*, 359–60.

29. Ibid., 214.

30. Pullman, *The Complete Jelly Roll Morton Library of Congress Interviews*, AFS 2488A.

31. Ibid.

32. Ibid., AFS 2488B.

33. Bricktop, *Bricktop*, 64.

34. Lomax, *Mister Jelly Roll*, 195.

35. Ibid., 196.

36. Pullman, *The Complete Jelly Roll Morton Library of Congress Interviews*, AFS 2488B.

37. Spikes, Interview, 156.

38. Lomax, *Mister Jelly Roll*, 201.

39. Ibid., 197.

40. Ibid.

41. Ibid., 198.

42. Ibid., 198–9.

43. Ibid., 198.

44. Spikes, Interview, 156.

45. Gushee, "New Orleans–Area Musicians," 16.

46. Pullman, *The Complete Jelly Roll Morton Library of Congress Interviews*, AFS 2489B; Lomax, *Mister Jelly Roll*, 197.

47. Lomax, *Mister Jelly Roll*, 197.

48. Ibid.

49. Morton, Notes to interviews with Alan Lomax, items 5.scr[ipt] and 18.scr.; Lomax, *Mister Jelly Roll*, 201–3. Not all of Morton's interviews were captured on audio recordings. The Library of Congress has preserved on microfilm a typescript of notes from interviews recorded stenographically. Thanks again to Lawrence Gushee for filling in this important gap in the audio recordings.

50. Gushee, "A Preliminary Chronology," 405.

51. Ibid.

52. Lomax, *Mister Jelly Roll*, 204.

53. Stoddard, *Jazz on the Barbary Coast*, 169–70.

54. Lomax, *Mister Jelly Roll*, 203. Twenty waitresses, according to Morton, Notes to interviews with Alan Lomax, item 5.scr.

55. Stoddard, *Jazz on the Barbary Coast*, 49.

56. Ibid., 50.

57. Morton, Notes to interviews with Alan Lomax, item 5.scr.

58. Quoted in Stoddard, *Jazz on the Barbary Coast*, 207–8.

59. Lomax, *Mister Jelly Roll*, 204.

60. Ibid., 204–5.

61. Stoddard, *Jazz on the Barbary Coast*, 170–3.

62. Russell, *Oh, Mister Jelly*, 117.

63. Lomax, *Mister Jelly Roll*, 206.

64. Morton, Notes to interviews with Alan Lomax, item 18.scr.

65. Lomax, *Mister Jelly Roll*, 206.

66. Spikes, Interview, 161.

67. Wright, *Mr. Jelly Lord*, 4; Gushee, "A Preliminary Chronology," 405. Gushee gives the name as Don Pasquall.

68. Miller, *"Such Melodious Racket,"* 71, nn. 11, 12; Gushee, "A Preliminary Chronology," 405.

69. "Some Letters," *Chicago Defender*, 9 September 1919, p. 9; Ragtime Billy Tucker, "Coast Dope," *Chicago Defender*, 31 July 1920, p. 4.

70. Morton, Notes to interviews with Alan Lomax, item 18.scr.

71. Gushee, "A Preliminary Chronology," 405.

72. Lomax, *Mister Jelly Roll*, 208.

73. Morton, Notes to interviews with Alan Lomax, item 18.scr.

74. Lomax, *Mister Jelly Roll*, 206.

75. Ibid., 207.

76. Ibid., 208.

77. Bricktop, *Bricktop*, 215.

78. Ibid.

79. Miller, *"Such Melodious Racket,"* 68.

80. Lomax, *Mister Jelly Roll*, 206–7; Gushee, "New Orleans–Area Musicians," 15.

81. Miller, *"Such Melodious Racket,"* 69.

82. Lomax, *Mister Jelly Roll*, 207.

83. Ibid.

84. Bricktop, *Bricktop*, 62.

85. Ibid., 72.

86. Ibid., 71.

87. Lomax, *Mister Jelly Roll*, 206.

88. Ibid., 217.

89. Ibid., 208–9.

90. Ibid., 209.

91. Morton, Notes to interviews with Alan Lomax, item 18.scr.

92. Lomax, *Mister Jelly Roll*, 209; Morton, Notes to interviews with Alan Lomax, item 18.scr.

93. Lomax, *Mister Jelly Roll*, 209.

94. Ibid., 216.

95. Ibid., 253.

96. Ibid., 153.

97. *California Eagle*, 1 July 1922, p. 7.

98. Gushee, "A Preliminary Chronology," 406.

99. Henry Villalapando Ford Collection (Ford Collection); Gushee, "A Preliminary Chronology," 406.

100. Gushee, "A Preliminary Chronology," 406.

101. Ibid., 406.

102. *Chicago Defender*, 24 February 1923, p. 8, and 17 March 1923, p. 8.

103. Lomax, *Mister Jelly Roll*, 209–10.

104. Ibid., 210.

105. Stearns, "Jelly Roll Morton—Grandpappy of the Piano," 12.

106. Morton, Notes to interviews with Alan Lomax, item 18.scr.

107. Lomax, *Mister Jelly Roll*, 52.

108. Morton, Notes to interviews with Alan Lomax, item 18.scr.

109. Lomax, *Mister Jelly Roll*, 210.

110. Morton, Notes to interviews with Alan Lomax, item 18.scr.; Lomax, *Mister Jelly Roll*, 210.

111. Ibid.

112. Morton, Notes to interviews with Alan Lomax, item 18.scr.

113. Lomax, *Mister Jelly Roll*, 210.

114. Morton, *Ferdinand "Jelly Roll" Morton*, 424.

115. Lomax, *Mister Jelly Roll*, 201.

116. Russell, *Oh, Mister Jelly*, 565, 564.

117. Gushee, "A Preliminary Chronology," 406; *California Eagle*, 15 July 1922, p. 7.

118. Spikes, Interview, 118–19.

119. Ibid., 116, 117, 118, 153.

120. *California Eagle*, 24 June 1921, p. 8.

121. *California Eagle*, 25 August 1921, p. 4.

122. Spikes, Interview, 116, 119.

123. Ibid., 152.

124. Bricktop, *Bricktop*, 62.

125. *California Eagle*, 23 September 1923, p. 6.

126. Spikes, Interview, 118.

127. Russell, *Oh, Mister Jelly*, 560.

128. Spikes, Interview, 118.

129. Ibid., 158.

130. Russell, *Oh, Mister Jelly*, 564.

131. *The New Grove Dictionary of Jazz*, 2d. ed., *s.v.* Oliver, King.

132. Lomax, *Mister Jelly Roll*, 198.

133. L. Williams, "Jelly Roll Morton," 12.

134. Spikes, Interview, 158.

135. Russell, *Oh, Mister Jelly*, 564.

136. Levin, "I Remember Buster Wilson," 6–7.

137. M. Williams, *King Oliver*, 19.

138. Levin, "I Remember Buster Wilson," 7.

139. M. Williams, *King Oliver*, 19–20.

140. Lomax, *Mister Jelly Roll*, 211.

141. Russell, *Oh, Mister Jelly*, 564.

142. Lomax, *Mister Jelly Roll*, 211.

143. Ibid., 211–12.

144. Ibid., 212.

145. Ibid.

146. Ibid., 217.

147. Ibid., 214.

148. Ibid., 212.

149. Stoddard, *Jazz on the Barbary Coast*, 98.

150. Spikes, Interview, 162–4.

151. Ibid., 146.

152. *California Eagle*, 13 December 1919, p. 4.

153. *California Eagle*, 20 December 1919, p. 4.

154. Stoddard, *Jazz on the Barbary Coast*, 110.

155. *California Eagle*, 10 January 1920, p. 4.

156. Lomax, *Mister Jelly Roll*, 212–13.

157. Ibid., 213.

158. Spikes, Interview, 149.

159. Ibid., 131.

160. Lomax, *Mister Jelly Roll*, 213–14.

161. Lawrence Gushee, e-mail to the author, 20 September 1997; *Talking Machine World* (15 May 1923): 120.

162. Lomax, *Mister Jelly Roll*, 225.

163. Ibid., 225–6.

164. Gushee, "A Preliminary Chronology," 406.

165. Lomax, *Mister Jelly Roll*, 217.

166. Ibid., 232.

167. Russell, *Oh, Mister Jelly*, 88–93.

168. Lomax, *Mister Jelly Roll*, 232–3.

169. Pullman, *The Complete Jelly Roll Morton Library of Congress Interviews*, AFS 2489B. Brackets in the original.

170. Lomax, *Mister Jelly Roll*, 200–201.

171. Ibid., 254.

172. Morton, *Ferdinand "Jelly Roll" Morton*, ix.

173. Blesh and Janis, *They All Played Ragtime*, 261; Lomax, *Mister Jelly Roll*, 352.

174. Pullman, *The Complete Jelly Roll Morton Library of Congress Interviews*, AFS 2488B.

175. Wright, *Mr. Jelly Lord*, 169.

176. Morton, *Ferdinand "Jelly Roll" Morton*, 216.

177. Ibid., 211.

178. Ibid., 79.

179. Ibid., 249, 259.

180. Lomax, *Mister Jelly Roll*, 352.

181. Blesh and Janis, *They All Played Ragtime*, 261.

182. Charters, *Nobody*, 116.

183. Lomax, *Mister Jelly Roll*, 348.

184. Ibid., 348–51.

4. THE SCRAPBOOK

1. Joe Marvin, letter to author, 16 March 1997.

2. Lomax, *Mister Jelly Roll*, 210.

3. Russell, *Oh, Mister Jelly*, 147.

4. Ibid., 172.

5. Lomax, *Mister Jelly Roll*, 251.

6. Ibid., 239.

7. Ibid., 236.

8. Russell, *Oh, Mister Jelly*, 147.

9. Lomax, *Mister Jelly Roll*, 284.

10. Morton, "I Created Jazz in 1902," cover. At this date, the title of the magazine was spelled as two words; later it was spelled as one.

11. Ford Collection; Cornwall's emphases.

12. Lomax, *Mister Jelly Roll*, 269.

13. Ibid., 269 ff.

14. Levin, "Untold Story of Jelly Roll Morton's Last Years," 41.

15. Lomax, *Mister Jelly Roll*, 214.

16. Bigard, *With Louis and the Duke*, 61.

17. Lomax, *Mister Jelly Roll*, 294.

18. Russell, *Oh, Mister Jelly*, 47.

19. Lomax, *Mister Jelly Roll*, 275.

20. Ibid., 279.

21. Ibid., 294.

22. Lomax, *Mister Jelly Roll*, 298; Morton, "Final Years of Frustration," pt. 1, p. 2.

23. Morton, "Final Years of Frustration," pt. 1, p. 3.

24. Ibid., 5; ellipses in the original.

25. Ibid., 5.

26. Ibid., pt. 2, p. 8.

27. Lomax, *Mister Jelly Roll*, 298–9.

28. Morton, "Final Years of Frustration," pt. 2, p. 5.

29. Lomax, *Mister Jelly Roll*, 300.

30. Ibid., 312.

31. Ibid., 260.

32. Ibid., 304.

33. Ibid., 250.

34. Ibid., 244.

35. Ibid., 260.

36. Barker, *A Life in Jazz*, 127–8.

37. Lomax, *Mister Jelly Roll*, 256–7.

38. Wright, *Mr. Jelly Lord*, 12.

39. Spikes, Interview, 35–6.

40. "Jelly Roll to Help BMI Get Negro Writers," 6.

41. Levin, "Untold Story of Jelly Roll Morton's Last Years," 38.

42. Lomax, *Mister Jelly Roll*, 215.

43. Ibid., 13.

44. Ibid., 310–11.

45. Barker, *A Life in Jazz*, 126–7.

46. Russell, *Oh, Mister Jelly*, 48.

5. LAST DAYS

1. Lomax, *Mister Jelly Roll*, 301–2.

2. Morton, "Final Years of Frustration," pt. 2, p. 8.

3. Lomax, *Mister Jelly Roll*, 300.

4. Ibid.

5. Ibid., 261.

6. Ibid., 302–3.

7. Ibid., 306.

8. Russell, *Oh, Mister Jelly*, 94, 567.

9. Morton, "Final Years of Frustration," pt. 2, p. 9.

10. Spikes, Interview, 35–6.

11. "Jelly Roll to Help BMI Get Negro Writers," 6.

12. Russell, *Oh, Mister Jelly*, 551.

13. Balliett, *American Musicians*, 26.

14. Russell, *Oh, Mister Jelly*, 147.

15. Ibid., 147–8.

16. Ibid., 145.

17. Ibid., 145–7.

18. Ibid., 557.

19. Levin, "The Saga of Jelly Roll Morton's Ill-Fated Final Recording Date," 38.

20. Russell, *Oh, Mister Jelly*, 556.

21. Ibid.

22. Ibid., 557.

23. Levin, "The Saga of Jelly Roll Morton's Ill-Fated Final Recording Date," 38.

24. Levin, "Untold Story of Jelly Roll Morton's Last Years," 41.

25. Ibid., 38.

26. Levin, "The Saga of Jelly Roll Morton's Ill-Fated Final Recording Date," 38.

27. William Russell Collection, *Jelly Roll Morton Manuscript Collection*.

28. McRae, "The Ghost of Jelly Roll," 14.

29. Reich, "'Lost' Scores Show a Jelly Roll Morton," 1.

30. Russell, *Oh, Mister Jelly*, 189–206.

31. Vappie, "Don Vappie and the Creole Serenaders."

32. Russell, *Oh, Mister Jelly*, 608–660.

33. Ibid., 579.

34. Ibid., 578.

35. Morton, "Final Years of Frustration," pt. 2, p. 8.

36. Ibid., 9.

37. Bryant et al., eds., *Central Avenue Sounds*, 216.

38. Ibid., 217.

39. Lomax, *Mister Jelly Roll*, 303.

40. Ibid., 306.

41. Ibid., 306–7.

42. Superior Court of the State of California in and for the County of Los Angeles, In the Matter of the Estate of Ferdinand Joseph Morton aka Ferd J. Morton, Deceased, No. P206, 148: 15 August 1941.

43. Hoefer, "'Jelly Roll' Rests His Case," 1.

44. Lomax, *Mister Jelly Roll*, 307.

45. Ibid., 308.

46. Balliett, *American Musicians*, 26.

47. Russell, *Oh, Mister Jelly*, 148.

48. Lomax, *Mister Jelly Roll*, 312.

49. "Bury Jelly Roll Morton on Coast," 13.

50. Ibid.

51. Smith, "The Strange Case of Jelly's Will," 9.

52. Lomax, *Mister Jelly Roll*, 38.

53. Russell, *Oh, Mister Jelly*, 507.

54. "Let Your Own Defend You," 1.

55. Russell, *Oh, Mister Jelly*, 507, 509.

56. Lomax, *Mister Jelly Roll*, 269.

57. Ibid., 270.

58. Ibid., 271.

59. Ibid.

60. Ibid., 274.

61. Russell, Letter to Floyd Levin.

62. Superior Court of the State of California in and for the County of Los Angeles. In the Matter of the Estate of Ferdinand Joseph Morton aka Ferd J. Morton, Deceased, 19 June 1944.

63. Lomax, *Mister Jelly Roll*, 260–1.

64. Ibid., 244.

65. Ibid.

66. Russell, *Oh, Mister Jelly*, 296.

67. Ibid., 300.

68. Ibid., 148.

69. Lomax, *Mister Jelly Roll*, 352–3.

BIBLIOGRAPHY

Balliett, Whitney. *American Musicians; Fifty-six Portraits in Jazz*. New York: Oxford University Press, 1986.

Barker, Danny. *A Life in Jazz*. New York: Oxford University Press, 1986.

Bigard, Barney. *With Louis and the Duke: The Autobiography of a Jazz Clarinetist.* Ed. A. Barry Martyn. New York: Oxford University Press, 1986.

Blesh, Rudi, and Harriet Janis. *They All Played Ragtime: The True Story of an American Music*. New York: Knopf, 1960.

Bontemps, Arna, and Jack Conroy. *Anyplace but Here*. New York: Hill and Wang, 1966.

Bricktop [Ada Smith Ducongé and James Haskins]. *Bricktop*. New York: Athenaeum, 1983.

Brown, Karen McCarthy. *Mama Lola: A Vodou Priestess in Brooklyn*. Berkeley and Los Angeles: University of California Press, 1997.

Bryant, Clora, et al., eds. *Central Avenue Sounds: Jazz in Los Angeles*. Berkeley and Los Angeles: University of California Press, 1998.

"Bury Jelly Roll Morton on Coast." *Down Beat* (1 August 1941): 13.

California Eagle. 1915–23.

Castleman, Deke. *Las Vegas*. Oakland, Calif.: Compass American Guides, 1992.

Charters, Ann. *Nobody: The Story of Bert Williams*. London: Macmillan, 1970.

Chicago Defender. 1915–1923.

De Barros, Paul. *Jackson Street after Hours: The Roots of Jazz in Seattle*. Seattle: Sasquatch Books, 1993.

de Graf, Lawrence B. "The City of Black Angels: Emergence of the Los Angeles Ghetto, 1890–1930." *Pacific Historical Review* 39 (1970): 323–52.

Dirty Dozen Brass Band. *The Dirty Dozen Brass Band Plays Jelly Roll Morton*. Columbia Records, 1993.

Ellison, Ralph. *Going to the Territory*. New York: Vintage, 1995.

———. *Shadow and Act*. New York: Random House, 1964.

Ford, Jeanne. Interview by author, 21–24 February 1997.

Ford, Mike. Interview by author, 21–24 February 1997.

Ford, Patti. Interview by author, 21–24 February 1997.

Foster, Pops. *Pops Foster: The Autobiography of a New Orleans Jazzman*. As told to Tom Stoddard, interchapters by Ross Russell. Berkeley and Los Angeles: University of California Press, 1975.

Gauthé, Jacques. Letter to Floyd Levin, 9 January 1999. Floyd Levin Archive, Studio City, California.

Griffin, Betty. Telephone interview by the author, 4 February 1997.

Gushee, Lawrence. E-mail to author, 20 September 1997. Subject: How Melrose got "Wolverine Blues."

———. E-mail to author, 20 November 1997. Subject: Marie Laveau.

———. E-mail to author, 16 January 1999. Subject: Harrison Smith.

———. "New Orleans–Area Musicians on the West Coast, 1908–1925." *Black Music Research Journal* 19, no. 1 (spring 1989): 1–18.

———. "A Preliminary Chronology of the Early Career of Ferd 'Jelly Roll' Morton." *American Music* 3 (1985): 389–412.

———. "Would You Believe Ferman Mouton (A Second Look)." *Storyville* (December 1981–January 1982): 56–9.

Haskins, Jim. *Voodoo and Hoodoo: Their Traditional Craft as Revealed by Actual Practitioners*. Chelsea, Mich.: Scarborough House, 1990.

Henry Villalapando Ford Collection (Ford Collection). Historic New Orleans Collection, New Orleans, Louisiana.

Hines, Duncan. *Adventures in Good Eating*. Ithaca, N.Y.: Duncan Hines Institute, 1946.

Hoefer, George, Jr. "'Jelly Roll' Makes His Case." *Down Beat* (1 August 1941): 1–4.

Howard, Paul. Interview by Patricia Willard and Buddy Collette, 8–9 May 1978. Jazz Oral History Project, Rutgers University Institute of Jazz Studies.

Hulsizer, Kenneth. "Jelly Roll Morton in Washington." In *This Is Jazz*, ed. Kenneth Williamson, 202–16. London: Newnes, 1960.

Hurbon, Laennec. "American Fantasy and Haitian Voodoo." In *Sacred Arts of Haitian Voodoo*, ed. Donald Consantino, 181–97. Los Angeles: UCLA Fowler Museum of Cultural History, 1995.

Hurston, Zora Neale. *Mules and Men*. New York: Harper, 1990.

"Jelly Roll to Help BMI Get Negro Writers." *Down Beat* (1 January 1941): 6.

Johns, Rose Mary. Telephone interviews by the author, 1, 5, 25 August; 22 September; 24 November 1996; 16, 22, 25 February; 24 March; 14 May 1997.

"Let Your Own Defend You." *California Eagle* (17 November 1938): 1.

Levin, Floyd. "I Remember Buster Wilson." *Jazzbeat* (fall 1986): 6–8.

———. "The Saga of Jelly Roll Morton's Ill-Fated Final Recording Date." *American Rag* (November 1997): 38.

———. "Untold Story of Jelly Roll Morton's Last Years." *West Coast Rag* (July 1991): 37–41.

Lomax, Alan. *Mister Jelly Roll: The Fortunes of Jelly Roll Morton, New Orleans Creole and "Inventor of Jazz."* New York: Pantheon, 1993.

Los Angeles County. Probate file, Ferdinand J. Morton aka Ferd J. Morton. No. 206, 148.

Marvin, Joe. Letter to author, 16 March 1997.

———. Telephone interview by the author, 20 March 1997.

McRae, Barry. "The Ghost of Jelly Roll." *Jazz Journal International* (August 1998): 14.

Metraux, Alfred. *Voodoo in Haiti*. Trans. Hugo Charteris. New York: Schocken Books, 1972.

Miller, Mark. *"Such Melodious Racket": The Lost History of Jazz in Canada, 1914 to 1949*. Toronto: Mercury Press, n.d.

Mintz, Sidney, and Rolph Trouillot. "The Social History of Haitian Voodoo." In *Sacred Arts of Haitian Voodoo*, ed. Donald Consantino, 123–47. Los Angeles: UCLA Fowler Museum of Cultural History, 1995.

Morrison, Van. *Van Morrison Glossary* Online. Netscape 2. 1 April 1997. Available http://www.harbout.sfu.ca/~hayward/va/glossary/jellyroll.html.

Morton, Ferdinand "Jelly Roll." *Ferdinand "Jelly Roll" Morton: The Collected Piano Music*. Ed. and transcribed by James Dapogny. Washington, D.C.: Smithsonian Institution, 1982.

———. "Final Years of Frustration (1939–1941)." Parts 1 and 2. *Jazz Journal* 21, no. 11 (1968): 2–5; no. 12 (1968): 8–9.

———. "I Created Jazz in 1902." *Down Beat* (August 1938): 3 ff; (September 1938): 4.

———. Interviews recorded by Alan Lomax, 23 May–14 December 1938. Library of Congress, Washington, D.C. Audiocassette copies of the entire series, music and spoken word, courtesy of Peter Pullman.

———. Notes to interviews with Alan Lomax, n.d. Items 5.scr. and 18.scr. Library of Congress, Washington, D.C.

———. *Winin' Boy Blues: Library of Congress Recordings Recorded by Alan Lomax.* Vol. 4. Rounder Records, 1993.

Murray, Albert. *Stomping the Blues.* New York: McGraw-Hill, 1976.

Paher, Stanley W. *Las Vegas: As It Began, as It Grew.* Las Vegas: Nevada Pub., 1971.

Pullman, Peter. *The Complete Jelly Roll Morton Library of Congress Interviews.* *American Folklore Society* (AFS), 2488 A and B, 2489 A and B. (Transcripts of Jelly Roll Morton's Library of Congress interviews. Copy mailed to author.)

Reich, Howard. "'Lost' Scores Show a Jelly Roll Morton Who Was a Step Ahead of His Time." *Chicago Tribune,* 1 May 1998, "Tempo" section, p. 1.

Rose, Al. *Eubie Blake.* New York: Schirmer, 1979.

———. *Storyville, New Orleans: Being an Authentic, Illustrated Account of the Notorious Red-Light District.* Alabama: University of Alabama Press, 1974.

Russell, William. Letter to Floyd Levin, n.d. With photocopy of RCA Records invoice to Harrison Smith, 31 August 1972. Floyd Levin Archive, Studio City, California.

———, ed. *Oh, Mister Jelly: A Jelly Roll Morton Scrapbook.* Copenhagen: Jazz-Media, 1999.

Sonnier, Austin, Jr. *A Guide to the Blues: History, Who's Who, Research Sources.* Westport, Conn.: Greenwood Press, 1994.

Smith, Harrison, as told to Bob Kumm. "The Strange Case of Jelly's Will." *Storyville* 25 (1969): 8–9.

Spikes, Benjamin "Reb." Interview by Patricia Willard, May 1980. Jazz Oral History Project. Rutgers University Institute of Jazz Studies.

State of California. Department of Public Health. Vital Statistics. Certificate of Death: Anita Julia Ford. Registration District No. 1901. Registrar's No. 7544. 24 April 1952.

————. Certificate of Death: Laura Hunter. District No. 1901. Registrar's No. 2351. 14 February 1940.

————. Certificate of Death: Ferdinand Morton. District No. 1901. Registrar's No. 9682. 10 July 1941.

Stearns, Marshal. "Jelly Roll Morton—Grandpappy of the Piano: Earl Hines Learning ABC's When Jelly Roll Cut QRS Piano Rolls." *Down Beat* (1 January 1938): 12.

Stewart, Rex. *Boy Meets Horn.* Ed. Claire P. Gordon. Ann Arbor, Mich.: University of Michigan, 1991.

Stoddard, Tom. *Jazz on the Barbary Coast.* Berkeley, Calif.: Heyday Books, 1998.

Superior Court of the State of California in and for the County of Los Angeles. In the Matter of the Estate of Ferdinand Joseph Morton aka Ferd J. Morton, Deceased. No. P206, 148: 1941–1966.

Tallant, Robert. *Voodoo in New Orleans.* Gretna, La.: Pelican, 1994.

Triem, Judith P. *Ventura County: Land of Good Fortune.* 2d ed. San Luis Obispo, Calif.: EZ Nature Books, 1990.

U.S. Bureau of the Census. 1900. United States Census. Enumeration district no. 31, sheet 2.

————. 1910. United States Census. Enumeration district no. 32, sheet 11A.

————. 1920. United States Census. Enumeration district no. 567, sheet 5.

Vappie, Don. "Don Vappie and the Creole Jazz Serenaders." Private recording sent by Vappie to author, n.d.

William Russell Collection. Jelly Roll Morton Manuscript Music Collection. Ed. Richard Jackson and Nancy Ruck. New Orleans: Historic New Orleans Collection, 1 October 1996.

Williams, Lowell W. "Jelly Roll Morton—Grandpappy of the Piano: Earl Hines Learning ABC's When Jelly Roll Cut QRS Piano Rolls." *Down Beat* (1 January 1938): 12.

Williams, Martin. *King Oliver.* New York: Barnes, 1960.

————. "The Roll." In *Jazz Masters of New Orleans,* 38–78. New York: Da Capo, 1967.

Wright, Laurie. *Mr. Jelly Lord.* Chigwell, England: Storyville, 1980.

INDEX

Composition: G&S Typesetters, Inc.
Text: 10/15 Janson
Display: Janson
Printing and binding: Thomson-Shore